LATIN AMERICAN TEXTUALITIES

Edited by
HEATHER J. ALLEN and
ANDREW R. REYNOLDS

LATIN AMERICAN TEXTUALITIES

History, Materiality, and Digital Media

THE UNIVERSITY OF
ARIZONA PRESS
TUCSON

The University of Arizona Press
www.uapress.arizona.edu

We respectfully acknowledge the University of Arizona is on the land and territories of Indigenous peoples. Today, Arizona is home to twenty-two federally recognized tribes, with Tucson being home to the O'odham and the Yaqui. Committed to diversity and inclusion, the University strives to build sustainable relationships with sovereign Native Nations and Indigenous communities through education offerings, partnerships, and community service.

© 2018 by The Arizona Board of Regents
All rights reserved. Published 2018
First paperback edition published 2025

ISBN-13: 978-0-8165-3771-6 (cloth)
ISBN-13: 978-0-8165-5532-1 (paper)
ISBN-13: 978-0-8165-3902-4 (ebook)

Cover design by Lisa Force

Publication of this book is made possible in part by financial support from West Texas A&M University and the University of Mississippi.

Library of Congress Cataloging-in-Publication Data are available at the Library of Congress.

Printed in the United States of America
♾ This paper meets the requirements of ANSI/NISO Z39.48-1992 (Permanence of Paper).

Contents

Acknowledgments   vii

Introduction: Textuality in Latin America   3
HEATHER J. ALLEN AND ANDREW R. REYNOLDS

PART I. READING HISTORY THROUGH TEXTUALITY

1. Writing Orality: Turning Quechua into a Language of Religious Conversion   27
   CATALINA ANDRANGO-WALKER

2. A Witch in the City: History and Textuality in the Nineteenth-Century Andes   46
   WALTHER MARADIEGUE

3. The Sudamericana Publishing House: Catalogs as Objects of Study   66
   JOSÉ ENRIQUE NAVARRO

PART II. TEXTUAL ARTIFACTS AND MATERIALITIES

4. Guaman Poma's Library: Costume Books and the Illustration of an Indigenous Manuscript   85
   GEORGE ANTONY THOMAS

5. *Rioplatense* Sound, Text, and Transmission in the
    Early Era of Sonic Reproducibility   108
    SAM CARTER

6. The Postcard Poetics of Nicanor Parra's *Artefactos*   128
    REBECCA KOSICK

7. Reading Images: Art, Aesthetics, and the Imagery of
    the Future in Argentine Science Fiction   151
    SILVIA KURLAT ARES

PART III. DIGITAL TEXTUALITIES, MEDIA, AND EDITING

8. Discourse or Data? Theorizing the Electronic Edition of
    Antonio de León Pinelo's 1629 Bibliography of the Indies   177
    CLAYTON MCCARL

9. Do Borges's Librarians Have Bodies?   197
    ZAC ZIMMER

10. Between Street and Book: Textual Assemblages and
    Urban Topologies in Graphic Fiction from Brazil   221
    EDWARD KING

    Afterword: Texts, Coding, and Translation   241
    SARA CASTRO-KLARÉN

    Contributors   *253*
    Index   *257*

Acknowledgments

WE WOULD FIRST LIKE TO acknowledge and thank the Publications Committee at the University of Arizona Press for supporting this project. In particular, Editor in Chief Kristen Buckles has been an enthusiastic advocate for this book from the beginning and we are so grateful for her continued encouragement. Stacey Wujcik has been extremely patient and instrumental in bringing this project to fruition. Additionally, we appreciate the anonymous reviewers' incisive comments, which helped shape *Latin American Textualities*. Generous institutional support from Jessica Mallard, Steve Severn, and the Joan Urban Williams Fund from West Texas A&M University and the Department of Modern Languages and College of Liberal Arts at the University of Mississippi helped make this publication possible. We would also like to thank Kendra Carter Reynolds for supporting the book's completion, and Scott Iverson for designing the volume's webpage and providing technical support.

LATIN AMERICAN TEXTUALITIES

Introduction

Textuality in Latin America

HEATHER J. ALLEN AND ANDREW R. REYNOLDS

IN THE PRESENT VOLUME, we understand "textuality" as the conditions in which a text is created, edited, archived, published, disseminated, and consumed. "Text" thus encompasses a broad variety of artifacts, from traditional printed matter such as grammar manuals and newspaper articles, to items we might consider newcomers or even interlopers in the textual world, including the phonograph, fashion illustrations, publishing house catalogs, postcards, graphic novels, and virtual databases and cataloging systems—all of which this volume's contributors examine.[1] Defined in this way, text and textuality point to the wide diversity in their manifestations throughout Latin America, and the inherent difficulties of cultural representation in the region's textual production. This heterogeneity is both a product of, and a contributing factor to, the evolution of the textual history of Latin America—a vast area with numerous indigenous cultures, geographical features, and particular regional histories, all subject to centuries of colonization that dramatically affected text production and consumption.[2] Accordingly, we argue that Latin American textual studies should not attempt to reconcile differences between referent and mode of production but rather account for and contextualize these systems of difference and set them apart as rich and essential sites of analysis for understanding historical and literary tensions in the region. We aim to do so by collecting perspectives across genre, period, and national lines, bringing together divergent representations of Latin American textual cultures.

The difficulty in producing texts that resemble any sort of universal form furthermore indicates how Latin American textualities can open the Anglo-centered academic field to new perspectives, particularly in relation to encounters between cultural systems around the world. Thus we also seek to create sites for dialogue between the broader fields of Latin American textual studies and (Anglo-centered) textual studies, which heretofore have been separate in part due to the language barrier—the former publishing largely in Spanish and the latter in English and French.[3] We are well aware that our edition is ambitious and partial and that there is much more work to be done, although in the past thirty years many scholars have produced increasingly more studies exploring textualities in Latin America.

While not all the examples of textuality presented in the first paragraph are unique to Latin America, others are indeed distinctive in that they arise out of a perceived need to overcome the region's colonial circumstances. Latin American print history, dominated by Western forms of production the Spanish colonizers introduced, continuously intersected with indigenous forms of discourse—from pictographic codices, to sculpture, textiles, and *khipus*. This intersectional process dramatically transformed concepts of history, representation, and expression throughout the hemisphere. Yet the oppressed indigenous groups whose forms of record-keeping were considered inferior by some colonizers began to incorporate and utilize dominant textualities to express themselves in writing, though often at the cost of further marginalizing or forgetting their own traditions of material communication.[4] Hence textual history in Latin America, from its "invention" in 1492, includes indigenous subjects frequently mediated by Western textualities.[5] Additionally, if we claim that material forms of text, textual production, and consumption, and the social dynamics of textual culture are essential to our sociohistorical understanding of the region—as book historians have successfully argued in the case of Europe[6]—then one that relies solely on Western textual forms is inescapably inadequate in depicting and including indigenous textualities, culture, and history. Thus it is all the more important to examine colonial processes and interrogate the dominant manifestations that people on the margins of society interacted with and brought into their own spheres of textual communication and representation.

In recent years, the rise of decolonial studies has attempted to recuperate these marginalized perspectives and reconsider the way scholars have traditionally studied the region from a Eurocentric slant that propagates Western viewpoints and modes of study. Walter Mignolo explains that the de-colonial option requires a different type of thinking . . . , a non-linear and chronological (but spatial) epistemological break; it requires border epistemology (e.g., epistemic disobedience), a non-capitalist political economy, and a plurinational (that, is non-mono-national) concept of the state. The de-colonial option opens up as a de-linking and negativity from the perspective of the spaces that have been silenced, repressed, demonized, devaluated by the triumphant chant of self-promoting modern epistemology, politics and economy and its internal dissentions.⁷

That is, adequately theorizing the region, with tensions between colonial authority and indigenous textualities, requires us to utilize a border-thinking that crosses back and forth between temporalities, geographic spaces, and cultures.

Cultural critic Antonio Cornejo Polar offers another way to conceptualize this challenge, arguing in his classic text on *indigenismo* and heterogeneity that Latin America does actually break from Western classification systems of nation, period, and genre. Instead, his concept of literary heterogeneity is characterized by "la duplicidad o pluralidad de los signos socio-culturales de su proceso productivo" (the duplicity or plurality of sociocultural signs and their processes of production).⁸ For Cornejo Polar, textual systems in the region are in continual conflict, which leads to what he terms a "desencuentro" (disagreement or misunderstanding) between textual production and Latin American society and culture.⁹ The consequences of this rupture have a representational effect in that the "desencuentro" extends to the "índole desigual del referente que se pretende revelar" (unequal nature of the referent that the text attempts to reveal).¹⁰ This plurality calls for a necessary contextualization of the many textualities that have occurred across Latin American cultures and a conscientious attempt to eschew singularities despite the imperial, homogenizing designs of Spanish colonization.

Cornejo Polar argues for an approach to Latin American studies that considers textuality as necessary in order to recognize the heterogeneity of cultural processes in the Americas. He explains that "a través de un análisis simple del proceso literario, que permita distinguir la producción, el texto resultante, su referente y el sistema de distribución y consumo, cabe precisar la distancia que separa a las literaturas homogéneas de las heterogéneas" (through a simple analysis of the literary process that permits one to distinguish its production, the resulting text, its referent and its system of distribution and consumption, the distance that separates homogeneous literatures from those that are heterogeneous should be noted).¹¹ For instance, the Peruvian critic sets the colonial chronicle apart as exemplary in its heterogeneity because it introduces Western forms of writing to the newly "discovered" Americas. The production of the chronicle results in a separation between the genre's textuality and the "New World" it attempts to describe: "el rey, la metrópoli, es *su* lector. En el otro extremo del proceso de producción de las crónicas está el referente, ese Nuevo Mundo que se presenta como realidad incontrastable y se propone como opaco o deslumbrante enigma" (the king and the metropolis is *its* audience. In the other extreme of the chronicle's production process is its referent, this New World that is presented as an incomparable reality yet at the same time is put forward as an opaque and spellbinding enigma).¹² The complexities of the colonial encounter, of Western systems of cultural production coming into contact with referents that are in many ways unrepresentable by those same systems, indicate a heterogeneity in the attempt to textually reconcile this encounter. It is heterogeneous in that the dissemination of texts depicting the New World to a royal audience speaks of the indigenous societies of the Americas while also formulating a construction based on separation and difference, a reality divergent from the one that is being represented.¹³ The production of the text, or the contexts of its construction, its readerships, and its material formats—in other words, its textuality—is a primary culprit of this disconnect between text and the representation of the region's cultural realities.¹⁴

Beyond the colonial period, textuality continues to be central in Latin American culture and society, as the region's critical and literary traditions demonstrate. Political thinkers, for example, used textual metaphors to conceptualize the genesis of nations. Ángel Rama consecrated the Latin American cosmopolis as *La ciudad letrada* (*The Lettered City*, 1984). José Martí explained that a well-edited book "dará a las ideas de poetas y letrados palacio, y no cárcel" (will provide the ideas of poets and the learned with a palace, and not a prison).¹⁵ José Enrique Rodó's *Ariel* (1900), an essay exhorting Latin American youth to study in the service of activism and nation-building, commences with a description of Prospero's books as "fieles compañeros" (faithful friends).¹⁶ Cultural thinkers similarly used such metaphors to contemplate how culture shaped the Latin American subject. Octavio Paz, for instance, described the metaphorical Mexican mask as an ancient text, "indescifrable a primera vista, como una piedra sagrada cubierta de incisiones y signos . . . y, más tarde, máscara, significación, historia" (indecipherable at first glance, like a sacred stone covered with incisions and signs . . . and, then, mask, signification, history).¹⁷ Other popular twentieth-century authors, too, theorized textuality in their fiction. Jorge Luis Borges's stories are filled with speculative explorations of complex textualities, from the infinite encyclopedic worlds of "Tlön, Uqbar, Orbis Tertius," to the creation of Pierre Bernard's new version of *Don Quijote* and the endless hexagonal libraries in "La biblioteca de Babel" ("The Library of Babel"; see chapter 9 in this volume). In the novel *Rayuela* (*Hopscotch*, 1963), Julio Cortázar introduced book consumption as a game and admonished the reader that "a su manera este libro es muchos libros" (in its own way this book is several books).[18] In Gabriel García Márquez's *Cien años de soledad* (*One Hundred Years of Solitude*, 1967), one of the first things that protagonist José Arcadio Buendía does upon the arrival of Melquíades, the librarian and keeper of the archive, is to close himself in a room and produce "un manual de una asombrosa claridad didáctica" (a manual with astonishing didactical clarity) to send to governmental authorities together with testimonial texts and "varios pliegos de dibujos explicativos" (various documents with explanatory drawings).[19] Prefiguring Márquez's Buendía and his compelling need to document everything in writing, literary historian Silvio Romero observes that in nineteenth-century Brazilian society, "in terms of copying, mimicry, and pastiches to impress the gringos, no people has a better Constitution on paper . . . , everything is better . . . on paper."[20]

While the previous examples show that text and textuality have been and continue to be major themes in Latin American intellectual discourse, the following section offers a more in-depth examination of the unique and complex nature of Latin American textualities through a close reading of how an infamous document has been edited since its inception.

The Uniqueness of Latin American Textualities: The Case of Sor Juana

Folio 174 of the "Libro de profesiones y elecciones de prioras y vicarias del convento de San Gerónimo" includes two brief professions of faith by the Mexican poet Sor Juana Inés de la Cruz (see figure I.1). The nun recorded one upon entering the convent in 1669. She then renewed in writing her devotion, signed in her own blood, shortly before her death over two decades later in 1694. She writes: "Yo Juana Ynés de la Cruz, religiosa profesa de este convento . . . ratifico mi profesión y vuelvo a reiterar mis votos" (I Juana Ynés de la Cruz, a professed religious woman of this convent . . . ratify my profession and again reiterate my

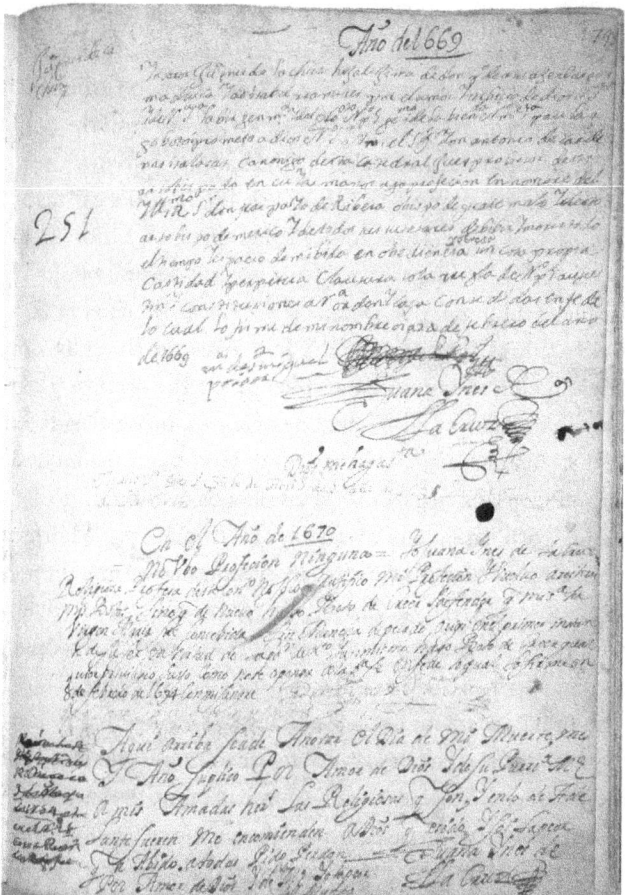

FIGURE I.1 Sor Juana Inés de la Cruz's professions of faith from 1669 and 1694 in the "Libro de profesiones y elecciones de prioras y vicarias del Convento de San Gerónimo." Benson Latin American Collection, University of Texas at Austin.

vows).[21] The legendary folio's textuality exemplifies the complexities inherent in Latin American textual production. Its physical attributes comprise the most readily evident elements of its textuality: disordered page numbers, the marginal label "Sor Inés de la Cruz" in the upper left corner calling attention to the famous signatory, dark blots of ink scattered across the page, the scratched-out signature of the first profession, the faint rusty red renewal of her Christian vows dated 1694 and labeled "con mi sangre" (with my blood). In addition to these inscribed characteristics, the textuality of the Sor Juana folio and the bound manuscript as a whole also encompasses its archival conditions (including its digital manifestations), production and dissemination, reproduction and editing (which began in 1586 and continues today), and consumption of the text throughout its existence.

The Sor Juana manuscript is preserved in the Benson Latin American Collection of the University of Texas at Austin. The codex was acquired by well-known Sor Juana scholar Dorothy Schons and then processed by the Benson Latin American Collection in 1994. The Instituto Mexiquense de Cultura (Mexican Institute of Culture) published the manuscript in 2013 in a facsimile volume edited by Guillermo Schmidhuber de la Mora. An open-access PDF copy of the complete manuscript is also available on the Benson Latin American Collection website.[22] Schmidhuber's facsimile edition omits the following textual elements of the manuscript added to the text after Schons acquired it: a paragraph-long description in English of the "Libro de profesiones" on the inside cover of the book; and, pasted opposite, an October 23, 1915, letter from Edwin A. Barber, the director of the Pennsylvania Museum and School of Industrial Art (now the Philadelphia Museum of Art) that addresses an inquiry regarding a Sor Juana portrait.[23]

Thus, although the edition describes itself as a "Facsímil del original conservado en la Biblioteca Benson de la Universidad de Texas en Austin" (facsimile of the original conserved in the Benson Latin American Collection),[24] the fact that Schmidhuber omitted parts of the text emphasizes his dominant role in the process of textual editing and reproduction. This gives rise to further questions, such as: What else is lost in the editorial process? How does the modern reprinting of a manuscript change the text? Because the Benson Latin American Collection's digitized copy contains high-resolution images of all pages (including the ones omitted in Schmidhuber's book edition), how does digital editing contrast with traditional textual editing particularly since, in this case, Schmidhuber's edition omitted textual elements of the manuscript that are helpful in understanding its transmission and history?

Archival materiality also points to the impact of authority and conditions of the archive on public access to the original text. As described on the Benson Latin American Collection's website, "the fragile nature of the document and the writing medium" of the text prohibits public viewing of the manuscript. Acquiring access to the original "Libro de profesiones" is a complex task reserved for a select group of academics with the ability and resources necessary to visit the archive.

Yet another component that certainly complicates and perhaps muddies the folio's consumption is the entry dedicated to the "Libro de profesiones" on the *Tex Libris* blog from the Office of the Director of the University of Texas Libraries.[25] The page briefly describes the confession folio and incorporates several digital elements that contribute to a reading of the text. The blog, produced in English and supported by a wealthy U.S. research university, contains an image of the Sor Juana folio and a brief commentary.[26] Questions of authorship arise as the blog content has its own author, signaled by a hyperlink for the author that leads to another webpage titled "All posts by Travis Willmann."[27] Three hyperlinks are present in the post's message: one leading to the Sor Juana poets.org webpage, and two others that link to internal library pages. Six tags categorize the post: "Blood," "Book of Professions," "Convent," "Dorothy Schons," "San Geronimo," and "Sor Juana Inés de la Cruz." These tags all link back to a "Tag Archives" webpage whose sole reference is the "Sor Juana's 'Book of Professions'" blog post. The tags also seem rather arbitrary. For example, other *Tex Libris* pages tag general terms such as "Archive," "Art," "Digitization," "Creativity," and even "Mexico," all of which could apply to the Sor Juana entry.[28] There is also a "Thought" section where readers can provide feedback to the blog content, and there is a comment from December 2014 that reads, "Love the Benson Collection! Studied and researched there when preparing my dissertation. Keep acquiring historic materials." The manuscript is represented by a digitized image of the Sor Juana folio and, when accessed, a scan of the page and caption is enlarged, making the text readable (it is unreadable in its original size on the webpage). The folio is captioned: "'Libro de professiones [*sic*] y elecciones de prioras y vicarias del convento de San Gerónimo, 1586–1713.' Ink and blood on paper. 8 × 12 inches. Dorothy Schons Papers, Benson Latin American Collection."

All of this digital archival information, of varying degrees of relevance for interpreting the folio, pushes up against further questions regarding the manuscript's textuality in relation to this digital manifestation: How does the digitized reference transform the text? How does it add to our understanding of the text? How does the folio's promotion help us read and understand the text's content differently from other versions? While we do not aim to provide answers in this introduction, in posing them we hope to make clear how digital representation complicates textuality and brings about new ways of reading, differing points of textual accessibility, new ways of studying the materiality of the text, and conflicting institutional and editorial control of how the text is defined and consumed. Understanding the Sor Juana folio in these diverging manifestations opens up several new perspectives for understanding the document.

Overview

Latin American Textualities is composed of contributions from investigators working in the fields of textual studies and Latin American cultures and literatures. They explore themes of textualities through a variety of theoretical lenses with a focus on the fundamental role that the text and its materiality, technological manifestations, and production has on Latin American culture, history, and identity. The volume is divided into three distinct sections: "Reading History Through Textuality," "Textual Artifacts and Materialities," and "Digital Textualities, Media, and Editing," bookended by this introduction by the editors and an afterword by Latin American literary scholar Sara Castro-Klarén.

Reading History Through Textuality

The studies in the book's first section support our claim that the foundation of textual culture studies in Latin America must be based on an understanding of the complexities of the region's history. Accordingly, chapter contributors elucidate the formation, continual renewal, and adjustment of histories by investigating a variety of materials, including grammars, catechisms, newspaper articles, chronicles, and publisher catalogs, from the sixteenth to twentieth centuries, from rural Peru to metropolitan centers throughout Latin America and beyond. These studies unmask power structures and relations as they describe how religious, political, and commercial figures attempted to construct and shape not only historical events but the narration of cultural encounters and how their own spheres of power would be perceived throughout history.

Catalina Andrango-Walker's chapter, "Writing Orality: Turning Quechua into a Language of Religious Conversion," shows how religious authorities tried to shape Quechua into a language of conversion via the publication of catechisms and other evangelization materials. She describes how during the first decade of the seventeenth century, the Jesuit convents in Lima, Cuzco, and Juli convened the best speakers of Quechua and Aymara to translate evangelizing materials and establish the standards for writing in these two languages. The resulting vocabularies and grammar books, she argues, go beyond a mere linguistic exegesis; in fact, the authors provided another way to approach the pre-Hispanic past as well as an additional means of understanding seventeenth-century colonial Peru. Taking into account the methods by which these authors understood, classified, and conceptualized the linguistic and cultural conventions of Quechua and Aymara, her study analyzes how these texts can be regarded as artifacts that not only helped cross the linguistic barrier between European and Andean cultures but also served as instruments of colonization and meaningful indicators of Andean political and social changes.

Moving forward in time to the late nineteenth century, in "A Witch in the City: History and Textuality in the Nineteenth-Century Andes," Walther Maradiegue explores the tragic burning of an accused witch in rural Peru, focusing on how elite journalists, writers, and politicians in the country's urban centers and beyond reframed the incident in diverse formats. The materiality of these texts, he demonstrates, not only altered how current events in the region were produced and consumed but also tied indigenous oral culture and the Quechua language to urban centers through repeated attempts to represent reactions to and commentary on the burning. Written in diverse genres including journalism, academic prose, law, and fiction, these texts were an opportunity to make claims about modernity, science, and civilization. Maradiegue argues that these written reactions to this event are key to understanding the production and circulation of texts in late nineteenth-century Peru in two ways. The first is related to their geopolitical distribution and flow, and allows us to rethink the role of the capital city versus the rural *provincias* (provinces), *el campo* (the country), and *la sierra* (the mountains)—via the dissemination and legitimization of ideas and information. The second scrutinizes nineteenth-century Andean literacy as a social practice strongly influenced by indigenous languages, orality, and so-called Andean Spanish.

Leaving nineteenth-century Peruvian elite textual production for twentieth-century Argentinian editorial marketing, in "The Sudamericana Publishing House: Catalogs as Objects of Study," José Enrique Navarro examines the 1950 and 1969 catalogs from the publishing house Sudamericana. Taking as a point of departure Pierre Bourdieu's theory of the cultural field, Navarro examines Sudamericana's role as an agent in the country's cultural and literary development. The catalog book descriptions—aimed at national and international booksellers, bookstores, and libraries—are far removed from the literary production of the books contained therein. Nonetheless, Navarro demonstrates how the publisher's image of the literary field affects how consumers perceive it and exerts control over the construction of literary history by including or excluding authors and texts from a system created in part by the publisher itself. He pays special attention to the various book series included in this understudied document, including books in translation, which sold worldwide. In doing so, he assesses the impact of Sudamericana's publishing policies on the production, circulation, and consumption of certain books, and consequently the consolidation of specific reading trends as well as the canonization of some authors over others in Argentina and beyond.

Textual Artifacts and Materialities

After considering Latin American history from a perspective rooted in textual materiality, the second section logically moves to an examination of specific textual artifacts. In doing so, it makes clearer the connections between text production (composition, printing, and dissemination) and objects not traditionally seen as "text." The collection of artifacts in this section depicts not only a rampant intertextuality, what Roberto González Echevarría titles a "clash of texts," but also a system of divergent media that discursively constructed the region across historical periods.[29] Arising from the study of what we call "textual artifacts," specific material examples of the vast textual history of the region, is a complex web where textual and media-based formats are combined, cultural histories come into contact, and print culture is transformed into a multifaceted transnational dynamic. Through a fusion of elements that seem ephemeral and even kitschy—such as Nicanor Parra's postcards discussed in chapter 8—the textual makeup of Latin America becomes more and more broadly defined as a heterogeneous archive sharing only the classification of text.

Beginning with the intersections between fashion illustrations and native and European historiographical conventions, in "Guaman Poma's Library: Costume Books and the Illustration of an Indigenous Manuscript," George Antony Thomas demonstrates how Felipe Guaman Poma de Ayala's *Primer nueva corónica y buen gobierno* (ca. 1615) provides ample evidence of the interactions between an indigenous author and European print culture, in particular how European costume books influenced the author's illustrations. Italian costume books, which often focused on descriptions of ancient rulers from imperial Rome, inspired his illustrated account of Inca rulers and their accomplishments. German and French costume books containing anti-Catholic descriptions of members of the clergy appear to be a model for the indigenous author's critical renditions of colonial Peruvian clergymen. These confluences not only suggest that Guaman Poma had access to books not usually on lists of titles in circulation in the colonies; they also demonstrate his modifications of European print culture conventions to create a uniquely indigenous chronicle.

Moving from the visual to the audible text, in "*Rioplatense* Sound, Text, and Transmission in the Early Era of Sonic Reproducibility," Sam Carter asks how the arrival of reproducible sound unsettled notions of textuality in Latin America. If Thomas Edison's phonograph—which the inventor understood primarily in terms of speech and dictation and, notably, not with respect to music as later users would—offered the possibility to reproduce sound by retracing indexical grooves, the textual object's status as a carrier of sonic significance was indelibly altered. While an object like the phonogram (a phonograph recording used in roughly the same way as a letter) never achieved any prominent position within the media landscape, it is still possible to detect how a variety of textual objects reacted to the arrival of reproducible sound. Focusing primarily on the Río de la Plata region—where we can find ample evidence of telephone, phonograph, and radio use and distribution—and drawing on both nineteenth- and twentieth-century examples, Carter's chapter argues that textual objects adopted a different stance toward their depiction of sound. Descriptive and evaluative rather than imitative, the incorporation of sound in these texts aims not at phonography—that is, at another version of writing sound—but rather at the preservation of subjective impressions of frequently ephemeral sonic events.

With Rebecca Kosick's chapter, "The Postcard Poetics of Nicanor Parra's *Artefactos*," we return to the visual text, but one that undermines and questions the very conventions governing its own textuality. As mentioned, she considers Chilean poet Nicanor Parra's 1972 collection of poetry, *Artefactos*, in light of its publication on and as 230 individual postcards in a box. These poems combine brief printed and handwritten phrases with illustrations by Guillermo Tejeda. Together, the text and images make use of popular, political, and borrowed speech and iconography to provoke readers and challenge the conventions of poetry and good taste. As a rejection of traditional poetic form and lyrical subjectivity, Parra's famous antipoems favored an irreverent, aggressively down-to-earth approach to poetry, something that, in the *Artefactos*, is both concentrated and exploded into many postcard-sized fragments. While scholars have commented on the relationship between the *Artefactos* and antipoetry, this chapter expands the critical reception of these poems to include a sustained focus on their materialization as postcards. In doing this, this study examines the interplay of text and image in the *Artefactos* and theorizes the poems' status as material "artifacts" that poetically capture not just the sights and sounds of lived experience but also the material structures of its popular communication.

Continuing this line of inquiry into the increasingly blurred distinction between art forms and media, between high and low cultural production, and also between the perception of centers and peripheries, in "Reading Images: Art, Aesthetics, and the Imagery of the Future in Argentine Science Fiction," Sylvia Kurlat Ares examines this phenomenon as manifested in twentieth-century Argentine science fiction comics. She posits that this porosity makes up the scaffolding of an aesthetic that operates from naturalism but with the instruments of pop surrealism, with the languages of pop and op arts and with the rigor of realism and cubism. Such complex operations can be traced both in book covers and magazine illustrations as well as in graphic novels, where the complexity of visual language disputes the space of political and ideological narratives. From the stunning images of the famed *Péndulo* magazine, to the visual universe of graphic novels by Ricardo Barreiro or Diego Agrimbau's imagery, Kurlat Ares shows how Argentine science fiction has reworked its relationship with art and literature as a way not simply to claim a space for itself in the cultural field but to rework Argentina's surrealist tradition. She further explores the construction of an aesthetic that draws on a variety of sources in order to think about relationships between different areas of cultural production, as well as aesthetic objects (and the media in which they are supported). In this way, she questions not only how science fiction has evolved and changed the relationships between different forms of art but how far different media and vocabularies have been merged into a common redefined cultural agenda after modernity.

Digital Textualities, Media, and Editing

The final section of this book traverses how digital media is revising Latin American cultural histories and artistic expression, whose textual forms have undergone continuous destabilization since pre-Columbian times. Latin American textual history and its transition into digital formats provide new and important perspectives on the complexities of imagining future textual formats and readerships. While digital textualities have transformed ways that people experience reading, textual production, book markets and promotion, and the availability and dissemination of texts around the world, digitization of the text has also made it possible for ever-increasing audiences to read and come to know Latin American literary and cultural production. For instance, many writers use social media not only to share their literature but to create new aesthetic spaces. Take, for instance, two examples from Mexican author Yuri Herrera's (1970–) Twitter account (see figures I.2 and I.3).

One way that Herrera uses his Twitter feed is for brief, fragmentary moments of literary expression. Upon posting a message through Twitter, his text is published electronically to over twelve thousand followers instantaneously. Textual production through Twitter can be performed using a cell phone, thus breaking down traditional writing processes and completely uprooting bookish materialities. In digital spaces, literary production and consumption become practices that can occur in infinite contexts, complicating notions of technique, audience, and literary networks. In this vein, the chapters in this section problematize linear models of digital editing via thinking through the digitization of complex nonlinear colonial manuscripts, explore how works like those of Jorge Luis Borges symbolically address issues relating to the mass storage of data information, and question whether transforming a street art project into a coffee-table book undermines the project's original nonlinear or narrative multiplicity.

In the opening chapter, "Discourse or Data? Theorizing the Electronic Edition of Antonio de León Pinelo's 1629 Bibliography of the Indies," Clayton McCarl explores conceptual and practical problems in electronic editions of early modern print bibliographies, with a focus on his own in-progress digital version of Antonio de León Pinelo's *Epítome de la biblioteca oriental i occidental,*

FIGURE I.2 "Bitterness is more Christmasy than any carol." Yuri Herrera, tweet, December 29, 2016.

nautica i geografica (1629), the first bibliography of the Americas. Conceived as an open-access, online resource, his project represents the first modern edition of the *Epítome*, usually consulted in rare book collections or facsimile. McCarl focuses on the dual nature of historical bibliographies as linear pieces of discourse (autobiographical, political, literary, etc.) and as nonlinear repositories of information. In doing so, he studies the complex relationship between bibliographies and "real" books, and considers the threat that the desire to normalize and correct may pose to the integrity of the text. He then addresses how these concerns have informed his approach to editing the *Epítome*. McCarl explains the TEI/XML-based encoding scheme developed to address the text's dual nature, and a prototype interface design that will allow the user to interact with the *Epítome* as discourse and a collection of bibliographical "facts." The chapter also considers how the encoding and interface highlight the *Epítome*'s precarious ties to bibliographical reality, a situation that León Pinelo laments. Far from undercutting the value of the *Epítome*, highlighting such fallibility underscores a central aspect of León Pinelo's project, a denunciation—articulated through bibliographic discourses—of the indifference of Spain's intellectual class to the complex realities of the overseas empire.

Continuing to imagine the digitization of text, Zac Zimmer's chapter, "Do Borges's Librarians Have Bodies?," examines how critics have read Argentine author Jorge Luis Borges's short story "The Library of Babel" as a prescient imagining of what we now call cyberspace. Zimmer notes, however, that little

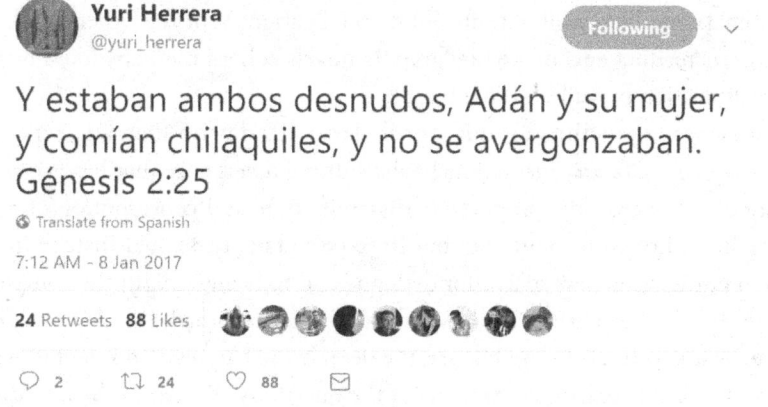

FIGURE I.3 "And they were both naked, Adam and his wife, and they ate *chilaquiles*, and they were not ashamed. Genesis 2:25." Yuri Herrera, tweet, January 8, 2017.

has been made of the Librarians who inhabit Borges's proto-data space. They very rarely appear, for instance, in the many and varied attempts to visualize the Library of Babel in digital media. From multimedia installations at Latin American book festivals to Jonathan Basile's libraryofbabel.info, it would seem that Borges's Librarians themselves are absolutely incorporeal. By tracing the material and digital texualities of a particularly viral topic of visualization, Zimmer's investigation follows Borges and critics who try to interpret his "Library of Babel" as an early cyberspace, as guides to navigating the impulse to transmute the entire human experience into information.

Taking up the theme of nonlinearity present in McCarl's and Zimmer's chapters, Edward King investigates this phenomenon in the ever more critically recognized graphic novel in his chapter, "Between Street and Book: Textual Assemblages and Urban Topologies in Graphic Fiction from Brazil." Its rise to popular and critical prominence in Latin America has coincided with the growing digitization of culture. The emphasis placed on materiality by the publication of increasingly elaborate long-form comic books in Brazil, Chile, and Mexico goes against the tendency toward dematerialization in contemporary culture, governed as it is by the logic of digital networks. However, the relationship between the contemporary Latin American graphic novel and digital culture is not simply that of an assertion of materiality in the face of its apparent erosion. Rather, the graphic novel form explores the new hybrid textualities emerging in digital media. On the one hand, graphic novels have reintroduced a plurality of image-word relations reduced and standardized by printing conventions. As a result, they function as a print corollary of the complex image-word combinations that proliferate in online publications. On the other hand, the nonlinear reading encouraged by graphic novels echoes the networked hypertextualities that prevail on the internet.

In bringing together a group of scholars with diverse thematic expertise, *Latin American Textualities* points to the cultural divergence that has existed in relation to the creation, production, dissemination, and consumption of texts. Our aim is not to recount the multifaceted details of textual history in the region but to open new spaces for dialogue and to bring to light the complexities of the Latin American historical condition to the broader academic field of textual studies. In exploring history, the deep textual archive, and digital manifestations of the text, we cover many of the questions relevant to the interdisciplinary aims of textual scholarship. It is our hope that this volume will provoke further interaction among scholars and students seeking to understand how

Latin American textualities form an integral part in comprehending culture and history in the Americas.

Notes

1. Our inclusive definition of "text" is similar to that of textual scholar D. F. McKenzie: "visual, oral, and numeric data, in the form of maps, prints, and music, of archives of recorded sound, of films, videos, and any computer-stored information, everything in fact from epigraphy to the latest forms of discography." McKenzie, *Bibliography and the Sociology of Texts*, 13.
2. For book-length studies on precolonial indigenous textualities of the Aztecs, Maya, and Inca, see Brokaw, *A History of the Khipu*; Hanks and Rice, *Word and Image in Maya Culture*; Hill Boone, *Stories in Red and Black*; Leibsohn, *Script and Glyph*; Marcus, *Mesoamerican Writing Systems*; and Salomon, *The Cord Keepers*. The study of colonial textualities is an important subfield within Latin American colonial literary research. On colonial manuscript production, see León-Portilla, *Tepuztlahcuilolli*; Magaloni, *The Colors of the New World*; and Mijares Ramírez, *Escribanos y escrituras públicas en el siglo XVI*. For book and print history during colonialism, see Hampe Martínez, *Bibliotecas privadas en el mundo colonial*; Johnson, *The Book in the Americas*; Lafaye, *Albores de la imprenta*; Leonard, *Books of the Brave*; Millares Carlo and Calvo, *Juan Pablos*; Peña Díaz, Ruiz Pérez, and Solana Pujalte, *La cultura del libro en la edad moderna*; Schons, *Book Censorship in New Spain*; Stols, *Antonio de Espinosa*; Thompson, *Printing in Colonial Spanish America*; Toribio Medina, *La imprenta en México (1539–1821)*; Torre Revello, *Orígenes de la imprenta en España y su desarrollo en América Española*; Torre Villar, *Breve historia del libro en México*; and Wroth, *Some Reflections on the Book Arts in Early Mexico*. The following works explore nineteenth-century textual cultures: Acree, *Everyday Reading*; Briggs, *The Moral Electricity of Print*; Masiello, *La mujer y el espacio público*; Prieto, *El discurso criollista en la formación de la Argentina moderna*; Rama, *The Lettered City*; Reynolds, *The Spanish American Crónica Modernista, Temporality, and Material Culture*; and Roldán Vera, *The British Book Trade and Spanish American Independence*. On twentieth-century and contemporary textualities, see Bilbija and Celis Carbajal, *Akademia Cartonera*; Bush and Gentic, *Technology, Literature, and Digital Culture in Latin America*; Epplin, *Late Book Culture in Argentina*; González, *Journalism and the Development of Spanish American Narrative*; Sarlo, *El imperio de los sentimientos*; and Wells, *Media Laboratories*.
3. There are a few scholarly groups based in English-speaking academia that focus on textual scholarship, including the Society of Textual Scholarship (STS), the Society for the History of Authorship, Reading and Publishing (SHARP), the Bibliographical Society of America, the Association for Documentary Editing (ADE), the American Printing History Association (APHA), and the Codex Foundation. These groups sponsor journals such as *Book History*, *Scholarly Editing*, and *Textual Cultures*. Each of these groups holds regular conferences and symposiums, and

although their missions are international in scope, there is a general lack of Latin American scholarship and perspectives on the field of textual studies within these organizations and their activities.

4. Other Europeans greatly admired indigenous writing systems. See Cañizares-Esguerra, *How to Write the History of the New World*, for an overview of the debate.

5. For an introduction to the interaction between European and indigenous writing systems in the early years of colonization, see Gruzinski, *La colonización de lo imaginario*; Hill Boone and Mignolo, *Writing Without Words*; and Mignolo, *The Darker Side of the Renaissance*.

6. For an introduction to European book history, see, among others, Chartier, *The Order of Books*; Eisenstein, *The Printing Revolution in Early Modern Europe*; and Febvre and Martin, *The Coming of the Book*.

7. Mignolo, "Introduction," 2.

8. Cornejo Polar, "El indigenismo y las literaturas heterogéneas," 12. All translations are ours unless otherwise indicated.

9. Cornejo Polar, "El indigenismo y las literaturas heterogéneas," 12.

10. Cornejo Polar, "El indigenismo y las literaturas heterogéneas," 12.

11. Cornejo Polar, "El indigenismo y las literaturas heterogéneas," 11.

12. Cornejo Polar, "El indigenismo y las literaturas heterogéneas," 13.

13. Beatriz Pastor makes a similar, if much simpler, observation in her discussion of Hernán Cortés's *Cartas de relación*, in which he resorts to fantastical language in an attempt to describe New World circumstances beyond the cosmovision of his intended European audience. Pastor, *The Armature of Conquest*, 98. Serge Gruzinski discusses Columbus's first encounters with Taino indians and the Spanish attempts to understand indigenous statues. Gruzinski calls them "puzzled observers" and argues that it was difficult for Columbus "to establish reference points outside of his own cultural background." Instead, the explorer was plagued with "perplexity and groping explanations." Gruzinski, *Images at War*, 7.

14. Horacio Legrás's entry "Text" in the *Dictionary of Latin American Cultural Studies* comments that Cornejo Polar's theory explains that in Latin America "we are faced with an equally variegated array of linguistic traditions, verbal formulas, and popular wisdom codified in songs, sayings, and proverbs. But this linguistic wealth is seldom integrated into a more general textuality, in part because they come from cultural (textual) spaces so heterogeneous that they cannot find a common ground even in such general notions as literature and culture. . . . Heterogeneity names this problem of the absence of a common ground that will allow different productions to meet in a common structure that is simultaneously able to respect the system of their differences." Legrás, "Text," 328–29.

15. Quoted in Agramonte, "Martí y el libro," 53.

16. Rodó, *Ariel*, 39.

17. Paz, *El laberinto de la soledad*, 144.

18. Cortázar, *Rayuela*, 111.

19. García Márquez, *Cien años de soledad*, 84. For an analysis of the archive, see González Echevarría, *Myth and Archive*, 23.
20. Romero, *Machado de Assis*, 142, quoted in Schwartz, "Brazilian Culture," 241.
21. "Libro de profesiones," 174. The book was in use at the convent between 1586 and 1713.
22. The document can be accessed at http://repositories.lib.utexas.edu/bitstream/handle/2152/16026/txu-oclc-34023032-01-05-r.pdf. The date of digitization is unknown.
23. Although these elements are omitted from the facsimile, this short description was added by the editor: "NOTA: La versión virtual de *El libro de professiones*, llevada a cabo por la Biblioteca Benson de la Universidad de Texas en Austin, incluye fotografías del material incorporado que es anterior al primer folio, como el exlibris de Dorothy Schons, información bibliotecaria del libro, una carta, todo lo que hace que el primer folio sea el número 6" (NOTE: The online version of *El libro de professiones*, completed by the Benson Library of the University of Texas in Austin, includes photographs of incorporated material before the first folio, such as the bookplate of Dorothy Schons, library information of the book, a letter, all of which makes the first folio page 6.) "Libro de profesiones," 70.
24. "Libro de profesiones," 59.
25. See Willmann, "Sor Juana's 'Book of Professions.'"
26. The description reads: "Sor Juana Inés de la Cruz (1651–1695) was one of [the] most illustrious Mexican writers and scholars of the colonial period. This page from the manuscript 'Book of Professions' of the convent of San Gerónimo in Mexico City, which Sor Juana entered in 1669, features a written affirmation of her religious vows, signed by the famous nun in her own blood. From the Dorothy Schons Papers at the Benson Latin American Collection."
27. Willmann is the communications director at the University of Texas Libraries.
28. There are also several social media links on the page that allow viewers to share the post on other electronic mediums. The tracking numbers next to each social media share link show that the post has had zero interactions across social media via the page's links as of May 2018.
29. González Echevarría, *Myth and Archive*, 11.

Works Cited

Acree, William. *Everyday Reading: Print Cultures and Collective Identity in the Río de la Plata*. Nashville, Tenn.: Vanderbilt University Press, 2011.

Agramonte, Roberto. "Martí y el libro." *Círculo: Publicación del Círculo de Cultura Panamericano* 15 (1986): 47–57.

Bilbija, Ksenija, and Paloma Celis Carbajal. *Akademia Cartonera: A Primer of Latin American Cartonera Publishers*. Madison: Parallel Press / University of Wisconsin Libraries, 2009.

Briggs, Ronald. *The Moral Electricity of Print: Education and the Lima Women's Circuit, 1876–1910*. Nashville, Tenn.: Vanderbilt University Press, 2017.

Brokaw, Galen. *A History of the Khipu*. Cambridge: Cambridge University Press, 2010.

Bush, Matthew, and Tania Gentic. *Technology, Literature, and Digital Culture in Latin America: Mediatized Sensibilities in a Globalized Era*. New York: Routledge, 2016.

Cañizares-Esguerra, Jorge. *How to Write the History of the New World*. Stanford, Calif.: Stanford University Press, 2001.

Chartier, Roger. *The Order of Books: Readers, Authors, and Libraries in Europe Between the Fourteenth and Eighteenth Centuries*. Translated by Lydia G. Cochrane. Stanford, Calif.: Stanford University Press, 1994.

Cornejo Polar, Antonio. "El indigenismo y las literaturas heterogéneas: Su doble estatuto socio-cultural." *Revista de Crítica Literaria Latinoamericana* 4, no. 7/8 (1978): 7–21.

Cortázar, Julio. *Rayuela*. Edited by Andrés Amorós. 1963. Reprint, Madrid: Cátedra, 2000.

Eisenstein, Elizabeth L. *The Printing Revolution in Early Modern Europe*. New York: Cambridge University Press, 2000.

Epplin, Craig. *Late Book Culture in Argentina*. New York: Bloomsbury, 2014.

Febvre, Lucien, and Henri-Jean Martin. *The Coming of the Book: The Impact of Printing, 1450–1800*. 3rd ed. London: Verso, 2010.

García Márquez, Gabriel. *Cien años de soledad*. Edited by Jacques Joset. 1967. Reprint, Madrid: Cátedra, 2002.

González, Aníbal. *Journalism and the Development of Spanish American Narrative*. Cambridge: Cambridge University Press, 1993.

González Echevarría, Roberto. *Myth and Archive: A Theory of Latin American Narrative*. Durham, N.C.: Duke University Press, 1998.

Gruzinski, Serge. *Images at War: Mexico from Columbus to* Blade Runner *(1492–2019)*. Translated by Heather MacLean. Durham, N.C.: Duke University Press, 2001.

———. *La colonización de lo imaginario*. Mexico City: Fondo de Cultura Económica, 2007.

Hampe Martínez, Teodoro. *Bibliotecas privadas en el mundo colonial: la difusión de libros e ideas en el virreinato del Perú (siglos XVI–XVII)*. Madrid: Iberoamericana, 1996.

Hanks, William F., and Don S. Rice, eds. *Word and Image in Maya Culture: Explorations in Language, Writing, and Representation*. Salt Lake City: University of Utah Press, 1989.

Hill Boone, Elizabeth. *Stories in Red and Black: Pictorial Histories of the Aztecs and Mixtecs*. Austin: University of Texas Press, 2008.

Hill Boone, Elizabeth, and Walter Mignolo, eds. *Writing Without Words: Alternative Literacies in Mesoamerica and the Andes*. Durham, N.C.: Duke University Press, 1994.

Johnson, Julie Greer. *The Book in the Americas: The Role of Books and Printing in the Development of Culture and Society in Colonial Latin America*. Providence: John Carter Brown Library, 1988.

Lafaye, Jacques. *Albores de la imprenta: El libro en España y Portugal y sus posesiones de ultramar (siglos XV y XVI)*. Mexico City: Fondo de Cultura Económica, 2002.

Legrás, Horacio. "Text." In *Dictionary of Latin American Cultural Studies*, edited by Robert McKee Irwin and Mónica Szurmuk, 321–30. Gainesville: University Press of Florida, 2012.

Leibsohn, Dana. *Script and Glyph: Pre-Hispanic History, Colonial Bookmaking and the Historia Tolteca-Chichimeca*. Washington, D.C.: Dumbarton Oaks, 2009.

Leonard, Irving A. *Books of the Brave*. Edited by Rolena Adorno. Berkeley: University of California Press, 1992.

León-Portilla, Ascensión H. de. *Tepuztlahcuilolli: Impresos en Nahuatl: Historia y bibliografía*. 2 vols. Mexico City: Universidad Nacional Autónoma de México, 1988.

"Libro de profesiones y elecciones de prioras y vicarias del convento de San Gerónimo." Dorothy Schons Papers, Benson Latin American Collection, University of Texas Libraries, University of Texas at Austin, 1586–1713.

Magaloni, Diana Kerpel. *The Colors of the New World: Artists, Materials, and the Creation of the Florentine Codex*. Los Angeles: Getty Research Institute, 2014.

Marcus, Joyce. *Mesoamerican Writing Systems: Propaganda, Myth and History in Four Ancient Civilizations*. Princeton, N.J.: Princeton University Press, 1992.

Masiello, Francine. *La mujer y el espacio público: El periodismo femenino en la Argentina del siglo XIX*. Buenos Aires: Feminaria Editora, 1994.

McKenzie, D. F. *Bibliography and the Sociology of Texts*. Cambridge: Cambridge University Press, 1999.

Mignolo, Walter. *The Darker Side of the Renaissance*. Ann Arbor: University of Michigan Press, 2003.

———. "Introduction: Coloniality of Power and De-Colonial Thinking." In *Globalization and the Decolonial Option*, edited by Arturo Escobar and Walter Mignolo, 1–22. New York: Routledge, 2010.

Mijares Ramírez, Ivonne. *Escribanos y escrituras públicas en el siglo XVI: El caso de la ciudad de México*. Mexico City: Universidad Nacional Autónoma de México, 1997.

Millares Carlo, Agustín, and Julián Calvo. *Juan Pablos: Primer impresor que a esta tierra vino*. Mexico City: Porrúa, 1954.

Pastor, Beatriz. *The Armature of Conquest: Spanish Accounts of the Discovery of America, 1492–1589*. Translated by Lydia Longstreth Hunt. Stanford, Calif.: Stanford University Press, 1992.

Paz, Octavio. *El laberinto de la soledad*. Edited by Enrico Mario Santí. Madrid: Cátedra, 2002.

Peña Díaz, Manuel, Pedro Ruiz Pérez, and Julián Solana Pujalte, eds. *La cultura del libro en la edad moderna: Andalucía y América*. Córdoba: Universidad de Córdoba Servicio de Publicaciones, 2001.

Prieto, Adolfo. *El discurso criollista en la formación de la Argentina moderna*. Buenos Aires: Editorial Sudamericana, 1988.

Rama, Ángel. *The Lettered City*. Translated by John Chasteen. Durham, N.C.: Duke University Press, 1996.

Reynolds, Andrew. *The Spanish American Crónica Modernista, Temporality, and Material Culture: Modernismo's Unstoppable Presses*. Lewisburg, Penn.: Bucknell University Press, 2012.

Rodó, José Enrique. *Ariel*. Madrid: Espasa Calpe, 1991.
Roldán Vera, Eugenia. *The British Book Trade and Spanish American Independence: Education and Knowledge Transmission in Transcontinental Perspective*. Hampshire, England: Ashgate, 2003.
Romero, Silvio. *Machado de Assis: Estudo comparativo de literatura brasileira*. Rio de Janeiro: Laemmert & C. Editores, 1897.
Saloman, Frank. *The Cord Keepers: Khipus and Cultural Life in a Peruvian Village*. Durham, N.C.: Duke University Press, 2008.
Sarlo, Beatriz. *El imperio de los sentimientos: Narraciones de circulación periódica en la Argentina, 1917–1927*. Buenos Aires: Grupo Editorial Normal, 2000.
Schons, Dorothy. *Book Censorship in New Spain*. Austin: University of Texas Press, 1949.
Schwartz, Roberto. "Brazilian Culture: Nationalism by Elimination." In *Latin American Cultural Studies Reader*, edited by Ana del Sarto, Alicia Ríos, and Abril Trigo, 233–49. Durham, N.C.: Duke University Press, 2004.
Stols, Alexandre A. M. *Antonio de Espinosa: El segundo impresor mexicano*. Mexico City: Biblioteca Nacional, 1962.
Thompson, Lawrence S. *Printing in Colonial Spanish America*. Hamden, Conn.: Shoestring Press, 1962.
Toribio Medina, José. *La imprenta en México (1539–1821)*. Santiago: Impreso en casa del autor, 1908.
Torre Revello, José. *Orígenes de la imprenta en España y su desarrollo en América Española*. Buenos Aires: Institución Cultural Española, 1940.
Torre Villar, Ernesto de la. *Breve historia del libro en México*. Mexico City: Universidad Nacional Autónoma de México, 1990.
Wells, Sarah Ann. *Media Laboratories: Latin Modernist Authorship in South America*. Evanston, Ill.: Northwestern University Press, 2017.
Willmann, Travis. "Sor Juana's 'Book of Professions.'" *Tex Libris* (blog), December 19, 2014. http://blogs.lib.utexas.edu/texlibris/2014/12/19/sor-juanas-book-of-professions/.
Wroth, Lawrence C. *Some Reflections on the Book Arts in Early Mexico*. Cambridge: Department of Printing and Graphic Arts, 1945.

PART I

Reading History Through Textuality

1

Writing Orality

Turning Quechua into a Language of Religious Conversion

CATALINA ANDRANGO-WALKER

In what sort of mind does it occur that innumerable people forget the language of their homeland and only speak in a strange, foreign tongue, and that they only rarely hear it and with great annoyance? When they are in their own homes dealing with things in their native language, who will surprise them? Who will denounce them? How will we obligate them to speak in Spanish?

—JOSÉ DE ACOSTA, *DE PROCURANDA INDORUM SALUTE*

WHEN FATHER JOSÉ DE ACOSTA urged parish priests in the New World to learn the languages of the native populations, he was referring to the extensive debates regarding linguistic barriers and the most appropriate manner to achieve an effective Christianization in the Andean region, which had begun in the first few decades after the arrival of the Spanish. These preoccupations are reflected in the appearance of instructional materials such as *cartillas*, *silabarios*, and other devotional texts translated into Quechua by the same evangelizers or other lettered men who learned Quechua and other native languages after they had arrived in Peru. In this chapter, I present an overview of the importance of the Quechua language to the success of the evangelization project. Then I study how, by using European conceptions of alphabetic letters as well as classical grammatical and rhetorical theory, Spanish missionaries coopted this language to use it as a vehicle of evangelization. I present two cases, that of Fray Domingo de Santo Tomás's *Grammática, o, Arte de la lengua general de los indios de los reynos del Peru* (1560) and Diego González Holguín's *Gramática y arte nueva de la lengua general de todo el Perú, llamada quichua* (1607), in order to show that both grammar books go beyond a mere exegesis of the language. In fact, the authors provide another way to approach

Andean culture by demonstrating the sophistication of Quechua and in so doing demonstrate the refinement of its native speakers. By accounting for the methods by which these authors understand, classify, and conceptualize the linguistic and cultural conventions of Quechua and also taking into consideration the limitations they encounter in conveying Christianity to Andean inhabitants, I propose that these texts can be regarded as artifacts that not only helped to diminish the linguistic barrier between European and native cultures but also served as instruments of colonization and meaningful indicators of Andean political and social change.

From the Language of Incan Power to the Language of Conversion

Realizing the necessity for indoctrinating priests to be able to communicate in the same language as their converts, in 1551 Archbishop Jéronimo de Loayza instituted a chair of Quechua in Lima's Cathedral. Years later, Viceroy Francisco de Toledo followed in Loayza's footsteps by establishing Quechua as a field of study in 1579 at the University of San Marcos.[1] In addition, Toledo created an ordinance that required students to pass a proficiency test in Quechua in order to earn a university degree or a priestly ordination. The development of these programs was possible in part thanks to the few existing printed materials on the language, particularly the works of the Dominican friar Domingo de Santo Tomás, such as his *Grammática, o, Arte de la lengua general de los indios de los reynos del Perú* and *Lexicón, o Vocabulario de la lengua general del Perú*, both published in Valladolid in 1560. These two books not only constituted the first printed pedagogies for teaching the language but also represent the earliest attempts to establish the norms for the Quechua language that are still extant today.

Although in some chronicles and other documents it is possible to find references to even older texts than those of Friar Domingo, these materials have yet to be located. For example, in the dedicatory letter to Viceroy Antonio de Mendoza in *Suma y narración de los incas* (*Narrative of the Incas*, 1557), its author, Juan de Betanzos, declares that prior to this work he has spent six years of his youth "[translating] and compil[ing] a book named Christian Doctrine, which covers Christian Doctrine and two vocabularies, one of words and the other of notions, whole prayers, conversations and confessionals."[2] At the same time, while speaking about the efforts of the evangelizers during their first decades in the Andean region, the Jesuita anónimo (the Anonymous Jesuit) observes that "although they arrived later, good workers were not missing among the Augustinians, particularly one, who not only worked, but also wrote in the language so that the newcomers could take advantage."[3] These notices point to the existence of even earlier translations of evangelizing documents, but we know about them only because of the above-mentioned testimonies.

The Third Council of Lima, which took place between 1582 and 1583, had a significant and decisive impact on the unification of catechization materials and especially in establishing the languages of evangelization. The council authorities published three works, *Doctrina christiana, y catecismo para instrucción de los indios* (1584), *Confessionario para los curas de indios* (1585), and *Tercero catecismo y exposición de la doctrina christiana, por sermones* (1585). These were printed in Spanish as well as Quechua and Aymara.[4] With these texts, the authorities of the council hoped that "the Indians would find consistency in all of them, and would not think that it was a different law, and a Gospel different from what some people would teach them."[5] Father José de Acosta supervised the impression of these books in the print shop that Italian Antonio Ricardo set up in the Jesuit convent, which, as Porras Borrenechea has pointed out, was transformed into "an academy of native languages."[6] The convent assembled the finest speakers of Quechua and Aymara for the translation of the texts, including *criollos*, *mestizos*, and Spaniards who were already familiar with native languages. From then on these books exercised a great deal of influence on the construction of Andean spirituality. Moreover, the canonical pastoral works of the Third Council continued to be instrumental for a long time; for instance, the *Confessionario* and *Tercero catecismo* remained in use until the nineteenth century.[7] The translations of the Christian prayers are still used even today.[8] Furthermore, in 1586 Ricardo's print shop produced *Arte y vocabulario en la lengua general del Peru llamada quichua, y en la lengua española*. Its anonymous author indicates that his work aims to complement the Third Council corpus, and in his dedication to the reader, he states, "It would take a lot of work . . . for he who wished to learn a foreign language (if every word were to be available, including those that were necessary in order to speak it) would have to go and ask about them several times, and of different people, because not only would it take a lot of time, but it would be an annoying and difficult job."[9] In this way, *Arte y vocabulario* reiterates once again the pressing necessity to unify the language through the norms that facilitate its learning.

Quechua and Aymara were selected to transmit the evangelizing teachings because they were spoken in the most influential political and economic centers of the Viceroyalty of Peru, as explained in the books themselves. So, for example, in "Anotaciones o scolios sobre la traducción," included in *Doctrina christiana*, the council authorities praised Quechua, the administrative language of the Incas, by referring especially to the "vocablos exquisitos" used in Cuzco.[10] A similar elegance of language was only comparable to the Aymara spoken in the area around Potosí, which was the most important mining center of the colonial period.[11] In "Anotaciones," the parameters for the translation that the authorities adopted are also explained in order for these two languages to be effective instruments of persuasion and religious conversion. This is different from the approach that was taken in Mesoamerica, in which, as Louise Burkhart explains, in order to translate the gospels into Nahuatl, "friars elicited and recorded native oratory, listed the figures of speech and adages contained therein and strove to master the elegant speaking style of the native orators."[12] In contrast, the dialectical richness and diversity of the Quechua and Aymara languages became an impediment that had to be overcome by standardizing not only their grammar but also their pronunciation and vocabularies.

In order to achieve this objective, the council authorities placed an emphasis on the search for an equilibrium between "the crude and corrupt manner of speaking that exists in some provinces: and the excessive curiosity, with which some in Cuzco, and in its surroundings use such exquisite and obscure words and manners of speech that go beyond the limits of the language, which is appropriately called Quichua."[13] The problem caused by "the great variety of words," which the council authorities qualified as "imperfection or barbarity," led to a search for uniformity by establishing "a common language, easy and proper, observing in its translation, the rule to interpret meaning for meaning, rather than word for word."[14] Something rather similar is specified for Aymara, although the emphasis is more on Quechua. Frank Salomon, while commenting on the translation methods adopted during the 1580s, confirms that "the infiltration of Quechua in the Andean region from Colombia to Bolivia and Argentina was in large part the result of efforts to simplify the communicative map by promoting the substitution of Quechua for various 'particular languages' (today generally extinct, but hardly documented)."[15] Indeed, the hierarchical structuring of these languages and their unification, to the detriment of their variants and—more than anything else—the other multiple languages spoken not only in the areas close to centers of power but also those further away, allowed the integration of a larger number of Andean inhabitants. At the same time, in order to facilitate the work of evangelization, the adoption of a more unified language eliminated the multiplicity of dialects at the expense of reflecting the cultural heterogeneity of the inhabitants of the region.

With the publication of the Third Council evangelization corpus, there began a period of greater dissemination of native languages among foreign missionaries, such that during the following decades, books on grammar and vocabulary, catechism manuals, and other religious texts in Quechua and Aymara began to appear, and—although to a much lesser extent—Catholic doctrine was also translated into other languages, such as Pukina, Mochica, and Guaraní. For example, *Symbolo catholico indiano*, by the Franciscan Luis Jerónimo de Oré (Huamanga, 1554–Concepción, 1630), was published in Lima in 1598; in this work, the author translates the Symbols of Faith, which until that time had been attributed to Saint Athanasius, into Quechua. Nine years later, Oré published *Rituale seu manuale Peruanum* in Naples. *Rituale* contains Biblical teachings not only in Quechua and Aymara but also in Pukina, Guaraní, Mochica, and Brasilica. The Franciscan author brought together important figures from diverse religious orders who dominated the language of each region, to include translations to administer the sacred sacraments in the different indigenous languages.[16]

Although the Dominicans and the Franciscans played an important role in the diffusion of native languages during the first few decades after the arrival of the Spaniards to the Andean region, it was the late-arriving Jesuits who distinguished themselves during the period of the council and in subsequent years. In the first decade of the seventeenth century, the results of these efforts can be seen reflected in the works of three members of that religious order: *Arte y grammatica muy copiosa de la lengua aymara* (1603) and *Arte breve de la lengua aymara* (1603) by Ludovico Bertonio; *Gramática y vocabulario de la lengua quichua, aymara y española* (1603) by Diego de Torres Rubio; and *Gramática y arte nueva de la lengua general de todo el Perú, llamada lengua quichua* (1607) and *Vocabulario de la lengua general de todo el Perú llamada lengua qquichua o del Inca* (1608) by Diego González Holguín. Of the three authors, only González Holguín published both works in Peru with Francisco del Canto's press.

Along with foundational works by Friar Domingo de Santo Tomás, the work of these three Jesuits contributed to the creation of a basis for standardized writing in the Quechua language. Moreover, beginning with the council texts they also played a central role in the establishment of norms for writing Aymara by following and at times adapting the rules of Latin and Spanish grammar.[17]

These three intellectuals developed their work in very similar circumstances: Spaniard González Holguín (Extermadura, 1560–Lima, ca. 1620) and Italian Bertonio (Rocca Contrada, 1552–Lima, 1625) arrived in the same vessel to Callao in 1581, almost at the same time that Torres Rubio (Alcázar de San Juan, 1547–Chuquisaca, 1638) landed in Peru. The three later coincided in the Juli mission, in the area around Lake Titicaca, where the Jesuits had established themselves in order to expand their missionary activity among the natives of Lupaca. Two decades after their arrival in Peru, each one became distinguished for their works on Quechua and, in the case of Bertonio, his work on Ayamara, languages that they had by then mastered.[18]

European Models to Establish the Rules of Grammar in Quechua

As it has already been explained by experts in the field of missionary linguistics, the efforts to create norms for indigenous languages did not occur inside a "linguistic vacuum." On the contrary, these authors based their texts on works of a theoretical character similar to those that would establish the rules for a standardization of Spanish, which began to appear in Spain near the end of the fifteenth century.[19] This allowed these religious scholars "to match the linguistic phenomena of the Amerindian languages with existing models or, in place of these, the development of new models."[20] At the same time, the use of these models allowed these intellectuals to establish once and for all the fact that Quechua "was a civilized language, not some conglomerate of barbarous communications incapable of giving linguistic shape to anything beyond what was accessible to the five senses."[21] Due to this effort, it became a language deemed worthy and appropriate for the transmission of divine knowledge to the natives.

From the end of the fifteenth century, the works of Antonio de Nebrija—*Introducciones latinas* (1481), *Gramática castellana* (1492), and *Diccionario latino-español* (1492), and their subsequent re-editions and adaptations during the centuries following their first appearance—enjoyed a widespread popularity in Spain. In addition, these works "provided the framework within which some seventy years later, the missionary friar Domingo de Santo Tomás . . . organized his Quechua grammar and lexicon."[22] Indeed, Friar Domingo, in his "Prologue to the Reader," paraphrases the words of Nebrija, who "says in the prologue of his work about the Latin language, that he has corrected it three times. . . . And so it is that I in such a way in the present bring this Artezillo to light: that he opens the door, not only for me, but also for those who understand the language better than me."²³ Furthermore, the friar addresses Philip II in the prologue and provides more indications that he will follow Spanish grammar rules, mentioning that Quechua can follow the precepts of Latin and Castilian, because this Andean

> language has an abundance of words, the convenience that they have with the things that they signify, the diverse manners and curious expressions, the soft and attractive sound on the ear at the pronunciation of them, the facility with which to write in our characters and letters: As easy and sweet is the pronunciation of our language, because it is ordered and adorned with the attributes of the noun, moods, tenses and persons of the verb. And briefly in many things and parts of speech, so in agreement with Latin and Spanish: and in its art and artifice, that it only seemed a prognostication, that the Spanish would have to possess it. A language, Your Majesty, so polished and abundant, regulated and enclosed beneath the rules and precepts of Latin such as this (as can be seen in this *Art*) is not barbarous, that is to say (according to Quintilliano, and other Latins) full of barbarisms and defects, without moods, tenses or cases, or order, rule, or concert, rather it is polished and delicate [to the ear] one can say.²⁴

In addition to highlighting the importance of this work as a contribution toward the process of evangelization, Friar Domingo presents the development of native inhabitants' polished language as evidence of their intellectual capabilities. He argues that their language could be regulated according to the same precepts as Latin.²⁵ In this way, the author associates the civility of the Andeans with the order and richness of their language that prior to the arrival of the Spaniards was also the language of an empire in expansion.²⁶

Nebrija's impact on Friar Domingo's work comes into view more clearly in the way he structures his grammar. The author assures the reader that "in this language as in Latin and others, there are eight parts of the sentence or of speech . . . because as it is said this *Arte* is principally made and ordered for ecclesiastical persons who have already mastered Latin." Additionally, he states that "it is understood that based on Antonio de Nebrija's grammar book and the grammar of the Latin language, they already know the definition and declaration of every one of the aforementioned eight parts."²⁷ Following these principles, Friar Domingo discusses in detail each part of speech in twenty-five chapters.²⁸ Explaining every part again provides the author with more opportunities not only to familiarize European audiences with Andean culture but also to show the level of organization and civility of the inhabitants of that region. For instance, while describing patronymic nouns, he states that

> just as the Latin and Spanish languages have names known as patronymics that are derived from parents, grandparents or brothers and passed on to sons and descendants, or else these names are derived from the lands where they live; such as Scipiones from Scipio, Catones from Cato, Romans from Rome; Mendozas, Guzmanes, Andalucians, etc. In the same way in this language of the Indians there are many patronymic nouns of all these kinds. For if a lord is famous for something, his children take his name, and not only the children, but all the descendants, from where they derive the lineages that are known as *ayllo* and *pachaca*.²⁹

The parallel that the author establishes with Latin and Spanish has as its objective a demonstration of the high degree of native rationality. Thus, in this case, with the reference to the *ayllo* (*ayllu*) and the *pachaca*, Friar Domingo shows the organization that the Incas implemented in the administration of their empire.³⁰

In this manner, the author provides the rules for the language, but at the same time, he tries to educate the European reader of his *Grammática* on the most relevant aspects of the Incan culture, such as the origin of the Incas. Friar Domingo expands on his understanding of patronymic nouns, pointing out that "everyone that descends from the first lord called Manco Capac calls himself Yngas, and this lineage contains other particular names and linages, the chief of which is called *capac ayllo*. . . . In Cuzco there are also two other principal linages, one called *Maras toco*, and the other called *Xutic ayllo*."³¹ The author then concludes that "the Indians of Cuzco believed that they both emerged from the two caves that are in the town of Pacaritambo from where they say the said Manco ynga emerged," referring in this way to the origin myths of the beginning and divine nature of the Incas.³² The friar also goes on to detail the political organization of the empire before the arrival of the Spaniards, naming the different provinces in which it was divided. As Sabine MacCormack points out, the author "demonstrated that political order, *policia*, was as rooted in the Andes as it was in the Old World."³³ Moreover, showing the high degree of organization of the Incas and their intellectual capacity allowed Friar Domingo to defend the natives from the Spaniards who considered them culturally inferior.

Although in *Grammática* Friar Domingo tries to explain every aspect of the language, at the same time, he recognizes the limits of Quechua to translate Christian concepts and the difficulty of imposing the precepts of a faith completely different from the natives' own religious beliefs. This becomes obvious at the end of his book, at which point the author presents a "Plática para todos los indios" (Sermon for all the Indians). The sermon, written in Spanish with a Quechua translation, aims to briefly explain the nature of the Christian God. As Juan Carlos Estenssoro has noted, this sermon "is the oldest extant text in Quechua and is the first example of a sermon written in Peru."[34] Besides its historical value, the sermon accounts for the way in which Friar Domingo understood the Andean culture and the adaptations he had to make to reach Andean audiences.

In the sermon, Friar Domingo does not begin with the creation of the world—in which the Christian listener is already familiar with the concept of God as a supreme and omnipotent being. Rather, he begins by explaining man's superiority with respect to animals. The establishment of this hierarchical order allows the friar to explain that when man dies, "only his body dies. But our soul and spirit . . . never die."[35] Continuing on the concept of life after death, he explains the difference between heaven and hell, placing the first as an ideal toward which to reach, the place where the soul is joined with God. The author uses native deities in order to explain that the Christian God created the sun, moon, stars, angels, the devil, man, and woman. He also makes clear that God created not only the Spanish people but also the Andeans and every other inhabitant on the earth.[36] It is important to note the inclusive manner Friar Domingo uses to describe creation and make the natives a part of it. He concludes his sermon by defining good and evil, and assuring the new converts that devils are the ones who "every day advise us to sin. . . . They put bad thoughts in your hearts, they tell you, Adore the sun, the moon, the rocks and idols."[37] Following Friar Domingo's defense of Quechua, this sermon demonstrates the capacity of this language to explain divine precepts to the natives, starting with elements that are familiar to them. In this way, the author introduces cultural concepts that are outside their culture and imagination.[38] At the same time, as MacCormack explains, the sermon also highlights "the limitations of translation," which oblige Friar Domingo to reorder "the story of salvation in light of what an anticipated Andean listener might most easily identify with."[39] Accordingly, the author translates concepts such as sin, heaven, hell, good, and evil into an Andean context.[40] As Regina Harrison points out, "The 1560 dictionary of

Santo Tomás contains 150 blank spaces where no Quechua word that represented the meaning of the Spanish vocabulary item was found."[41] In addition to Christian concepts, most unavailable translations are related to words for food, metals, commerce, governance, rituals, and philosophical essences.[42]

The grammar books of later decades take into account these limitations of translation, and, in spite of continued evidence of Nebrija's influence, his texts were no longer as central as in the work of Friar Domingo. For example, neither the anonymous author of the 1586 grammar book nor González Holguín mentions Nebrija.[43] González Holguín's work also conveys the new direction of Quechua grammar. For instance, the "natural order" that Nebrija makes compulsory in his grammar book, which consists of going in ascending order from the letter to the sentence, is not valid for the Jesuit priest, "because this structure is adequate to explain a known and spoken language."[44] The advances in the study of linguistics in the sixteenth century, such as those suggested in Francisco Sánchez de las Brozas's (el Brocense) *Minerva sive de causis linguae latinae* (1587) and *Mercurius maior sive grammaticae institutiones* (1546) by Italian Augustinus Saturninus, placed "the sentence, *oratio*, [as] the basic unit of grammatical analysis, rather than beginning, as Nebrija had done, with sounds, letters, and parts of the speech."[45] These developments are also reflected in González Holguín's *Gramática*. In this way, in the form of a dialogue between a student who asks questions to his professor, from its beginning the author in *Gramática* teaches the learner how to form clauses and later full sentences by avoiding studying the parts of speech in an isolated manner.

Unlike Friar Domingo, González Holguín's conception of Quechua grammar no longer depends on Latin, although frequently he makes comparisons to help the student understand concepts that are already familiar to him. For example, when he talks about adjectival moods, he tells his student that "because all of the genitives in this language are like Hebrew, and the names of material out of which are made artificial objects such as *qullqui aquilla*, a silver cup, turn into adjectives, as in Latin."[46] Throughout his book, the author insists on deviating from the rules of Latin to establish the norms for Quechua and to maintain its purity. Furthermore, González Holguín differs with Friar Domingo in several aspects; for instance, the author explains in great detail the ayllu system, pointing out that "*ayllo* is the relatives' common name. *Aylloy* means my relative, or *ayllo maciy, ayllocuna*, or *ayllo pura*, which means the ones related to each other, or *ayllomaciycuna*, or *maciypura, cispantin ayllo*, to designate close relatives, or *khaylla ayllo pura*."[47] To this list, the Jesuit author adds at least nine more designations to name blood relatives. The extensive detail about the ayllu, which most authors including Friar Domingo treat only superficially, shows the complexity of the Quechua language.⁴⁸ Since these structures do not follow the pattern of Latin grammar, González Holguín begins his exposition by stating the necessity to understand them on their own, pointing out as well his great effort to include all the distinctions about such complicated material.⁴⁹

The explanation about the organizational system of the Incas and the complexity of kinship relationships, such as blood relatives, as well as in-law relatives, spiritual relatives, and so on, is only the preamble to talk about patronymic nouns. Unlike Friar Domingo, González Holguín contends that there are no such nouns in Quechua since

> we cannot say that family names or nicknames, whether of an entire linage, such as (*Incaroca*), or of groups such as (*Hanan Cuzco, Hurin Cuzco*), or of the provinces, like (*Cuntinsuyo, Collasuyo*), or ancient nicknames like (*Quispipuma Huaman*) are patronyms. For these names do not follow the rule that is given in the grammar books, that they must be terms derived by means of some addition or extension from other kinship terms, using a particle for this purpose, such as the Latin particle (*des*) in (*Aeneas, Aeneades*) to designate to those of the lineage of Aeneas. Neither are constructed with an adjectival noun derived from a proper name, such as (*Saturnia proles*, descendants of Saturn). In Quechua we do not find any correspondence with this, but there are names and surnames. Also, patronymic nouns are not indispensable, since they are not common to other languages other than in Latin and Greek.⁵⁰

In this manner, González Holguín looks for original ways to explain the complexities of the Andean system of kinship, at the same time making evident that not everything fits the patterns of the Latin or Spanish languages but realizing that Quechua linguists have to look for ways to explain an original reality, independent of the Western tradition.

Accordingly, in the fourth part of his *Gramática*, a section that is designed to teach the elegance of the language, González Holguín provides sentence-forming and word-order rules. He indicates that the first rule is to "flee from the mode of speaking Spanish, because it disposes the sentence and its parts opposite of this language. Example: I'm going to the church to hear the sermon of the Holy Sacrament, the Indians begin at the point where the romance ends, and end where it begins [as they would say] of the Holy Sacrament the sermon to go the church I am."⁵¹ By including a series of examples of this type, the author illustrates the differences in structure of the two languages, thus educating the student of Quechua in the art of composition. But at the same time, he warns that another second law is to avoid the manner of speech of the *indios ladinos*. The main reason for this has to do with the fact that in order to show that they know how to speak Castilian, the ladinos have abandoned the pure manner of their own language and mix it with Spanish. The Jesuit priest observes that "they made many mistakes that they do not speak well their language, nor imitate well Spanish."⁵² González Holguín demonstrates how the language would suffer from these processes of change due to the political circumstances of its speakers. Overall, the author depicts the anxiety of the natives to integrate into a new system by adopting the language of the conquerors. The infiltration of Spanish into Quechua adds to the problems that regional variants of the language already presented for the cultivators of Quechua.

In spite of their careful emphasis on the linguistic aspects of the languages, the work of both Friar Domingo and González Holguín is characterized by the way in which they reflect a process of change in the Andean region. In the case of the contamination of the language that bothered González Holguín, Friar Domingo also points out the changes in Andean society, which are a product of the natives' exposure to Spanish culture. Upon indicating the complexity of "translating some words that the natives use, which are impossible to explain correctly, or express in the vocabulary of this language," he refers to the terminology the natives used to take an oath, which was different from those used by the Christians.⁵³ According to Friar Domingo, the natives did not know how to swear by God or by heaven, and he considered the natives' oaths to be "of a curse and that they weren't swearing to God, or by God, or by the sun, or the moon, rather . . . if I lie may the earth eat me (*ñoca llullapti, pachamicuancmancha*). They would more briefly say oaths such as these (*yndipas, quillapas, pachapas, micuancmancha*), which is to say, may the sun kill me, may the moon drown me, may the earth swallow me but it's true what I am saying."⁵⁴ Later, the author recounts with satisfaction that since the arrival of the Christians, this is changing because the natives had adopted their manner of taking an oath. However, to his sorrow, the natives had also taken up several of the Spaniards' bad habits. Friar Domingo recounts an anecdote about his meeting with a native chief; when he asked if he was already a Christian, the chief explained: "Although I am not completely one, but I am already beginning to be, he told me, I know how to swear to God, and play cards a little bit, and I'm beginning to steal."⁵⁵ The friar immediately laments the manner in which the natives had begun copying Christian modalities, believing "that being a Christian was nothing more than what they commonly witnessed Christians doing."[56] In this manner, the author accounts not only for the attempts of religious transformation but also for the changes that were already discernible in Peruvian society due to the adoption of foreign customs and habits.

In spite of their differences in approach, both authors write about the Andes while in the Andes and in doing so they use their own experience to textualize an oral language and culture. Therefore, their grammars invite the contemporary reader toward an approach that is more than linguistic in nature. Friar Domingo shows his experience as a missionary; in fact, the defense of native rationality in the dedication to King Philip II is part of a much more extensive debate. It is necessary to place this passage among his constant complaints about the abuses of the Spaniards, who in their conquest depopulated the Andes.[57] González Holguín, instead, forms part of a much more elaborate machinery established by the Jesuits. Moreover, the journey previously undertaken by lettered men, who complained for having to write about a culture without letters, and the Third Council of Lima shaped his work. This fact helped him not only to translate orality but also to give a more accurate depiction of the complexities of Andean people. Furthermore, these authors learned that the largest inconvenience to translate biblical knowledge to Quechua resided in cultural differences, particularly the Spaniard's lack of experience to understand a culture different from those of the Mediterranean, with which they had had to grapple until then.[58] However, beyond this, both authors point out the social changes that came about as a result of the natives' necessity to adapt to a new hegemonic order. Consequently, the grammar books go beyond their purpose of being tools for religious conversion, thereby allowing a reading of Andean history through the same textual production of the Quechua language.

Notes

I would like to thank Heather Allen and Andrew Reynolds for their careful reading and thoughtful comments. Also, many thanks to John Walker, Elisabeth Austin, and Anna Pope for helping me edit this article. All translations are mine unless otherwise indicated.

1. Rodolfo Cerrón-Palomino, *Castellano andino*, 143, provides more details about the establishment of the chairs of Quechua. For more information about Arzobispo Loayza, see Castro Pineda, *La cátedra de lengua quechua en la catedral de Lima*.

2. Betanzos, *Narratives of the Incas*, 3.
3. Anonymous Jesuit, *Relación de las costumbres antiguas*, 185.
4. For more information about the Third Council, see Lisi, *El tercer concilio limense*.
5. Catholic Church and Acosta, *Doctrina christiana*, n.p. The "Epístola del concilio" is located at the beginning of *Doctrina christiana*.
6. Porras Barrenechea, introduction to González Holguín, *Vocabulario de la lengua general*, vii. Guibovich Pérez, "The Printing Press in Colonial Peru," 168, summarizes Jesuit efforts to establish a print shop in Lima; as a result, in 1581 Italian printer Antonio Ricardo arrived in that city. However, the first texts from this press, that is, the ones ordered by the Third Council of Lima, began to appear only three years later when, finally, Ricardo obtained permission for the print shop to begin operation.
7. Estenssoro, *Del paganismo a la santidad*, 248.
8. Durston, *Pastoral Quechua*, 104. For more detailed information about Ricardo's role as a printer in Peru and especially about his responsibilities as the printer of the Third Council corpus, see Medina, *La imprenta en Lima*, 1:4–29. See also Guibovich Pérez, "The Printing Press in Colonial Peru," which offers more details regarding Ricardo's collaboration with the Third Council.
9. Anon., *Arte y vocabulario*, n.p.
10. Catholic Church and Acosta, *Doctrina christiana*, 74.
11. Catholic Church and Acosta, *Doctrina christiana*, 78.
12. Burkhart, *The Slippery Earth*, 12.
13. Catholic Church and Acosta, *Doctrina christiana*, 74.
14. Catholic Church and Acosta, *Doctrina christiana*, 74.
15. Salomon, "La textualización de la memoria," 231.
16. For an extensive study of Oré's life, see Cook, "Luis Jerónimo de Oré," his introduction to *Relación de la vida y milagros*, and his article "Viviendo en las márgenes del imperio." See also my book, *El símbolo católico indiano (1598) de Luis Jerónimo de Oré*.
17. Hamerly, *Artes, Vocabularios*, 53.
18. For more detailed information about these three Jesuit linguists, see Porras Barrenechea's introduction to *Vocabulario de la lengua general de todo el Perú llamada lengua quichua o del Inca*, 15–18.
19. Dedenbach-Salazar Sáenz, "La descripción gramatical," 294; Segovia Gordillo, "La gramática y arte nueva," 91–92.
20. Dedenbach-Salazar Sáenz, "La descripción gramatical," 295.
21. MacCormack, *On the Wings of Time*, 177.
22. MacCormack, *On the Wings of Time*, 174.
23. Santo Tomás, *Grammática* (1560), n.p. For a deep study of Nebrijas's contributions to the expansion of the Spanish language and the connections he perceived between language and empire, see Mignolo, "On the Colonization of Amerindian Languages."
24. Santo Tomás, *Grammática* (1560), n.p.

25. Santo Tomás, *Grammática* (1560), n.p.
26. The defense of the natives' intellectual capabilities associated with the sophistication of their language is an argument that Peruvian Luis Jerónimo de Oré used later in *Symbolo catholico indiano*, where he assures that Cuzco's Quechua is comparable to what the Ionic dialect was for Athens and what Latin was for Rome (*Symbolo catholico indiano*, 33v). Inca Garcilaso de la Vega in *Comentarios reales* expands on this topic, showing also how Quechua was the language of the conquerors; see especially the first four chapters of the seventh book (*Royal Commentaries of the Incas*, 402–11).
27. Santo Tomás, *Grammática* (1560), 2–2v.
28. In each chapter, Friar Domingo develops topics such as orthography; nouns; pronouns; verbs; participles; infinitives; gerunds; prepositions; adverbs; interjections; conjunctions; relative pronouns; comparative, superlative, and diminutive names; patronymics; adverbs of place; numerals; syntax; particular terms that native speakers use; special ways of speaking; particles; and accents. For an in-depth study of the content of each chapter, see Cerrón-Palominos's introduction in the 1995 edition of Santo Tomás, *Grammática*.
29. Santo Tomás, *Grammática* (1560), 56v.
30. According to the Inca organization system, ten grown men with their respective households formed a group called *chunca*, and ten *chuncas* formed a bigger organization called *pachaca*. Zuidema, *The Ceque System of Cuzco*, 200.
31. Santo Tomás, *Grammática* (1560), 56v.
32. Santo Tomás, *Grammática* (1560), 57.
33. MacCormack, *On the Wings of Time*, 183.
34. Estenssoro, *Del paganismo a la santidad*, 34.
35. Santo Tomás, *Grammática* (1560), 87v.
36. Santo Tomás, *Grammática* (1560), 92v.
37. Santo Tomás, *Grammática* (1560), 94v.
38. As Gerald Taylor has noted, in the sermon there are certain words that do not have an equivalent in Quechua, such as *Dios, caballo*, and *cristiano*. Taylor, *El sol, la luna y las estrellas no son Dios*, 20.
39. MacCormack, *On the Wings of Time*, 181.
40. For a more extensive study of the sermon, see Taylor, *El sol, la luna y las estrellas no son Dios*, 19–29.
41. Harrison, "The Language and Rhetoric," 12.
42. Harrison, "The Language and Rhetoric," 12.
43. As a student at the Universidad de Alcalá de Henares, González Holguín must have been familiar with Nebrija's books, as well as with other linguists of that time. For a deeper study of González Holguín and Nebrija's influence on his work, see Segovia Gordillo, "La gramática y arte nueva." See also Beyersdorff, "The Meeting of Two Imperial Languages," for more biographical information about the author.
44. Segovia Gordillo, "La gramática y arte nueva," 95.
45. MacCormack, *On the Wings of Time*, 195.

46. González Holguín, *Gramatica*, 4.
47. González Holguín, *Gramatica*, 96v. The current accepted spelling is *ayllu*, while Friar Domingo and Gonzalez Holguín use *ayllo*.
48. The difference in the depth with which the authors discuss certain topics is also clear in the way they discuss interjections. Friar Domingo states that there is nothing particularly interesting to notice because the natives express their emotions with corporal effects, using their eyes, their fingers, and other parts of their bodies. In contrast, González Holguín offers twenty-seven interjections. For more details, see Cerrón-Palomino's 1995 introduction to Santo Tomás, *Grammática*, xl.
49. González Holguín, *Gramática*, 96–96v.
50. González Holguín, *Gramática*, 99.
51. González Holguín, *Gramática*, 119. The author also strays from the Latinization of the language in other aspects; for example, in Quechua a concordance between noun, adjective, or number does not exist, nor is there one between a verb and its subject, or between a noun and an adjective.
52. González Holguín, *Gramática*, 119.
53. Santo Tomás, *Grammática*, 67.
54. Santo Tomás, *Grammática*, 67–67v.
55. Santo Tomás, *Grammática*, 68.
56. Santo Tomás, *Grammática*, 68.
57. Lisi, *El tercer concilio limense*, 247. For more information about Friar Domingo's missionary activities, see Cerrón-Palomino's 1995 introduction to Santo Tomás, *Grammática*. See also Urbano, López-Ocón, and Hehrlein, "Historia y difamación."
58. MacCormack, "'The Heart Has Its Reasons,'" 445–46.

Works Cited

Acosta, José de. *De procuranda Indorum salute: Predicación del evangelio en las Indias*. Introduction, translation, and notes by Francisco Mateos. Madrid: Colección Españas Misionera, 1952.

Andrango-Walker, Catalina. *El símbolo católico indiano (1598) de Luis Jerónimo de Oré: Saberes coloniales y los problemas de la evangelización en la región andina*. Frankfurt: Iberoamericana Editorial Vervuert, 2018.

Anonymous. *Arte y vocabulario en la lengua general del Peru llamada quichua, y en la lengua española: El mas copioso y elegante que hasta agora se ha impresso*. Lima: Imprenta de Antonio Ricardo, 1586.

Anonymous Jesuit. *Relación de las costumbres antiguas de los naturales del Perú*. In *Crónicas peruanas de interés indígena*, edited by Francisco Esteve Barba, 153–89. Biblioteca de autores españoles 209. Madrid: Ediciones Atlas, 1968.

Bertonio, Ludovico. *Arte breve de la lengua aymara para introducción del arte grande de la misma lengua, compuesta por el P. Ludovico Bertonio Romano de la compañia de Iesus en la Provincia del Piru, de la India Occidental*. Rome: Luis Zannetti, 1603.

———. *Arte y grammatica muy copiosa de la lengua aymara: Con muchos y varios modos de hablar para su mayor declaracion, con la tabla de los capitulos y cosas que en ella se contienen. Compuesta por el P. Ludouico Bertonio Romano de la Compañia de Iesus en la prouincia del Piru, de la India Occidental.* Rome: Luis Zannetti, 1603.

Betanzos, Juan de. *Narrative of the Incas.* Translated by Roland Hamilton and Dana Buchanan. 1557. Reprint, Austin: University of Texas Press, 1996.

Beyersdorff, Margot. "The Meeting of Two Imperial Languages in the Quechua-Spanish Vocabulario of Diego González Holguín." In *Andean Oral Traditions*, 257–82. Boon: BAS, 1994.

Burkhart, Louise M. *The Slippery Earth: Nahua-Christian Moral Dialogue in Sixteenth-Century Mexico.* Tucson: University of Arizona Press, 1989.

Castro Pineda, Lucio. *La cátedra de lengua quechua en la catedral de Lima.* Lima: Imprenta de la Universidad Nacional Mayor de San Marcos, 1963.

Catholic Church and José de Acosta. *Confessionario para los curas de indios con la instrucion contra sus ritos: Y exhortacion para ayudar a bien morir: Y summa de sus privilegios; y forma de impedimentos del matrimonio compuesto y traduzido en las lenguas Quichua, y Aymara. Por autoridad del Concilio Provincial de Lima, del ano de 1583.* Lima: Imprenta de Antonio Ricardo, 1585.

———. *Doctrina christiana, y catecismo para instruccion de los indios, y de las de mas personas, que han de ser enseñadas en nuestra sancta fé: Con vn confessionario, y otras cosas necessarias para los que doctrinan, que se contienen en la pagina siguiente.* Lima: Imprenta de Antonio Ricardo, 1584.

———. *Tercero cathecismo y exposicion de la doctrina christiana, por sermones: Para que los curas y otros ministros prediquen y enseñen a los Yndios y a las demas personas.* Impresso con licencia dela Real Audiencia, en la Ciudad de los Reyes. Lima: Imprenta de Antonio Ricardo, 1585.

Cerrón-Palomino, Rodolfo. *Castellano andino: Aspectos sociolingüísticos, pedagógicos y gramaticales.* Lima: Pontifícia Universidad Católica del Perú, Fondo Editorial, 2003.

Cook, Noble David. "Luis Jerónimo de Oré: Una aproximación." In *Symbolo catholico indiano*, edited by Antonine Tibesar, 35–63. 1598. Reprint, Lima: Australis, 1992.

———. *Relación de la vida y milagros de San Francisco Solano.* Lima: Pontificia Universidad Católica del Perú, Fondo Editorial, 1998.

———. "Viviendo en las márgenes del imperio: Luis Jerónimo de Oré y la exploración del *Otro*." *Histórica* 32, no. 1 (2008): 11–38.

Dedenbach-Salazar Sáenz, Sabina. "La descripción gramatical como reflejo e influencia de la realidad lingüística: La presentación de las relaciones hablante-enunciado e intra-textuales en tres gramáticas quechuas coloniales y ejemplos de su uso en el discurso quechua de la época." In *La descripción de las lenguas amerindias en la época colonial*, edited by Klaus Zimmermann, 291–320. Frankfurt: Iberoamericana Editorial Vervuert, 1997.

Durston, Alan. *Pastoral Quechua: The History of Christian Translation in Colonial Peru, 1550–1650.* Notre Dame, Ind.: University of Notre Dame Press, 2007.

Estenssoro, Juan Carlos. *Del paganismo a la santidad: La incorporación de los indios del Perú al catolicismo, 1532–1750.* Translated by Gabriela Ramos. Lima: Instituto Francés de Estudios Andinos, 2003.

González Holguín, Diego. *Gramática y arte nueva de la lengua general de todo el Peru, llamada lengua quichua.* Lima: Imprenta de Francisco del Canto, 1607.

———. *Vocabulario de la lengua general de todo el Perú llamada lengua quichua o del Inca.* Edited by Raúl Porras Barrenechea. 1608. Reprint, Lima: Imprenta Santa María, 1952.

Guibovich Pérez, Pedro. "The Printing Press in Colonial Peru: Production Process and Literary Categories in Lima, 1584–1699." *Colonial Latin American Review* 10, no. 2 (2001): 167–88.

Hamerly, Michael. *Artes, Vocabularios, and Related Ecclesiastical Materials of Quichua/quechua, Aymara, Puquina, and Mochica Published During the Colonial Period: A History and a Bibliography.* Aachen, Germany: Shaker Verlag, 2001.

Harrison, Regina. "The Language and Rhetoric of Conversion in the Viceroyalty of Peru." *Poetics Today* 16, no. 1 (1995): 1–27.

Lisi, Francesco Leonardo. *El tercer concilio limense y la aculturación de los indígenas sudamericanos: Estudio crítico con edición, traducción y comentario de las actas del concilio provincial celebrado en Lima entre 1582 y 1583.* Salamanca: Universidad de Salamanca, 1990.

MacCormack, Sabine. "'The Heart Has Its Reasons': Predicaments of Missionary Christianity in Early Colonial Peru." *Hispanic American Historical Review* 65, no. 3 (1985): 443–66.

———. *On the Wings of Time: Rome, the Incas, Spain, and Peru.* Princeton, N.J.: Princeton University Press, 2007.

Medina, José Toribio. *La imprenta en Lima (1584–1824).* Vol. 1. Santiago de Chile: Impreso y grabado en casa del autor, 1904.

Mignolo, Walter D. "On the Colonization of Amerindian Languages and Memories: Renaissance Theories of Writing and the Discontinuity of the Classical Tradition." *Comparative Studies in Society and History* 34, no. 2 (1992): 301–30.

Nebrija, Antonio de. *Diccionario latino-español.* Salamanca, 1492.

———. *Gramática castellana.* Salamanca, 1492.

———. *Introducciones latinas.* Salamanca, 1481.

Oré, Luis Jerónimo de. *Rituale seu manuale Peruanum et forma brevis administrandi apud Indos sacramenta per Ludovicum Hieronymum Orerium, elaborata.* Napoli, 1607.

———. *Symbolo catholico indiano en el qual se declaran los mysterios de la fè contenidos en los tres symbolos catholicos, Apostolico, Niceno, y de S. Athanasio: Contiene assi mesmo vna descripcion del nueuo orbe, y delos naturales del: Y vn orden de enseñarles la doctrina christiana en las dos lenguas generales, quichua y aymara, con vn confessionario breue y catechismo dela communion: Todo lo qual esta approbado por los reverendissimos señores arçobispo delos Reyes, y obispos del Cuzco, y de Tucuman.* Lima: Imprenta de Antonio Ricardo, 1598.

Salomon, Frank. "La textualización de la memoria en la América Andina: Una perspectiva etnográfica comparada." *América Indígena* 54, no. 4 (1994): 229–61.

Sánchez de las Brozas, Francisco. *Minerva sive de causis linguae latinae.* Salamanca, 1587.

Santo Tomás, Domingo de. *Grammática, o, Arte de la lengua general de los indios de los reynos del Perú*. Valladolid, Spain: Imprenta de Francisco Fernández de Córdova, 1560.

———. *Grammática, o, Arte de la lengua general de los indios de los reynos del Perú*. Edited by Rodolfo Cerrón-Palomino. Cuzco: Centro de estudios regionales andinos "Bartolomé de las Casas," 1995.

———. *Lexicón, o Vocabulario de la lengua general del Perú*. Valladolid, Spain: Imprenta de Francisco Fernández de Córdova, 1560.

Saturninus, Augustinus. *Mercurius maior sive grammaticae institutiones*. Basel, Switzerland: Oporinus, 1546.

Segovia Gordillo, Ana. "La gramática y arte nueva de la lengua general de todo el Perú (1607) de González Holguín y las gramáticas de Nebrija (H. 1488–1492)." *Anuario De Lingüística Hispánica* 26 (2010): 90–114.

Taylor, Gérald. *El sol, la luna y las estrellas no son Dios: La evangelización en quechua, siglo XVI*. Lima: Instituto Francés de Estudios Andinos, 2003.

Torres Rubio, Diego de. *Gramática y vocabulario de la lengua quichua, aymara y española*. Rome: Luis Zannetti, 1603.

Urbano, Henrique, Leoncio López-Ocón, and Yacin Hehrlein. "Historia y difamación: El cabildo de la Plata contra Domingo de Santo Tomás." *Revista Andina* 6, no. 2 (1988): 165–205.

Vega, Garcilaso de la. *Royal Commentaries of the Incas, and General History of Peru*. Part 1. Edited by Harold V. Livermore. Austin: University of Texas Press, 1970.

Zuidema, R. Tom. *The Ceque System of Cuzco: The Social Organization of the Capital of the Inca*. Translated by Eva M. Hooykaas. Leiden, Netherlands: E. J. Brill, 1964.

2

A Witch in the City

History and Textuality in the Nineteenth-Century Andes

WALTHER MARADIEGUE

O NE DAY IN EARLY 1888, some Peruvian cities were astonished and scandalized after reading that in a small village in the distant highland Andes, a woman was accused of being a witch and of poisoning a man to death, and then burned alive by an enraged crowd acting in concert with a group of authorities and a Catholic priest who did not allow a legal trial. This was a terrible case that made these urban populations wonder about the limits of savagery. Reading about terms such as an *india* woman, bloodthirsty masses, a witch, and fire brought back to urban memory the fact that its country was composed of more than just thriving cities. There were unknown rural places, peoples not completely understood, a nation apparently not completely built.

The place where the burning of Benigna Huamán happened, the incident motivating this chapter, is the Andean town of Bambamarca. Although involved in the burgeoning local mining industry, Bambamarca was hardly part of the urban imagination of the lettered elites from Cajamarca, Trujillo, or Chiclayo as the journalistic reports analyzed in this chapter prove. The first of these texts was published just four days following Huamán's trial and they did not stop until at least forty years later, which speaks of the relevance given to this case. This particular case, due to either its high diffusion or the spectacular nature of the events described, produced an unprecedented reaction within intellectual groups. This intervention was expressed in printed works diverse in the number of fields and places of production, as well as in the agendas individual authors sought to elaborate in their texts. Furthermore, many of the articles examined in this chapter demonstrate the limits of the printed letter when it comes to producing "scientific" knowledge based on the analysis of newsworthy events such as Huamán's death, and why print textuality has always needed to incorporate other media and sources of knowledge in order to legitimize itself.

That so many intellectuals representing so many fields of knowledge felt compelled to discuss this case suggests that they needed to analyze and interpret social events that captivated public attention, and felt a desire to construct them as social fables according to their class terms and interests. In this sense, Benigna Huamán's story is crucial and revealing, for it includes and problematizes many of the important ideologies of *fin de siglo* modernity. The complexity and heterogeneity of the terms and strategies traced by each of the authors give clues that allow one to examine the different regional discourses of modernity produced in the nineteenth-century Andes in their intricate constitutions and intrinsic contradictions.

This chapter analyzes some of the approximately twenty sources compiled about this case. These texts are representative, for they cover different fields of knowledge—journalism, law, and fiction—and because they collectively suggest that intellectual groups relied on nonprinted and nonintellectual sources of knowledge for the reification of their scientific authority. At the same time, these works show an anxiety to present this event as controlled and domesticated, without complete success.

As previously announced, all the articles researched here describe the burning alive of a woman named Benigna Huamán in the main plaza of Bambamarca, a sentence that was carried out without any official trial. These events happened over the course of three or four days, in March 1888, although the exact date varies depending on the source. The ambiguity surrounding the information given by many of the texts that narrate Benigna Huamán's death might speak first of a lack of accurate information coming from Bambamarca but also as a strategic choice that gave individual authors the opportunity to develop their own arguments. Because it is almost impossible to construct one single version of the execution, I examine the ways in which these authors sought to construct a sense of verisimilitude, while at the same time delegitimizing other printed texts that might contradict or distort the reality each author constructs. And as the reader will find, the participation of indigenous languages and indigenous uses of the Spanish language were central in these projects and debates.

The struggles for verisimilitude and realism were happening not just in the realm of the printed letter but in a technological landscape inhabited by different media, including orality and popular memory, among others. However, this analysis does not ignore the political context in which the "lettered city" sought to control and domesticate other technologies and media through complex processes of presumed translations, transcriptions, and compilations of "popular" or "indigenous" traditions.[1] These processes of domestication—domestication of a "savage" event, domestication of a problematic feminine figure—are at the same time manifestations and evidences of the limits of the printed text to enunciate and name the semiotic spaces it claims to master. A critical reading of these texts should discover an independent space that reveals the limits these discursive products are trying to hide. The references all these texts make to highland geographical landscapes as locations where civilization has not yet arrived and where education and law are crucially needed show that the physical exteriority of these intellectual writers borders with what Mirko Lauer calls "psychological hinterland," a space behind and beyond which "there is nothing."[2] The set of discourses made about this case refers to these hinterlands, which constitute in themselves a totality, a sphere of sense that at the same time ends at a border. However, every space beyond this border, by being talked about, must also be constituted by language, a language stimulated and limited by the rules of the printed text.[3] In this sense, these texts demonstrate that what we might know as hegemonic Andean textual systems during the late nineteenth century in fact consisted of continuous language struggles where the "empty" and the "savage" spaces outside the *criollo*-imagined nation periodically manifested, and proposed continuous challenges to the printed letter. And, as we will see, one of the presumed ways these challenges were contested was the fictitious incorporation of other subaltern traditions of communication.

As Peruvian scholar Antonio Cornejo Polar explained, the incorporation of nonlettered traditions in Peru first responded to a certain consciousness of the limitations and restrictions that intellectual groups felt in order to propose the reformulation of a sense for a national history.[4] It has been historically difficult for intellectuals to characterize the information coming from subaltern groups as either "popular" or "indigenous," and even harder to delineate limits for interaction and exclusion between these sources and those coming from "enlightened" criollo groups. Especially evident in the newspaper articles about this case are complex processes of resemantization that are a product of the hierarchical structures the printed letter constructs, with itself in a position of authority in this hierarchy.

The administration, naming, and control of orality and the voice were indisputable elements of many criollo projects. As Ana María Ochoa Gautier elaborates, the nineteenth century should be seen as a contested site of different acoustic practices, rather than just the history of the constituency of the printed letter's hegemony, a view that might open a number of opportunities for listening to the silenced voices of the "other."[5] Nevertheless, voice should be understood in a metaphorical or sensorial way, not solely understanding orality as the other pole of writing but as a social practice that involves speaking and listening. In the case examined, these practices also involved the incorporation of the Quechua language in the ways nineteenth-century journalists described and transcribed it. Especially important are certain terms that come from Quechua and have been incorporated into popular spoken Spanish, which certainly trouble the conception of a "refined" language. These incorporations have been often studied in the work of *indigenista* writers such as Clorinda Matto de Turner's 1889 *Aves sin nido* or Enrique López Albújar's 1920 *Cuentos andinos*. In most cases these incorporations are seen as manifesting the problematic ways in which these writers understood and dealt with the limitations of Western writing conventions for expressing empathy and knowledge of Quechua as well as Andean Spanish.

The Newspaper and the Perversions of a Modern Inquisitor

A couple of days after the execution, Bambamarca was still quivering. The *prefecto* (local authority) wrote a report directed to the regional authorities signed by fifteen people who included the *regidores* (members of the municipal council) and the Catholic priest of the town, Celedonio Vargas. But when the news arrived in Trujillo and Chiclayo, the most important cities of the northern Andes at that time, the story became notorious everywhere. The fifteen signatories were arrested and put on trial, although only the priest was condemned to prison. At least three judicial reports were written: the mentioned report by the prefecto of Bambamarca in March 1888, another report made by the prefecto of the province of Pataz during the same month, and the *Causa célebre* prepared by the priest's lawyer during the trial in Lima in 1893.[6]

The story's notoriety was not limited to judicial circles. In fact, it was consumed and reimagined by different circles as many newspapers took up the story. Articles were published a few weeks after in *El Tiempo* and *El Deber* in Trujillo, *El Fénix* and *La Provincia* in Chiclayo, and *El Comercio* and *El Nacional* in Lima. The case also attracted wide interest outside Peru: *La Estrella de Panamá*, the *New York Times*, the *New York Herald*, the *Brooklyn Daily*, and the *Vossische Zeitung* in Berlin all published reports of this story within a year of the actual event. Many of these articles also made references to other versions published in Argentina, Ecuador, and Italy. The importance of journalistic interest in this case, as well as positioning it as an issue of national and historic significance, confirms Benedict Anderson's argument about the importance of the press as a means of affirming the nation as a community discursively linked by a historical past, drawn together in a determined territory, and destined to a common future.[7] While Anderson focuses on the analysis of the newspaper as the main way for propagating national ideals, he also argues that other types of printed texts, like magazines and other regional publications, played an important role in this task. Regional publications refer to printed works such as pamphlets or short books produced by local printing houses that, because of their small print run, often circulated only in one city and small surrounding towns. The term "magazine" (*revista*) refers to periodical publications, usually printed weekly or monthly, in which a group of authors addresses different genres in terms of science, arts, and letters. The main audience of many late nineteenth-century Peruvian regional publications was a local lettered elite, including the authors themselves, as well as other literate readers outside the region who would consume these publications in circuits of exchange of intellectual works. In the case of northern Peruvian coast publications, these circuits were commonly shaped and restricted by economic and transportation networks in which the authors, commonly belonging to the same economic elite consuming these publications, were also involved.

The importance of printed texts like these periodicals lay precisely in their capacity for reaching regional audiences, and addressing them in region-specific cultural and linguistic terms. In these publications, it is easier to appreciate elements such as the complicated processes of transcription of local dialects, the mutual and continuous influence between Spanish and indigenous languages, and the heterogeneous production and circulation of texts in a region like the northern Peruvian Andes, which at the time was experiencing accelerated processes of urbanization and rural industrialization. In many cases, these periodicals served as the printed voice of the region's economic elite and intellectuals like José María Rodríguez, who in 1895 wrote a so-called historic novel titled *Benigna Huamán, o la Bruja de Bambamarca*. Writing about its publication, the newspaper *El Deber* stated that "el autor ha procurado convertir la aridez del relato tomado de los mismos autos criminales, en un cuadro animado que lejos de perjudicar a la verdad, la presenta en sus condiciones naturales" (the author has tried to convert the aridity of the account taken from the criminal edicts into a lively portrait that far from harming the truth, presents it in its natural conditions).[8]

It is worth drawing attention to how information about the case traveled among cities and newspapers. In an attempt to trace circuits of information and knowledge, we can see that some versions are only replicated in Trujillo and Panama, others in Cajamarca, Chiclayo, and New York, and just some of them included Lima as a place of shared information. The June 6, 1889, *New York Herald* explained that "a Correspondent writes as follows from Trujillo." *La Estrella de Panamá* transcribed an article from the December 22, 1892, *La Provincia* in Chiclayo. And on May 28, 1888, the *Daily Star and Herald*, also from Panama, presented to its readers another transcription of a governmental report, preambled by opinion.

> Tienen ya conocimiento nuestros lectores del crimen perpetrado en Bambamarca (Perú). . . . No publicamos el acta con que el cura y sus autoridades del pueblo de Bambamarca dan fe del horroroso crimen que cometieron, porque indudablemente se sublevaría el espíritu de nuestros lectores al ver que todavía existen seres a quienes domina . . . la más supina ignorancia, la perversión de todo sentimiento humanitario, la perversión que solo por la práctica de todos los vicios se puede adquirir, diabólicas dotes que concurren todas en el moderno inquisidor. . . . Pero accediendo a una solicitud que del Perú se nos hace, damos publicidad a los siguientes documentos oficiales.

> [Our readers already have knowledge of the crime perpetrated in Bambamarca (Peru). . . . We are not publishing the report with which the priest and authorities of the town of Bambamarca give account of the horrendous crime they committed because the spirit of our readers would revolt for seeing that there still exists beings dominated by . . . the utter ignorance, the perversion of every humanitarian emotion, the perversion that can be acquired only through the practice of every vice, all these diabolical qualities that conjoin in the modern inquisitor. . . . But

consenting to a request made to us from Peru, we are publishing the following official documents.]

This time the transcribed *Actas* apparently do not come from a newspaper but were directly written by the subprefecto of the province of Pataz and directed to a higher governmental authority. These citations involve a newspaper in Panama that received and consumed articles from different Peruvian cities, while being part of different circuits of consumption and exchange of information and opinions. This points to the fact that during the late nineteenth century there existed important networks of train lines and ports that in many cases did not include Lima as a destination but traveled directly to the Northern Hemisphere. These sources also show how the incorporation of non-Spanish voices and imprecise sources of information were strategically posted to boost the authority of certain newspapers to develop arguments about this case. Just one month after the events in Bambamarca, *La Estrella de Panama* echoed the information compiled by *El Nacional* from Lima: "Con el rubro de triste acontecimiento, dice El Nacional de Lima: 'En carta fechada en Huamachuco hallamos, con este encabezamiento, un párrafo que sin comentario transcribimos en seguida" (With the title of sad occurrence, El Nacional from Lima says: 'In a letter dated in Huamachuco, we found with this heading a paragraph that, without comment, we transcribe as follows) (*La Estrella de Panamá*, April 28, 1888). After narrating some of the events in exuberant and somewhat perverse detail (e.g., that Huamán was given twenty-five lashings every fifteen minutes), the article moves to an also abundant description of the priest's character.

> Dos hombres que se quejaron de este crimen, los mandó tomar el cura Celedonio Vargas y les dio 25 latigazos. . . . En el pueblo de Mollepata, donde antes era cura este individuo, nos dicen que una vez, porque un conejo llamado *cuí* por aquí, había nacido sin pelo, lo puso en el altar mayor, y después de exorcizarlo, lo sacó en procesión y lo quemó en la plaza, diciendo que era el demonio.[9]

> [Two men who complained of this crime, were arrested by order of the priest Celedonio Vargas and received 25 lashings. . . . In the town of Mollepata, where this individual was priest, they tell us that one time, a rabbit, that is called *cuí* here, was born hairless, and the priest put it at the main altar, and after exorcizing it, he placed it in a religious procession and burned it at the square, saying that it was the devil.]

Four years after these events, the curiosity and fascination about Huamán and the priest had not ceased. Another newspaper from Panama transcribed a note, this time coming from Chiclayo.

> Como los detalles de este crimen no eran conocidos, he aquí cómo los refiere un testigo ocular, según dice *La Provincia* de Chiclayo en uno de sus más recientes números: 'Se encuentra en esta ciudad, desde hace algún tiempo, un individuo que, nos asegura, presenció el acto de quemar viva a la infeliz víctima del Presbítero Vargas. (*Daily Star and Herald*, December 20, 1892)

> [As the details of this crime were not known, this is how an eyewitness describes them, according to Chiclayo's *La Provincia* in one of its latest editions: "An individual who, assures us, witnessed the burning of Priest Vargas's poor victim, has been staying in this city for some time."]

These citations and analyses should make us rethink the highest importance of urban centers and their apparent hegemonic relationship with the provinces when trying to support arguments related to the invention or imagining of nationhood, modernity, or science. Moreover, I would like to understand this new urban distribution not just as geographical expansion but as a set of heterogeneous dialogical spaces where each of them conceived particular dynamics of production and consumption of knowledge. This idea could be complemented with a diverse understanding of what literacy could mean and how it could be expressed. I understand literacies as different processes of writing, reading, and the diverse ways of incorporating the visual, the sensorial, and the aural.[10] In this sense, literacies might be as diverse and specific as the amount of systems of meaning inhabiting a "national" territory.

This conception of literacies helps us reflect on what a city is and where it begins and ends. We could think of a city as a geographical space, and also as a social constellation built on an ideology of the supremacy of the lettered word, and ruled by a circle of *letrados* as controllers and producers of consciousness and cultural models for the configuration of public ideologies, as defined by Ángel Rama's *La ciudad letrada*.[11] I contend that a group of intellectual letrados saw in the Bambamarca event an occasion to argue that acts such as the burning alive of an india were senseless in at least two ways. First, any magic activity such as witchcraft was incompatible with the scientific progress taking place in Peruvian society, therefore witchcraft should be conceived as a sham. Second, many authors in Trujillo and Lima saw in the series of documents produced by the authorities of Bambamarca a pretext for highlighting the social conditions of what they called "regiones tan apartadas de los centros de civilización" (regions distanced from the centers of civilization).[12] The urban lettered elites saw in this case that local authorities were incapable of governing the faraway Andean towns in ways compatible with discourses of progress and modernity of the Peruvian state.

In our case, the agents of the printed word dwell in geographies as diverse as Bambamarca, an Andean hacienda, Lima, or New York. An alternative understanding of literacies proposes new ways of approaching the questions of what a text is and how history is written in terms of media, agents, networks of circulation, and the cultural traditions it might incorporate. These methodological paths have been followed by many interesting studies in the fields of anthropology and the analysis of early colonial texts but still present epistemological challenges for the study of the late nineteenth and early twentieth centuries because the abundance of textual production contrasts with the lack of possibilities of listening to other voices.[13] One of the texts forming part of this abundance is the one discussed in the following section, followed by an analysis of the possibilities for finding footprints of these complementary literacies during a time when the lettered city sought to prove its highest hegemony.

Fuegos brujos, and How to Deal with Savagery

In his story "La hechicería y sus consecuencias," contained in the book *Cuentos, tradiciones, leyendas y costumbres quechuas*, published in Lima, Francisco Nestárez deals with the Bambamarca case in a way that presents peculiar conceptions of criminality, civilization, and the problematic inclusion of subaltern voices in a textual narrative. This book is, as the title affirms, a compilation of nineteen texts covering diverse genres. Some of them narrate pre-Columbian myths, like "La serpiente monstruosa de Poyoc" or "El Landaruto." Others describe experiences or adventures the author claims to have had during his "viajes difíciles por el territorio nacional" (difficult travels through the national territory) ("Dedicatory"), such as "El eucaliptus filósofo" or "En busca de matrimonio." What these stories have in common is that they take place in the northern Peruvian Andes, "por las diferentes regiones del Río Marañón" (through the different regions of the Marañon River).[14]

At first glance, *Cuentos* presents itself as a compilation of texts in different genres that seeks to be a legitimate source of scientific knowledge about both the Andes and the Bambamarca events. The Bambamarca story's placement in the book can be seen as strategic, after the author's constant claims throughout the book of having acquired experience and knowledge during his travels that allowed him to deliver a final verdict about Huamán's death. He also does so by claiming the authority to propose an analysis of the Bambamarca case and consequently to include statements about science and criminality. We should also remember the importance that both travel as experience and the travelogue as a genre had for the constitution of lettered authority in turn-of-the-century Latin America. These two categories link to travel as a late nineteenth-century European "invention" for acquiring knowledge about the exotic, and to the expedition as a colonial enterprise after which the explorer subject felt to have the authority to speak for and to rule those exotic territories.[15]

Nestárez's interest in discussing Benigna Huamán's case reinforces the idea of the significance given to this case—a significance that echoes the high importance nineteenth-century Latin American republics gave to textual production for the collective imagination of the nation and of modern cities. As Julio Ramos explains, in Latin America the literary discourse introduced a space for the transmission of models, norms, limits, and symbolic frontiers.[16] An important component of these discourses was the modeling of citizenship, as well as its paradigms of conduct, race, science, and an apparent harmonious balance between the local and the global. Thus, Nestárez's work becomes a contribution to the establishment of these paradigms, a contribution that saw in the Bambamarca story a superb tool for its purposes.

These narratives evidence the importance given to the act of locating the Bambamarca events in a topography that mingles geography, the masses, and criminality in order to project the inverse values of individualism and reason in the inhabitants of the main Peruvian cities. In *Ficciones somáticas*, Gabriela Nouzeilles analyzes the debates that took place in late nineteenth-century Argentina on the impact of naturalist fictions in the construction of the nation and of a national art.[17] These debates were constantly aware of the effects naturalist rhetoric might have in the ongoing project of literarily disciplining the public in benefit of the nation. Within these debates, the production of these types of narratives relies on the moral and political potential of stories like Bambamarca's and their capacity for generating *useful* knowledge—useful for scientific progress and the agenda of modernity. The political dimension of these debates reveals that these texts were not a mechanical response to the urban demand for information. The specificity of these types of narratives also resided in the specific articulation between fable, politics, and knowledge implicit in narratives like Nestárez's.[18] It was also important for these groups of intellectuals to center the responsibility for specific crimes on identifiable and individual characters, and not nameless crowds. In this way, the fable would blame and punish individuals, strengthening the pedagogic character of the events and therefore more effectively shaping a modern urban audience.

Many letrados saw in this event an opportunity to address contemporary key issues such as civilization and science. But at the same time, it provoked anxiety in these groups, which saw in it a public incident that needed to be ideologically domesticated in front of the national urban masses so it did not disrupt the modernization that many of the main Peruvian cities were allegedly accomplishing. The story "La hechicería y sus consecuencias" deserves attention as this is a discussion on Benigna Huamán's death, as well as because this is the only story in Nestárez's book composed of two distinguishable parts. In the first part, the authorial narrator develops an analysis of witchcraft and a narration of contemporary witchcraft practices in the Northern Peruvian Andes. The story explains why he considers these practices as shams, and the *indios* trusting in it as naïve. The second part of the text presents a so-called copy of the *Acta* prepared by Isidoro Torres, prefect of Bambamarca who, after Huamán's death, sent it to the regional authorities. This copied *Acta* contains another copy of a different *Acta* signed by ten authorities of Bambamarca, which describes and testifies to the fatal burning of Benigna Huamán.

I call the narrator of the first part of "La hechicería y sus consecuencias" an *authorial narrator* because of the hybrid nature of this text. As previously explained, while the stories contained in Nestárez's book have either an omniscient or a testimonial narrator, this story begins with the rhetoric of an essay: "Algo que no debe pasar desapercibido dentro las páginas de este libro" (Something that should not be overlooked inside the pages of this book).[19] Then it shifts to an omniscient narrator: "Cuando ha llegado la noche, procurando no ser vista por persona alguna, coloca dentro de un cuerno de res" (When the night has arrived, trying not to be seen by anyone, she places inside a bull horn) (156), and finishes without conclusions, just as the closing of the "copied" *Acta* ends with a parenthetical clarification: "(Redacción y ortografía auténticos)" (Authentic writing and orthography) (162). These characteristics make it difficult to conceive that the narrator is the same one from the other texts forming part of the book, for this story constructs a particular narrator that seems at times to be the author, and at other times the omniscient narrator.

In "La hechicería y sus consecuencias," we have a story, written almost forty years after the events in Bambamarca, that interprets and copies the *Actas* written just four days after Benigna Huamán's death. These texts perform a rewriting or resignification of the copied *Actas*, reverse their arguments, and posit the story's final goal as a shifting responsibility for the events, originally attributed by the authorities of Bambamarca to the figure of Benigna Huamán, to those authorities themselves.

While this text is presented as one work, an initial reading suggests the question of understanding it as an individual narrative with a unique author, or as three different texts juxtaposed in one story: Nestárez's story and the two copies of the *Actas*. Of concern is the way the first part of the text conditions the reading of the first and second *Acta* and affects how they are interpreted. Thus, a reading that conceives an authorial narrator with multiple voices in a hybrid text is more fitting for this chapter.

Concerning the question of authorship, I follow Natalie Zemon Davis's discussion about sixteenth-century letters of remission in France written by scribes through the mediation of lawyers, with additional input from the person asking remission from the king. For Davis, authorship of these letters is better understood as emerging from an exchange among several people's perspectives about events, points of law, and narrative style.[20] This understanding of authorship helps observe how in "La hechicería y sus consecuencias," the proposed authorial narrator alternates references to different voices while claiming authorship of the text and at the same time stating that this authorial narrator is copying another text. In this way, an authority is constructed, where knowledge of literary and oral narrative traditions must be demonstrated in order to present both a self-made narration of contemporary witchcraft and a trustworthy narration of the events related to Huamán's death: as he states, "para confirmar los hechos, *copiamos* más abajo, el acta" (to confirm the incidents, we *copy* the report below) (155). Furthermore, the first *Acta* written by the prefect of Bambamarca is presented in its "authentic writing and orthography" (162). The sequence of transcriptions, I suggest, responds to Nestárez's arrogation of authorship and authority to stating the false nature of witchcraft as well as the wrongdoing of the Bambamarca authorities.

The insistence in making clear the original nature of the presented *Actas* prompts a reading of them as exact transcriptions. Then, inside the first *Acta* itself, it is interesting to note the multiple voices in the text. First we read the *teniente alcalde* (deputy mayor) of Bambamarca, Isidoro Torres, asserting, "[Yo] certifico: en cuanto puedo y a lugar de derecho" ([I] state, in my capacity and according to law) (157) that this is an "acta verificada por todos los vecinos" (report verified by all the neighbors) (158). In other words, the text is presented as Nestárez's transcription of Torres's *Acta*, where the latter also transcribes a second *Acta* apparently accepted and signed by "todos los vecinos."

One might conclude at first glance that this text has as many narrative agendas as it has authors. I would like to propose that these multiple voices are also subordinated to one another. First, Isidoro Torres's transcription constantly presents the incineration as a collective act, without a unique or distinguishable perpetrator. Since the beginning of the narration presented by the second transcribed *Acta*, we see "reunidos [a] todos los ciudadanos de la población, mayores y menores" (gathered all the citizens, old and young) (157) and "constituido [a] todo el pueblo en dicho lugar público" (all the townsfolk congregated in that public place) (157). Then, after finding Benigna Huamán guilty of the "delito criminal de hechicería" (criminal felony of witchcraft) (158), "el pueblo gritó: que sea quemada en la plaza, como en efecto se hizo" (the townspeople yelled: to burn her at the square, as it was effectively done) (160). This citation intends to present the events as motivated by an anonymous crowd, while the persons signing the *Acta* just appear as public servants of the people's desires: "la voz del pueblo ha sido justo [*sic*] y parece que la justicia ha castigado los hechos de este modo. Hemos quedado satisfechos, dando satisfacción al orden y a la Vindicta pública" (the voice of the people has been just and justice has punished the deeds in this way. We are now satisfied, giving satisfaction to the public order and vindication) (161). The authorities of the town are presented as satisfying public demands, while the main responsibility remains in "el pueblo" or "la justicia," as ambiguous as these terms might sound.

The statement that the incineration was both a popular claim and the voice of justice is complemented by the role Benigna Huamán plays in the narration. At the beginning of the *Acta*, the signers give account of how "se le encontró a Benigna Huamán, detenida en la cárcel" (Benigna Huaman was found, detained in prison) (158). It is unclear who the agent in this sentence is: who put Huamán in jail? This citation helps the story begin with no identifiable perpetrators. But the detail deserving more attention is contained in the following lines.

[Benigna Huamán] salió de la cárcel y marchó al lugar del martirio.... Habiéndole examinado el Alcalde Municipal y Teniente Gobernador que dijera quiénes eran las compañeras o discípulas antes de entrar al fuego expresó estas palabras: Yo misma me quemaré y no las demás. Como que ella misma quiso ser quemada, sin haberle empujado nadie, le abrazó el fuego y expiró. (160)

[(Benigna Huaman) left the prison and walked to the place of martyrdom.... After the Municipal Mayor examined her and the Governor asked her who her colleagues and disciples were, she pronounced these words: I myself will burn and not the others. This is how she herself chose to be burned, without anyone pushing her, the fire burned and she expired.]

As explained before, at one moment the *Acta* signatories (the Bambamarca authorities) claim that justice was served with the incineration because it followed the will of the people. But now, the *Acta* explains that Huamán herself chose to enter the bonfire. It also implies that one of the reasons for this immolation was her refusal to denounce her female colleagues and disciples. A first look tells of a contradiction between the official version the signers of the *Acta* wanted to give about the justice of the incineration and Huamán's accepted incineration. Thus, the overall purpose of the *Acta* is to appear as though its signers are nonperpetrators of the incineration, and solely witnesses of the legal course of the events.

Therefore, it is important to remember that in the first level of transcription, we see the *Acta* signed by a group of the town's male authorities constructing a narrative where the execution is presented as consequence of a collective petition, where it is not clear who the perpetrator was: "the townsfolk," "justice," or "she herself"; anyone but the Bambamarca authorities. The second *Acta* constantly argues about the role of the authorities in following the voice of justice and the people. Then, in the few lines of the first *Acta* by Isidoro Torres, he is also performing a "fiel copia del original" (exact copy of the original) (162).

However, this text is submissive to another text. The supra-text is the story titled "La hechicería y sus consecuencias," where Nestárez claims to be that author as well as the rigorous transcriber of Isidoro Torres's *Acta*. Together authorship and authority of transcription strengthen Nestárez's authority to both scrutinize the *Acta* and state a position not just about this specific event but also about witchcraft as a social practice in the Andes.

Before going to Nestárez's proper claims in this text, it is interesting to note that the work both *Actas* perform in search for authenticity and legality is appropriated and resignified by Nestárez. This is achieved by transcribing the *Actas* but also with the story's statement that Huamán's execution report constitutes an "acta criminal y torpe" (criminal and carelessly written report) (155). While it is not clear why this *Acta* is *torpe* (careless), saying that this is an *Acta criminal* certainly overthrows the arguments of Isidoro Torres and the authorities of Bambamarca even before the *Actas* are presented, and readers are influenced in their own judgments about who were the real perpetrators of Huamán's death.

When affirming that Isidoro Torres's *Acta* is resignified by Nestárez, I also suggest that the *Actas* lose their capacity for stating moral or ethical points of view and become documents from which the 1929 readers can only extract distorted information. For this reason, knowledge and authority are necessary conditions for stating scientific claims in the text. There is one main association readers are expected to make by reading Nestárez's story, concerning the depiction of witchcraft as a false activity. To assert the falseness of witchcraft, Nestárez presents a contemporary case at the beginning of his story—María Martina Echavarría as representative of false *brujería*: "diversos casos de la *llamada* hechicería, que *tanto creen* los indios, se practica, por las diferentes regiones del Río Marañón. Dominados de estas creencias *candorosas*, son graves los actos de inhumanidad que, en varias ocasiones, se han llevado a cabo contra los *supuestos* brujos" (different cases of the *so-called* sorcery, that the indios *believe in so much*, is practiced through the different regions of the Marañon River. Guided by these naïve beliefs, many inhuman acts have been fulfilled oftentimes against the *presumed* wizards) (155; emphasis added).

While Nestárez's sources regarding Echavarría's acts are unclear, we might infer his information comes from his wanderings around the northern Andes, described in the prologue of the book. Denouncing witchcraft as false implies that the indios who believe in it are perceived as careless. This idea is broadened throughout Nestárez's story, for it also includes the authors of the legal *Actas*. By saying that "para confirmar el hecho, copiamos más abajo; el acta criminal y torpe por la que se deduce fué [*sic*] quemada una pobre mujer" (to confirm the fact, we copy below: the criminal and carelessly written report through which it is deduced that a poor woman was burned), not only the *Actas* but especially their authors are considered as "*torpe(s)*" (155).

The adjectives Nestárez's story uses to describe Benigna Huamán, the indios, and the authors of the *Acta* are worth focusing on. They are among the story's strategies to appear more "scientific," in terms of the theoretical principles and cognitive structure included in positivist essays of the early twentieth century. In the *Acta*, Benigna Huamán is portrayed as a *bruja* (witch) or *hechicera* (sorcerer), but in Nestárez's story she is a "pobre mujer" (poor woman) (155), while Maria Martina Echavarría, who is depicted as a swindler, is just "una mujer" (a woman) (156). The reluctance to call these two women brujas or hechiceras responds to the story's agenda of demonstrating that witchcraft, and therefore every magic religious practice, is a sham. Examining the spectacular nature of the events narrated during the so-called scams, we find Echavarría's acts depicted as theatrical rather than professional.

> La *pretendida* bruja, está *a la caza* de alguien que contraiga alguna enfermedad. Cuando ha llegado la noche . . . coloca dentro un cuerno de res, un pequeño envoltorio que debe contener estiércol de acémilas, distintas hierbas, cabellos y pedazos de ropa de la pretendida víctima. Más tarde, si el enfermo váse agravando . . . esta *supuesta* hechicera, envía algún comisionado a la choza del enfermo, a fin de que los parientes sean convencidos de que se trata de grave caso de brujería. . . . Aceptada la curandera, ésta sólo aparece en la choza del enfermo, cuando *se entera de que puede salvar*. . . . Y es entonces cuando, en compañía de los parientes . . . *aparatosamente* desentierra el cuerno de la puerta de la choza, que ella, con anterioridad había enterrado, y salta luego el mal! (156–57; emphasis added)
>
> [The *so-called* witch, is *awaiting* someone to catch an illness. When the night arrives . . . she puts inside a bull horn, a small package that must contain mule dung, different herbs, hairs and pieces of clothing of the desired victim. Later, if the sick person gets seriously ill . . . this *presumed* sorcerer, sends some messenger to the sick person's hut, so that the relatives can be convinced that this is a serious case of witchcraft. . . . When the healer is accepted, she appears at the sick man's hut only *if she determines that he can heal*. . . . This is when, together with the relatives . . . she *dramatically* unearths the bull horn at the hut's door, that she had previously buried, and the malady is released!]

While Nestárez's story is designed to resemble a scientific essay, a narrative like the one quoted above—more evocative of a short story—was indispensable for these pretensions. In this narration, the author seems to know everything happening at the woman's home and in the sick man's hut. He knows what

María Echavarría did the night before the "healing," and during the day when the man was still sick. This narrative becomes methodologically effective for the argument the entire story builds.

After the description of Echavarría's scams, the combination of the first-person plural and brief sentences akin to those of a legal document give the impression that the author is not just expressing his opinion but also asserting legal and scientific statements. This maneuver coincides with a claim of authority that explains what the consequences of witchcraft are, as the title of the text promises.

What is Nestárez's position toward the Bambamarca events? I observe two arguments in this story. First, any magical practice should be considered fraudulent and thus any instance of alleged witchcraft in Bambamarca is therefore a product of the interaction between swindler women and naïve indios. Second, Benigna Huamán's death was utterly senseless, and any other punishment would have sufficed to obtain justice. In consequence, Nestárez's story considers the burning of a woman as a criminal act perpetrated by the Bambamarca authorities, and transfers the idea of criminality from the murdered woman to the representatives of the state in this town.

As a whole, in "La hechicería y sus consecuencias" the *Acta*'s arguments fulfill the task of recasting the paradigm of the *indio torpe* (careless indio)—"creencias candorosas"—so important for racist discourses in Latin America, and of converting this paradigm into one of an *indio impostor* (imposter Indian man); and, as an evil simile, one of an *india impostora* (imposter Indian woman). In this logic, the execution finds a place within the systems of meaning in effect at that time and that took part in the construction of Latin American nations.

Nestárez's book and its authorial narrators could be read as positivist science applied to knowledge *about* the indios. By alternating pre-Columbian myths and the author's experiences and legal texts, this book becomes a sort of epistemological machine capable of identifying, classifying, and excluding the bodies marked by stigmas of gender, racial, and economic distinction. This classification, as shown above, begins by associating the character of the indios with the savage, desolated, and steep geography of the Andes.

When employing the term "epistemological machine," I consider the possibility that Nestárez's text represents an exemplary case and contradicts the arguments of the Bambamarca authorities as a means for stating models of the modern urban behavior in terms of civilization and legality. The articulation of criminality in this text is expressed in at least three characters: a woman

(Huamán or Echavarría), the authorities, and the masses. This articulation contributes to the modeling of the modernizing cities as social organisms while at the same time locates these characters within a broader narrative that defines the national through its relationship with bigger Latin American models of science, gender, and race, based on the criteria for the validation of Western science.

From this perspective, while Nouzeilles's somatic fictions "dealt with an inevitable concern with the figure of the pragmatic colonized: the mestizo or racially impure,"[21] scrutinizing Huamán's death as a somatic fable (not necessarily a fiction) resolves previous tensions between the documentary and somewhat realistic rhetoric of the legal documents, and the scientific and civilizing one of the authors this chapter has scrutinized. These solutions manifest in the criminal and bestial character of the burning, which does not need a realist rhetoric to be effective. Instead, the scientific discourse and its specific rhetoric allow Nestárez's text to appeal to a realist narration, where the anecdotic meets the aesthetic.

Nevertheless, this chapter has also tried to unveil the "scientific" or "documentary" nature of these texts as the product of processes of appropriation, resignification, and rewriting of diverse textual forms, especially indigenous technologies of information. This set of textual forms goes beyond the printed letter and includes other technologies of communication, other material supports, as well as other linguistic traditions that consider the problematic coexistence of the "refined" Spanish language and other regional dialects. A case like the one studied here, where the presence of the printed letter might seem overwhelming, could lead one to be oblivious of those other analytical elements that played a crucial role in the constituency of this incident as a social fable. A case happening in what seems to be a distant Andean town can therefore also become a milestone for the writing of national histories and for the establishing of those groups who claim the privilege to write them.

Notes

1. By "technology," I recast Walter Ong's analysis of writing and orality as technologies for the transmission of information. Ong, *Orality and Literacy*.
2. Lauer, *Andes imaginarios*, 60. All translations are mine unless otherwise indicated.
3. See also Josefina Ludmer's discussion on the Gaucho genre and the ideological constitutions of territories in nineteenth-century Argentina. Ludmer, *El género gauchesco*.

4. Cornejo Polar, *La formación de la tradición literaria en el Perú*, 158.
5. Ochoa Gautier, *Aurality*, 4.
6. Palacios, *Causa célebre*. *Causa célebre* is a legal term in Spanish referring to a legal case that gained wide renown.
7. Anderson, *Imagined Communities*, 12.
8. *El Deber*, March 21, 1895.
9. *Cuí* is an inexact spelling of *cuy* (guinea pig).
10. Rappaport and Cummins, *Beyond the Lettered City*, 5.
11. Rama, *La ciudad letrada*, 30.
12. Rodríguez, "Proceso célebre," 5.
13. For two examples of these studies, see Salomon and Niño-Murcia, *The Lettered Mountain*; and Rappaport, *Cumbe Reborn*.
14. Nestárez, *Cuentos*, 155.
15. This link was already prominently proved by José de la Riva-Agüero on his travel throughout the Peruvian central and southern Andes in 1912. Riva-Agüero, *Paisajes peruanos*.
16. Ramos, *Desencuentros de la modernidad*, 8.
17. Nouzeilles, *Ficciones somáticas*, 13.
18. Nouzeilles, *Ficciones somáticas*, 14.
19. Nestárez, *Cuentos*, 155. Page references appear parenthetically hereafter.
20. Davis, *Fiction in the Archives*, 25.
21. Nouzeilles, *Ficciones somáticas*, 27.

Works Cited

Anderson, Benedict. *Imagined Communities: Reflections on the Origin and Spread of Nationalism*. Rev. ed. New York: Verso, 2006.

Cornejo Polar, Antonio. *La formación de la tradición literaria en el Perú*. Lima: Centro de Estudios y Publicaciones, 1989.

Davis, Natalie Zemon. *Fiction in the Archives: Pardon Tales and Their Tellers in Sixteenth-Century France*. Stanford, Calif.: Stanford University Press, 1987.

Lauer, Mirko. *Andes imaginarios: Discursos del indigenismo 2*. Cusco: Centro Bartolomé de las Casas; Lima: Sur, 1997.

López Albújar, Enrique. *Cuentos andinos*. Lima: Juan Mejía Baca, 1965.

Ludmer, Josefina. *El género gauchesco: Un tratado sobre la patria*. Buenos Aires: Eterna Cadencia, 2012.

Matto de Turner, Clorinda. *Aves sin nido*. Lima: PEISA, 1984.

Nestárez, Francisco. *Cuentos, tradiciones, leyendas y costumbres quechuas*. Lima: Talleres gráficos de la Penitenciaría, 1929.

Nouzeilles, Gabriela. *Ficciones somáticas: Naturalismo, nacionalismo y políticas médicas del cuerpo (Argentina 1880–1910)*. Rosario, Argentina: Beatriz Viterbo, 2000.

Ochoa Gautier, Ana Maria. *Aurality: Listening and Knowledge in Nineteenth-Century Colombia*. Durham, N.C.: Duke University Press, 2014.

Ong, Walter. *Orality and Literacy: The Technologizing of the Word.* New York: Routledge, 1991.
Palacios, Fernando. *Cause célebre: Informe del Dr. Sr. Fernando Palacios ante la Excelentísima Corte Suprema de Lima, por la combustion de la india llamada Bruja Benigna Huamán en el Pueblo de Bambamarca.* Lima: n.p., 1893.
Rama, Ángel. *La ciudad letrada.* Hanover, N.H.: Ediciones del Norte, 1984.
Ramos, Julio. *Desencuentros de la modernidad en América Latina: Literatura y política en el siglo XIX.* Mexico City: Fondo de Cultura Económica, 1989.
Rappaport, Joanne. *Cumbe Reborn: An Andean Ethnography of History.* Chicago: University of Chicago Press, 1994.
Rappaport, Joanne, and Thomas Cummins. *Beyond the Lettered City: Indigenous Literacies in the Andes.* Durham, N.C.: Duke University Press, 2012.
Riva Agüero, José de la. *Paisajes peruanos.* 1956. Reprint, Lima: Instituto Riva Agüero, 2012.
Rodríguez, José María. *Benigna Huamán, o la Bruja de Bambamarca.* Trujillo, Peru: Talleres Diario El Deber, 1895.
———. "Proceso célebre." *Diario El Deber* (Trujillo, Peru), March 21, 1895.
Salomon, Frank, and Mercedes Niño-Murcia. *The Lettered Mountain: A Peruvian Village's Way with Writing.* Durham, N.C.: Duke University Press, 2011.

3

The Sudamericana Publishing House

Catalogs as Objects of Study

JOSÉ ENRIQUE NAVARRO

TO THE MEMORY OF ENRIQUE FIERRO (1941–2016)

DESPITE THE FACT THAT publishing houses are widely recognized as agents of culture, their catalogs and archives have not received adequate critical attention. This may be due to a variety of interrelated reasons. First, with the exception of commemorative publications, publishers' catalogs are, obviously, tools of advertisement, at least in part.[1] Likewise, due to internal and external factors, such as changes in collections and price inflation, they tend to become ephemera. This has often led to publishers' catalogs being neglected as objects of study. Working with catalogs is not always easy, given that precisely because of their commercial and temporary character, not many libraries house this kind of document. Moreover, only a limited number of libraries preserve the archives of publishing companies, taking into account that when the latter disappear—or when they are acquired by other firms—most of their historical archives (correspondence, original manuscripts, catalogs, etc.) are usually destroyed.[2]

Even with all these restrictions, some scholars have been able to research these archives and produce seminal works in the field of the history of publishing and editorial policies in Argentina. In the 1980s Jorge B. Rivera wrote several monographs analyzing the professionalization of the writer and the development of Argentina's cultural industry since its independence in 1810 until 1970.[3] After reviewing several publishers' catalogs, Rivera laid out some general characteristics of the Argentine publishing industry and book market between 1930 and 1970, such as the transition from mass publications of foreign authors in translation to the preference for national authors.

In 1995 Leandro de Sagastizábal published *La edición de libros en la Argentina*, a brief monograph that traces the history of the Argentine publishing industry and its most notable milestones. Sagastizábal's study also starts in the early nineteenth century and ends at the beginning of the 1970s. Undoubtedly, one of the greatest contributions of Sagastizábal's work is the study of individual publishing houses by combining the analysis of their catalogs, public statistical data, and, in some rare cases, internal production reports from those same houses. The critic used this same method in his introduction to the volume commemorating the fiftieth anniversary of the founding of the University of Buenos Aires Press (Editorial Universitaria de Buenos Aires or Eudeba), which Sagastizábal directed from 2002 to 2005.

However, the work that has relied most on the catalog as a source of information and study is the influential *Editores y políticas editoriales en Argentina, 1880–2000*. In his prologue, the editor, José Luis de Diego, points out various methodological tensions that his colleagues and he himself had to face. For the purposes of this chapter, two of these tensions are particularly relevant. The first is the conjugation of quantitative elements, associated with the development of the book as an industry—such as new titles published per year, average first print runs, or total book sales—with qualitative ones that allow for evaluating the cultural impact of certain editorial policies.[4] This is precisely the main purpose of this chapter: to examine the catalogs of the publishing house Sudamericana and the influence of its publications in the Argentine cultural field between 1939 and 1969. The second tension to which Diego refers is the necessary balance between the reference to collections, titles, and authors that form the catalog and the proposal of interpretative hypotheses, thus avoiding falling "into the mere reference to a series of catalogs."[5] Such a tension was extreme in the case of the volume directed by Diego, given that each chapter analyzed a particular time period of Argentine publishing and cultural fields using multiple publishers' catalogs as references. In contrast, by limiting the subject matter of the present chapter to one publishing house, the reference to the catalogs will be more extensive and will also consider some elements previous critics have not always paid adequate attention to, such as their format, presentation, and indexes. In brief, the following pages consider publishers' catalogs as texts and as cultural artifacts, and examine them as both bibliographic and historic documents. Consequently, this work is based on the joint observation of a series of texts, Sudamericana's catalogs, and the contexts in which they appeared; that is, the 1940s to the end of the 1960s in Argentina. A contextualized reading of the catalogs will provide a better understanding of both their relevance as objects of study and the role of literary translation as a necessary step for the publication of certain Spanish American authors by Sudamericana that will later become part of the canon. Thus, the present work combines a text-based analysis of the publisher catalogs with an observation of the material conditions of cultural production.

Sudamericana from Its Foundation to 1950: Translation Matters

The history of the publisher Sudamericana illustrates perfectly some of the periods the Argentine book industry has gone through, starting with its so-called golden age during the second third of the twentieth century until the purchase of local publishing houses by international multimedia groups in more recent years. Founded in 1939, Sudamericana began with a board of directors composed of a group of Argentine and Spanish intellectuals and financiers. Some of those intellectuals were Victoria Ocampo—publisher of the legendary literary magazine *Sur*—and avant-garde poet Oliverio Girondo. Among the businessmen, the Catalan politician, businessman, and lawyer Rafael Vehils stands out. Many of the intellectuals left Sudamericana soon after issues emerged regarding the publication of "their friends, poets and writers, but with no business sense."[6] It was then that Rafael Vehils hired a Catalan printer, publisher, and bookseller named Antonio López Llausás.

Both Vehils and López Llausás had been members of the Barcelona Book Chamber board, but at different times. Vehils was its secretary in the early 1920s, before moving to South America in 1924. Meanwhile, López Llausás served as vice president of the chamber until it was seized by anarchist militias in 1936, when he went into exile in France. At Sudamericana, López Llausás acted as executive manager, and another Spaniard, Julian Urgoiti, as editorial manager. Urgoiti had been in charge of the Argentinie branch of the Spanish publisher Calpe (later Espasa-Calpe) before joining Sudamericana. He was also the brother of Nicolás Urgoiti, founder of the powerful industrial paper company Papelera Española, and director of both the influential newspaper *El Sol* and the publishing house Calpe.

One feature of Sudamericana worth mentioning, at least in its beginnings as an organization, is that it was fostered by the establishment of affiliative relationships. According to critic Edward Said, one characteristic of affiliative relationships is that their members are part of a community that shares certain ideas, values, and a given concept of the world, and whose ties, far from being based on blood relationships, are built on consensus, collegiality, and class, among others.[7] In this regard, the affiliative relationships in Sudamericana would constitute a sort of brotherhood that would compensate a work and social structure affected by migration and exile. Later, Sudamericana became a family company. López Llausas's son, Jorge López Llovet, joined Sudamericana but died unexpectedly soon thereafter. As a consequence, Gloria López Llovet, López Llausas's granddaughter, took over the house from 1979 until its purchase in 1998 by the German media conglomerate Bertelsmann.

Regarding its editorial policy, it is paradoxical to note that while one of Sudamericana's founding objectives was to make Latin American authors well known,[8] literary works in translation prevailed in its catalog until the late 1940s. The decision to publish so many foreign authors had as its ultimate purpose that of occupying a more prominent position in the transatlantic book market. This struggle for the Spanish-language book market began in the late nineteenth century, when Spain came to terms with the loss of its former colonies.[9] After independence, the former American colonies broke off relations with their erstwhile metropolis, paving the way for French and German publishers to become the main suppliers of Spanish-language books in the new republics. The Spanish publishing industry had to wait for the outbreak of World War I to regain control of the book market across the Atlantic. Nevertheless, its supremacy was never total, as it had to compete in some territories, such as Argentina, with a flourishing local publishing industry. In any case, Spain's dominant position only lasted for two decades, until the beginning of the Spanish Civil War. Many factors played against the Spanish publishing industry, such as the paper shortage in Europe; the shrinkage of the local reading public; the lack of human, technical, and economic resources; and the heavy burden of Francoist censorship. For all these reasons, many European and American writers who had previously published in Spain decided to sell their translation rights to Argentine houses.[10]

The wars in Spain and Europe were a necessary but insufficient condition for the development and growth of the Argentine cultural industry between 1938 and 1955; that is, during its so-called golden age.[11] Also, the increase in literacy levels boosted the growth of the middle class in Argentina. Weakened foreign competition, combined with a growing readership inside the country, led to an eightfold increase in editorial production during that period. This unprecedented growth in book publishing matches the Argentine tango, comics, and cinema booms. The country's most outstanding authors of the period (e.g., Aníbal Troilo, Enrique Santos Discépolo, Héctor G. Oesterheld, Hugo Pratt, Mario Soffici, and Leopoldo Torre Nilsson) found a growing and expectant audience.

Several statistics show how, starting in 1938, Argentina ceased to be simply a host country to become a producer and distributor in its own right. For example, while in 1920 half of Spain's publishing production was sold in Latin America, two decades later, during the postwar period, 80 percent of the books that circulated in Spain were printed in Argentina.[12] The figure that symbolizes as few others the drift in power from the Spanish to the Argentine publishing industry is Joaquin Oteyza. He was born in Madrid in 1889 and devoted his entire life to book trading in Spain and America. In his biography there are two outstanding milestones. In 1935 in Buenos Aires he opened the biggest warehouse of Spanish books in America, with funds mainly from consolidated publishers such as Sopena, Gili, and Salvat. In 1944, nine years later, in spite of the publishing slowdown suffered in Spain, he opened an Argentine book warehouse in Madrid whose first shipment consisted of more than three hundred tons of books.[13]

Argentine publishers stocked not only Spain but also Latin America with translations. Reaching such a vast reading public required overcoming the various dialectal varieties of Spanish, and this was only possible through the widespread use of a neutral, flat Spanish in translations.[14] On the other hand, and as far as Sudamericana is concerned, such foreign markets' acceptance of Argentine books justified the owners of Sudamericana opening first Edhasa (Editora y Distribuidora Hispanoamericana, Sociedad Anónima) in Barcelona in 1946, and, three years later, Hermes in Mexico. In the beginning, both companies merely functioned as distributors. Edhasa, for example, distributed Sudamericana's catalog in Spain, as well as the catalogs of its competitors Emecé and the Mexican Fondo de Cultura Económica. There are other facts that could explain the creation of these two companies in the second half of 1940. While López Llovet relates the creation of Edhasa and Hermes to political issues, in particular the "rising of Peronism," Dalla Corte and Espósito link it to the economic threat that loomed over Argentina's economy with the outbreak of World War II. This would be the reason behind Sudamericana's increasing capital and purchasing one of the most prominent bookstores in Buenos Aires, the Librería del Colegio.[15]

In any case, Sudamericana's important work was reflected in its catalog. The comparison between the number of titles listed in 1942 and in 1950 is revealing. The first one, published after four years of activity, had 80 titles, 24 of which were works from local authors.[16] The general catalog of 1950 included 396 references, an increase in titles of approximately 500 percent. The number of existing collections is also enlightening. In 1942, there were eight: "Horizonte" (Horizon), "Ciencia y Cultura" (Science and Culture), "Breviarios del Pensamiento Filosófico" (Compendium of Philosophical Thought), "Enciclopedia Agropecuaria" (Agriculture Encyclopedia), "Colección Infantil" (Children's Collection), "Credo de Pensadores" (Thinkers Creed), "Autores Argentinos," and "Sur"; a ninth collection was also announced that year, the "Biblioteca de Orientación Económica" (Library of Economic Orientation).[17] By 1950, these exceeded thirty.

Although it has not been possible to examine any catalogs prior to the 1950 edition, existing information about the catalogs published in the 1940s provides enough insight to reach a few preliminary conclusions regarding Sudamericana's editorial policy and the role of translation at the time. For example, there were two collections that published translated literature: "Horizonte" and "Sur." The former, dedicated to contemporary novels, released forty-five titles in 1945, of which only one was signed by an Argentine author (*Las águilas* [1943], by Eduardo Mallea) and another one by the Spanish writer Pío Baroja (*Laura o la soledad sin remedio* [1939]). Another novel from Mallea, *La bahía del silencio*, was released in 1940 but was not included in the "Horizonte" collection.[18] Regarding the "Sur" collection, it reprinted works originally published by a homonymous publishing house that specialized specifically in avant-garde literature in translation.[19] As a result of an agreement between the two publishers, Sudamericana reprinted, for example, Jorge Luis Borges's translation of Virginia Woolf's *Orlando*. Sudamericana also acquired the translation rights to other works not previously published by Sur. Such is the case of *The Wild Palms*, by William Faulkner, which was translated by Borges himself. It was these and other publishing jobs that nurtured the professionalization of Argentine writers.[20]

Several reasons gave rise to this preference for publishing translated works. As already mentioned, there was a pan-Hispanic book market that Spanish publishing houses no longer satisfied. But it is also true that Argentine writers had not yet gained local readers' trust. That is one of the conclusions Adolfo Prieto reached in his 1956 study, *Sociología del público argentino*.[21] Nevertheless, some publishing houses, such as Losada, opted for publishing Latin American authors. This statement may seem odd, because it is known that Losada published and recovered the work of many Spanish writers who were banned by the Franco regime, such as authors referred to as the Generation of '27. However, as Fernando Larraz shows in his study of Losada's pocket collection, "Biblioteca Contemporánea," comparing the number of authors according to their origin and not the number of titles published by each one, the difference between them is scant: 35 percent Spaniards compared to 30 percent Latin Americans. The number of authors who were published in translation is even smaller, 25 percent.[22] Following French sociologist Pierre Bourdieu, it is possible to assert that, by publishing a large number of foreign contemporary authors, several Argentine houses, such as Emecé, Losada, and Sudamericana, ended up occupying close positions in the local publishing field, and that subsequent differences in their publications policies, shown in their catalogs, were a desire to change their position in that field, so they could differentiate or individualize themselves in the eyes of booksellers, writers, readers, and so on.[23] For example, while all three of these houses published contemporary literature in translation practically from their start-up, Losada ended up suffering from its firm adherence to realist, committed literature.[24] Larraz dates Losada's decline to 1955, after the resignation of Guillermo de Torre as editorial director.[25] By contrast, that same year, Sudamericana, considered more eclectic and even commercial in its publications policies, hired Paco Porrúa as literary advisor in substitution of Julián Urgoiti. Porrúa contributed to the renovation of Sudamericana's catalog. He is associated with the discovery of Julio Cortázar and Gabriel García Márquez, among others. Finally, Emecé is remembered as a publisher, among others, of the collection of detective novels *El Séptimo Círculo* (The seventh circle), directed by Jorge Luis Borges and his longtime friend Adolfo Bioy Casares. Both would later become Emecé authors. The abovementioned changes in the publications policies can be traced back by analyzing and comparing the catalogs published before and after 1950. This exercise will shed light on the impact that literary translations had on the emergence of a number of renowned Spanish American authors in the 1950s and 1960s, many of whom were published by Sudamericana.

The 1950 and 1969 Sudamericana Catalogs

A perusal of the Sudamericana catalogs provides insight into some of the house's publishing policies, as well as the position it held in Argentine publishing and the cultural field from 1939 to 1969. One paradox worth highlighting when comparing the information in the catalogs from the 1940s with those of the 1950s and of 1969 is that of the disappearance of collections specifically dedicated to Argentine literature. Sagastizábal mentions the existence in 1942 of a collection titled "Autores Argentinos," which is later eliminated from the 1945 catalog.[26] Likewise, the 1969 catalog no longer mentions the "Narrativa Argentina" collection, which, Diego states, included major midcentury literary works from Argentine writers such as *Adan Buenosayres* (1948), by Leopoldo Marechal; *El túnel* (whose first edition was published in 1948 by the Sur publishing house), by Ernesto Sabato; *Bestiario* (1951), by Julio Cortázar; and *Misteriosa Buenos Aires* (1969), by Manuel Mújica Laínez.[27] These omissions may be due to the internal structure of the two catalogs, whose content was organized by subject instead of by collections, with only a few exceptions. Thus, when presenting its literary works, the 1950 catalog opens with a brief introduction to the "Horizonte" collection, followed by an annotated list of the eighty-three titles comprising it. The catalog then presents eleven works under the section "Other Novels." It follows the same system with its compilations of books of short stories, poetry, and theater—nine, fifteen, and nine works, respectively: it organizes them by subject with no mention of any specific collections, if any did indeed exist.

The 1969 catalog reinforces this organization by subject matter. As stated in its prologue, the different collections and publishing projects are grouped into broad sections, each with its appropriate subcategories, to offer booksellers and readers a clear, organized look at its extensive offerings.[28] The literature section, which once again opens the catalog and takes up almost half of its pages, is divided into novels, short stories, biographies, essays, theater, poetry, travel, history, literary criticism, and anthologies, as well as the "Colección Diamante," which consists of luxury editions of complete or selected works. The "Horizonte" collection seems not to have been deemed worthy of either space or presentation here, although the brief text introducing the novel category does mention it. This text also notes the "El Espejo" collection, describing it as a recent creation and one especially aimed at publishing "Latin American authors, who are becoming increasingly highly regarded."[29] Some titles appear along with an *H* or an *E* to indicate that they belong to one of these two collections. A count of the works marked in this way reveals that almost 70 percent of the fiction—novels or short stories—belongs to the "Horizonte" collection (177 of the 260 fiction works listed in the catalog). Only 10 percent, or 25 works, are from the "El Espejo" collection. The remainder, less than 60 books, belong to other collections, including, one supposes, "Narrativa Argentina." What is baffling is that the "Horizonte" collection is included within the general literature section, with its titles sprinkled among those from other collections, while the "Sur" collection, with only 35 books divided between fiction and essays, enjoys its own section in the catalog, listed under "Miscellany." One wonders, then, why the "Horizonte" collection was not recognized individually as a relevant category, when the remaining works from other collections could have been listed under "Other Novels," as they were in the 1950 catalog.

The answer to this question may be gleaned by analyzing other aspects of the Sudamericana catalogs, such as the indexes at the back of the publications and the illustrations included with the works presented. When studying the 1923 catalog put out by Calpe publishers, Juan Miguel Sánchez Vigil considers that Calpe gave priority to works over writers when it included an index of titles but not of authors.[30] Following this same criterion, it could be concluded that Sudamericana gradually placed greater emphasis on the authors than on the works themselves. Indeed, the 1950 catalog concludes with three indexes, one each for authors, titles, and subject matter, while the 1969 catalog omits the one on titles. Also supporting this hypothesis is the fact that by 1950, most of the images included alongside the commentary on the works consisted of photographs of the authors rather than reproductions of book jackets. This is especially evident among works of literature. For example, only eleven of the eighty-two books from the "Horizonte" collection reviewed in the catalog are shown with their book jackets; the others appear with a photograph as a heading for the commenting text.

The 1969 catalog underwent a number of significant design changes compared to the 1950 edition, possibly due to the constant increase in the number of titles published—climbing from 400 in 1950 to over 1,200—and to the competition of other mass media, particularly television, which robbed the average citizen of some of the time that he or she had previously spent reading books. Consequently, the 1969 catalog was no longer the "Reading Catalog," as boasted in the 1950 preface.[31] The first difference that someone would notice on first glance between the two editions is the number of books listed per page, which rose from two to ten and required a drastic reduction in the length of the blurbs (see figures 3.1 and 3.2).[32] This is why the 1950 descriptions and comments were replaced in 1969 with two or three sentences composed in a marked advertising style. Printing more titles per page also limited the number of illustrations that could be incorporated, and by 1969, photographs of authors and book jackets no longer accompanied each title listed, replaced by a scant two illustrations per page, that is, two for every ten book titles. Thus, a mere

FIGURE 3.1 Pages from the 1950 Sudamericana catalog. *Catálogo General no. 5* (Buenos Aires: Sudamericana, 1950).

forty-four illustrations appeared with the 250 novels offered in the 1969 catalog, only twenty-one of which were photographs of writers. While this would seem to contradict the thesis previously stated—that the use of photographs reflected the priority given to the authors rather than works—it is important to note that a third of these photographs illustrated extensive biographies of the house's prominent authors. Some were major figures of the so-called Boom of the Latin American narrative in the 1960s, such as Julio Cortázar or Gabriel García Márquez, while others were pre-Boom authors who also began to enjoy more attention, including Leopoldo Marechal and Ernesto Sabato.[33] Of the fourteen authors reviewed, two are Colombian—García Márquez, mentioned earlier, and Germán Arciniegas—and the others are equally divided between Argentine and non-Spanish-language authors.[34] Most of the Latin Americans

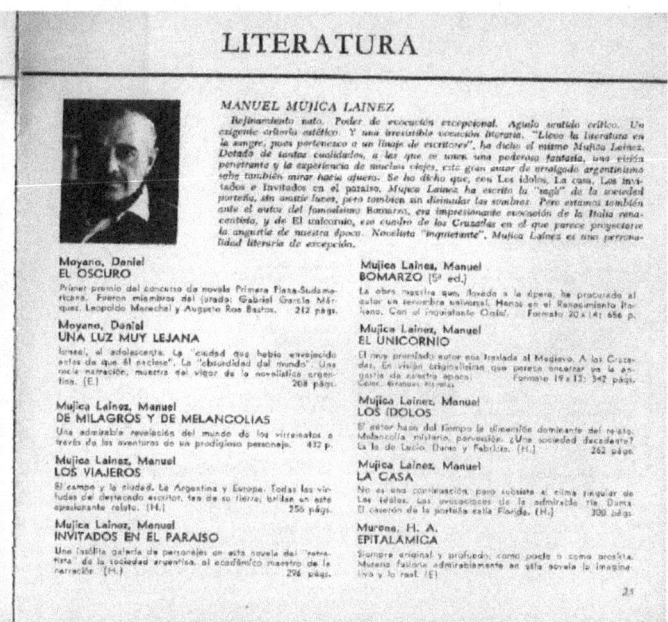

FIGURE 3.2 Pages from the 1969 Sudamericana catalog. *Catálogo General de la Editorial Sudamericana, 1939–1969* (Buenos Aires: Sudamericana, 1969).

have in common that they had not been published in the "Horizonte" collection. In fact, as Larraz states, two-thirds of this collection's titles are translated works.[35] All of the above leads to the conclusion that the purpose of grouping the vast majority of fiction collections under the general category of "novel" or "short story" and draining away such collections as "Horizonte" and "Narrativa Argentina" was to place greater emphasis on Latin American writers, who became very successful with the popularity of the Boom.

However, it would be incorrect to assume that the Sudamericana catalog suddenly became populated by local authors in the 1960s. Rather, it was a gradual process, one that began in 1945, was consolidated during the 1950s—coinciding with the recovery of the Spanish publishing industry and the growth of publishing in other Latin American countries—and gained steam during the Boom of the Latin American narrative in the 1960s. As previously stated, the 1945 catalog contained fiction from only three South American authors: two novels by Argentine Eduardo Mallea; and short story collections by Pablo Rojas Paz, also from Argentina, and the Uruguayan Juana de Ibarbourou. The

1950 catalog already exhibited evidence of this change. It included, together with the previous catalogs, a number of Argentine and Latin American writers whom we can only consider to be modest compared to the many authors in translation: Germán Arciniegas, Leonidas Barletta, Carmen Gándara, Felisberto Hernández, Leopoldo Marechal, Manuel Mújica Laínez, and Ernesto Sabato. Julio Cortázar published *Bestiario* the following year (although sales were scant, as with Marechal's *Adán Buenosyares*), Silvina Bullrich's pen was added to Sudamericana in 1958, Daniel Moyano published his first novel in 1966, and García Márquez, as is well known, published *Cien años de soledad* in 1967. These writers were featured in the 1969 catalog, along with other writers who were making a name for themselves, such as Carlos Fuentes and Mario Vargas Llosa, as well as such debut authors as Juan José Saer.

Sudamericana's poetry publishing followed a similar pattern from the 1940s to 1969. Of the twelve poets that appeared in the 1950 catalog, nine were Argentine: Francisco Luis Bernández, Fermín Estrella Gutiérrez, Orlando Franco, Oliverio Girondo, Leopoldo Marechal, Enrique Molina, Helena Muñoz Larreta, Silvina Ocampo, and Juan Rodolfo Wilcock. Of these, five were published between 1940 and 1946, and the other four between 1949 and 1950. This indicates that in the field of poetry, at least at Sudamericana, the catalog was already showing its preference for homegrown authors, with numbers that continued to grow considerably after 1949. Later, as previously indicated, their prominence was even greater: of the thirty-four poets listed in the 1969 catalog, twenty-eight were Argentine, the most important of whom were César Fernández Moreno, Alberto Giri, and Alejandra Pizarnik.[36]

The increasing share of Argentine authors listed in the Sudamericana catalog was due in part to stronger competition from the publishing industry in other countries, such as Mexico or, to a much lesser extent, Venezuela. The houses of these countries began to publish works and authors in translation formerly distributed by Argentine publishers. However, this outburst in the number of local writers being published arose as the consequence of the predominance of works in translation in Sudamericana's collections in the 1940s. The effect of translation was twofold. On the one hand, some writers relied on translations or related editorial activities for their livelihoods. But translating, editing, or proofreading foreign avant-garde literature served them also as a sort of exercise in style, whereby these authors learned, adapted, and adopted pioneering literary techniques, experimental narrative structures, and in some cases a whole new vocabulary. On the other hand, it was thanks to the introduction to avant-garde writers translated into Spanish during previous decades that the public was able to begin to appreciate works written by its compatriot authors. Thus, *Sur* magazine's translations of experimental works, which were later reprinted by Sudamericana in the 1940s, paved the way for, some years later, a growing number of university- and high school–educated readers who were able to enjoy more sophisticated books. As Naomi Lindstrom indicates, it is only at the end of the 1940s that many features of avant-garde movements finally came into their own in the Argentine literary world.[37] As previously mentioned, publishers such as Losada that opted for literary continuity and traditional realism began to lose ground,[38] while those who placed their bets on antirealist literature, including Sudamericana and Emecé, remained strong. Undoubtedly, the success of certain Argentine authors who are today considered essential reading is due not only to their inherent value but also to two phenomena—the proliferation of translated works and the Boom in Latin American fiction—in which the literary and publishing worlds went hand in hand.

Notes

1. For one of these exceptions, see *50 años de libros para todos*, a catalog published in 2008 in commemoration of the fiftieth anniversary of the founding of the University of Buenos Aires Press, known as Eudeba. Here we consider the definition of a publishers' catalog proposed by Juan Manuel Sánchez Vigil as a "memory or inventory of the collections of a publisher with the description of its contents, whose purpose is its presentation and promotion." Sánchez Vigil, "La editorial CALPE," 263. Unless otherwise stated, all translations are mine.
2. In the Spanish-language book industry, the archives of the historic house Salvat were destroyed after it was acquired in 1988 by the French publishing group Hachette. Salvat, Interview, 131. On some occasions, the former owners cannot publicly denounce the destruction of historical archives without violating the confidentiality clause included in the purchase agreement.
3. Strictly speaking, the first history of the Argentine publishing industry, *Libreros, editores e impresores de Buenos Aires*, by Domingo Buonocore, came out in 1944. Other classic monographs that deal with the history of the book and the publishing industry in Argentina were published in the first half of the 1960s. However, their authors—Raúl Bottaro and Eustasio A. García—based their analyses mainly on statistical data, disregarding publishers' catalogs or publishing policies as elements worth considering. See Bottaro, *La edición de libros en Argentina*; and García, *Desarrollo de la industria editorial argentina*. Jorge B. Rivera takes these works as a starting point for his studies *El camino hacia la profesionalización (1810–1900)*, *La forja del escritor profesional (1900–1930)*, *El auge de la industria editorial (1930–1955)*, and *Apogeo y crisis de la industria del libro: 1955–1970*. These monographs,

originally published in 1981 by Centro Editor de América Latina as dossiers of its acclaimed collection "Capítulo: La historia de la literatura argentina," were later compiled in the volume *El escritor y la industria editorial* by Atuel. The most recent edition, in digital format, is available on the website of Red de Historia de los Medios (http://rehime.com.ar).

4. Diego, *Editores y políticas editoriales en Argentina*, xi.
5. Diego, *Editores y políticas editoriales en Argentina*, xii.
6. López Llovet, *Sudamericana*, 29.
7. Said, "Secular Criticism," 19–20.
8. López Llovet, *Sudamericana*, 9.
9. Dalla Corte and Espósito, "Mercado del libro y empresas editoriales," 262.
10. Willson, "Traducir lo nuevo," 5.
11. Beginning and end dates of this fruitful publishing period in Argentina are not clearly established. Thus Sagastizábal estimates its beginning around 1936 (*La edición de libros en la Argentina*, 75), perhaps following Rivera's criteria, who proposed 1936–56 (*El escritor y la industria editorial*, 577) as the golden age of the Argentine cultural industry. Taking 1936 as the starting year is debatable for two reasons, one chronological and the other statistical. On the one hand, although the military uprising took place in Spain around mid-July 1936, and most of the Catalan publishers, mainly exporters, were collectivized in the following months, it seems difficult to argue that its effects could be felt already before the end of that year. In fact, existing statistics data deny that there was a substantial growth in the number of titles or copies published until 1938. See Bottaro, *La edición de libros en Argentina*, 31; García, *Desarrollo de la industria editorial argentina*, 105; and Rivera, *El escritor y la industria editorial*, 582. Fernando Larraz, who establishes the peak of the Argentine book industry between 1937 and 1951, may be considered more accurate ("Política y cultura," 1). Similarly, Diego dates it around 1938 to 1955 (*Editores y políticas editoriales en Argentina*, 91).
12. Rivera, *El escritor y la industria editorial*, 578–79.
13. Mangada and Pol, *Libreros y editores*, 195.
14. Willson, "Traducir lo nuevo," 136. This flat Spanish is still used nowadays in books translated and published in Spanish and then exported to Latin America. See Marín, "El español de todos y de nadie."
15. López Llovet, *Sudamericana*, 43; Dalla Corte and Espósito, "Mercado del libro y empresas editoriales," 280. Anti-Peronism was common among the managers of the main Argentine publishing houses, such as Losada, Sur, Emecé, Rueda, and Paidós. Giuliani, "Los editores y la irrupción del Peronismo," 5–6.
16. Sagastizábal, *La edición de libros en la Argentina*, 108.
17. Sagastizábal, *La edición de libros en la Argentina*, 108.
18. Diego, *Editores y políticas editoriales en Argentina*, 96.
19. Victoria Ocampo founded the literary magazine *Sur* in 1931. Two years later, she created the publisher of the same name for the purpose of offsetting the magazine's expenses with the sale of translation rights. Willson, "Los editores españoles," 146.

20. For example, Eduardo Mallea was in charge of three literary collections of the house Emecé: "Quimera," "Cuadernos de la Quimera," and "Grandes Novelistas." Larraz, "Los exiliados y las colecciones editoriales," 140.
21. Diego, *Editores y políticas editoriales en Argentina*, 114.
22. Larraz, "Política y cultura," 7. These percentages did not change much over time. The analysis of the number of authors published in this collection until 1961 provides the following figures: 42 percent are Spanish authors, 40 percent are Latin Americans, and 18 percent are foreign authors in translation. Larraz, "Los exiliados y las colecciones editoriales," 135.
23. Bourdieu, "A Conservative Revolution in Publishing," 135, 125.
24. Diego, "La literatura latinoamericana," 152.
25. Larraz, "Guillermo de Torre," 65.
26. Diego, *Editores y políticas editoriales en Argentina*, 96.
27. Diego, *Editores y políticas editoriales en Argentina*, 96.
28. *Catálogo General de la Editorial Sudamericana*, 5.
29. *Catálogo General de la Editorial Sudamericana*, 7.
30. Sánchez Vigil, "La editorial CALPE," 270.
31. *Catálogo General no. 5*, 4.
32. Before 1950 only one book was featured per page. Nevertheless, as the 1950 catalog states in its prologue, the amount of text accompanying each work has not changed compared to previous catalogs. *Catálogo General no. 5*, 5.
33. The publication of a series of Spanish American novels in a short period of time, such as Mario Vargas Llosas's *La ciudad y los perros* (*The Time of the Hero*, 1963), Julio Cortázar's *Rayuela* (*Hopscotch*, 1963), and Gabriel García Márquez's *Cien años de soledad* (*One Hundred Years of Solitude*, 1967) prompted a worldwide interest in Spanish American narrative and literature, labeled as the "Boom." A great deal has been written about the weight of extra literary factors in the outbreak of the Boom, particularly the success of the Cuban Revolution as well as the marketing strategies employed by certain publishing houses on both shores of the Atlantic. A fuller discussion would need more space than is available here, and would shift radically the focus of the present work, which is the study of Sudamericana's catalogs from the early 1940s to the late 1960s. A complete analysis of the Boom of the Spanish American literature and their publishers would require a study of the catalog and editorial policies of many other houses, such as the abovementioned Losada and Emecé, the Spanish publisher Seix Barral, or the Mexican publishing house Fondo de Cultura Económica.
34. The featured authors were as follows: in the section "Literatura," Silvina Bulrich, Julio Cortázar, Lawrence Durrell, Gabriel García Márquez, Eduardo Mallea, Manuel Mújica Laínez, Roger Peyrefitte, Simone de Beauvoir, Aldous Huxley, Lin Yutang, Salvador de Madariaga, and Leopoldo Marechal; in the section "Ciencia y Técnica," zoologist Julian Huxley (Aldous Huxley's brother); in the section "Grandes Obras" (Great Works), historian Will Durant and philosopher José Ferrater Mora; and in the section "Libros de Bolsillo" (Paperbacks), Germán Arciniegas and Ernesto Sabato.

35. Larraz, "Los exiliados y las colecciones editoriales," 137.
36. The number of studies and anthologies on Argentinian poetry published between 1955 and 1970 is remarkable. Examples include *Poesía argentina del siglo XX*, edited by Juan Carlos Ghiano (1957), *Antología de poesía nueva en la República Argentina*, edited by Juan Carlos Martelli (1961), *Antología de la poesía argentina contemporánea*, edited by César Rosales (1964), *La realidad y los papeles: Panorama y muestra de la poesía argentina*, edited by César Fernández Moreno (1967), and *Antología lineal de la poesía argentina*, edited by César Fernández Moreno and Horacio Jorge Becco (1968).
37. Lindstrom, *Twentieth-Century Spanish American Fiction*, 108.
38. Diego, "La literatura latinoamericana," 152.

Works Cited

50 años de libros para todos. Buenos Aires: Eudeba, 2008.

Bottaro, Raúl H. *La edición de libros en Argentina*. Buenos Aires: Troquel, 1964.

Bourdieu, Pierre. "A Conservative Revolution in Publishing." Translated by Ryan Fraser. *Translation Studies* 1, no. 2 (2008): 123–53.

Buonocore, Domingo. *Libreros, editores e impresores de Buenos Aires*. Buenos Aires: El Ateneo, 1944.

Catálogo General de la Editorial Sudamericana, 1939–1969. Buenos Aires: Sudamericana, 1969.

Catálogo General no. 5. Buenos Aires: Sudamericana, 1950.

Cortázar, Julio. *Rayuela*. Buenos Aires: Sudamericana, 1963.

Dalla Corte, Gabriela, and Fabio Espósito. "Mercado del libro y empresas editoriales entre el Centenario de las Independencias y la Guerra Civil española: La editorial Sudamericana." *Revista Complutense de Historia de América* 36 (2010): 257–89. doi:10.5209/rev_RCHA.2010.v36.12.

Diego, José Luis de, dir. *Editores y políticas editoriales en Argentina, 1880–2000*. Buenos Aires: Fondo de Cultura Económica, 2006.

———. "La literatura latinoamericana en el proyecto de Losada." In *La otra cara de Jano: Una mirada crítica sobre el libro y la edición*, 141–64. Buenos Aires: Ampersand, 2015.

Fernández Moreno, César, ed. *La realidad y los papeles: Panorama y muestra de la poesía argentina*. Madrid: Aguilar, 1967.

Fernández Moreno, César, and Horacio Jorge Becco, eds. *Antología lineal de la poesía argentina*. Madrid: Gredos, 1968.

García, Eustasio A. *Desarrollo de la industria editorial argentina*. Buenos Aires: Fundación Interamericana de Biblioteconomía Franklin, 1965.

García Márquez, Gabriel. *Cien años de soledad*. Buenos Aires: Sudamericana, 1967.

Ghiano, Juan Carlos, ed. *Poesía argentina del siglo XX*. Mexico City: Fondo de Cultura Económica, 1957.

Giuliani, Alejandra. "Los editores y la irrupción del Peronismo (1945–1947)." Paper presented at the Primer Congreso de Estudios sobre el Peronismo: La primera década.

Facultad de Humanidades, Universidad Nacional de Mar del Plata, November 6–7, 2008. *Red de Estudios sobre el Peronismo.* http://www.peronlibros.com.ar/sites/default/files/pdfs/giuliani.pdf.

Larraz, Fernando. "Guillermo de Torre y el catálogo de la editorial Losada." *Kamchatka: Revista de Análisis Cultural* 7 (2016): 59–71. doi:10.7203/KAM.7.768.

———. "Los exiliados y las colecciones editoriales en Argentina (1938–1954)." In *El exilio republicano español en México y Argentina: Historia cultural, instituciones literarias, medios*, edited by Andrea Pagni, 129–44. Frankfurt: Iberoamericana Editorial Vervuert, 2011.

———. "Política y cultura: Biblioteca Contemporánea y Colección Austral, dos modelos de difusión cultural." *Orbis Tertium* 14, no. 15 (2009): 1–10.

Lindstrom, Naomi. *Twentieth-Century Spanish American Fiction.* Austin: University of Texas Press, 1994.

López Llovet, Gloria. *Sudamericana: Antonio López Llausás, un editor con los pies en la tierra.* Buenos Aires: Dunken, 2004.

Mangada, Alfonso, and Jesús Pol. *Libreros y editores (1920–1960): Joaquín de Oteyza: Biografía de un empresario del libro.* Madrid. Paraninfo, 1996.

Marín, Maribel. "El español de todos y de nadie." *El País*, August 26, 2016. http://cultura.elpais.com/cultura/2016/08/26/babelia/1472199140_766881.html.

Martelli, Juan Carlos, ed. *Antología de poesía nueva en la República Argentina.* Buenos Aires: Anuario, 1961.

Prieto, Adolfo. *Sociología del público argentino.* Buenos Aires: Leviatán, 1956.

Rivera, Jorge B. *El escritor y la industria editorial.* Buenos Aires: Atuel, 1988.

Rosales, César, ed. *Antología de la poesía argentina contemporánea.* Buenos Aires: Ministerio de Relaciones Exteriores y Culto, 1964.

Sagastizábal, Leandro de. *La edición de libros en la Argentina: Una empresa de cultura.* Buenos Aires: Eudeba, 1995.

Said, Edward W. "Secular Criticism." In *The World, the Text, and the Critic*, 1–30. Cambridge, Mass.: Harvard University Press, 1983.

Salvat, Juan. Interview by Emiliano Martínez. In *Conversaciones con editores: En primera persona*, edited by Felicidad Orquín, 99–137. Madrid: Siruela, 2007.

Sánchez Vigil, Juan Miguel. 2006. "La editorial CALPE y el Catálogo general de 1923." *Documentación de las Ciencias de la Información* 29 (2006): 259–77. doi:10.5209/rev_DCIN.2006.v29.20059.

Vargas Llosa, Mario. *La ciudad y los perros.* Barcelona: Seix Barral, 1963.

Willson, Patricia. "Los editores españoles y la traducción en la Argentina: Desembarco en tierras fértiles." In *El exilio republicano español en México y Argentina: Historia cultural, instituciones literarias, medios*, edited by Andrea Pagni, 145–58. Frankfurt: Iberoamericana Editorial Vervuert, 2011.

———. "Traducir lo nuevo." *Lenguas Vivas* 1 (2001): 4–9.

PART II

Textual Artifacts and Materialities

4

Guaman Poma's Library

Costume Books and the Illustration of an Indigenous Manuscript

GEORGE ANTONY THOMAS

IN AN ESSAY WRITTEN TO ACCOMPANY the 1992 exhibition organized by the Americas Society titled *Guaman Poma de Ayala: The Colonial Art of an Andean Author*, John Murra speculates on the possible sources for *El primer nueva corónica y buen gobierno* (1615?) and contemplates the location and type of library used by Felipe Guaman Poma de Ayala to compose his magisterial work.[1] At one point Murra suggests that "somewhere—most likely in Cuzco—someone had accumulated a library of historical and ecclesiastic sources that became available to a young Andean man of no special status in colonial Huamanga or Cuzco during the second half of the sixteenth century."[2] Murra eventually concludes that the most likely library would be that of the canon of the Cuzco cathedral, Cristóbal de Albornoz.[3] While it may be impossible to provide conclusive evidence of such an association or to prove that Guaman Poma was able to gain access to other collections of books, another vein of inquiry relates not to the locations or owners of these possible libraries but rather to the types of books consulted. It is certain that Guaman Poma perused a variety of sources in order to compose his manuscript, and one of the illustrated European genres that he might have encountered is the costume book.[4]

The nature of Guaman Poma's interactions with European print matter brings to the fore a neglected topic within the field of the history of the book in colonial Latin America: the circulation and appropriation of books among indigenous readers. Although the *Nueva corónica* has been heralded primarily as a source of information on Andean history and culture, it also provides ample evidence of the interactions between an indigenous author and European print culture. As Murra recounts in his essay on Guaman Poma's library, a number of scholars have revealed how textual and pictorial references in the manuscript demonstrate a familiarity with locally printed works and imported best sellers.[5] Nevertheless, despite what one art historian has characterized as a glut of scholarship on the drawings in the *Nueva corónica*, examining the influence of European printed images on Guaman Poma's illustrations will help expand our understanding of colonial Peruvian print culture and indigenous interactions with the world of print.[6] The present study seeks to remedy a gap in current scholarship by following this line of inquiry. In addition to isolating the types of books that Guaman Poma could access, an analysis of the influence of costume books on the *Nueva corónica* will help provide an understanding of how illustrations were employed in early modern books and illuminate Guaman Poma's artistic practice in relation to early modern print culture.

One of the most striking elements of Guaman Poma's manuscript is the large number of illustrations it contains. While these pictorial elements are somewhat common in manuscripts produced by indigenous authors in pre-Hispanic and colonial Mesoamerica, they are relatively rare in Andean cultural production. This practice was most likely influenced by the large variety of lavishly illustrated books that were printed in sixteenth-century Europe. In order to catalog particular categories of information, these graphic compilations in a number of fields of knowledge often contained a large number of images: illustrations of flora and fauna, anatomy diagrams, maps of cities, or depictions of foreign dress. Although there are few records of the circulation of many of these types of books in the Spanish American colonies, this chapter will explore how one variety of this genre, the costume book, is likely to have influenced the *Nueva corónica*. Often labeled with the German moniker *trachtenbuch*, costume books contain illustrations and descriptions of the clothing of particular nations, regions, or cities. Sixteenth-century costume books were primarily published in Italy, France, Germany, and the Low Countries. These abundantly illustrated books usually include depictions from four continents: Europe, Asia, Africa, and America. This global picture is then subdivided into national and regional costume, with a particular focus on the most famous regions and cities of Europe (see figure 4.1).

While the costume book may often borrow images from a variety of historical and ethnographic texts, some unique elements relating to their format and composition suggest that Guaman Poma would have been familiar with

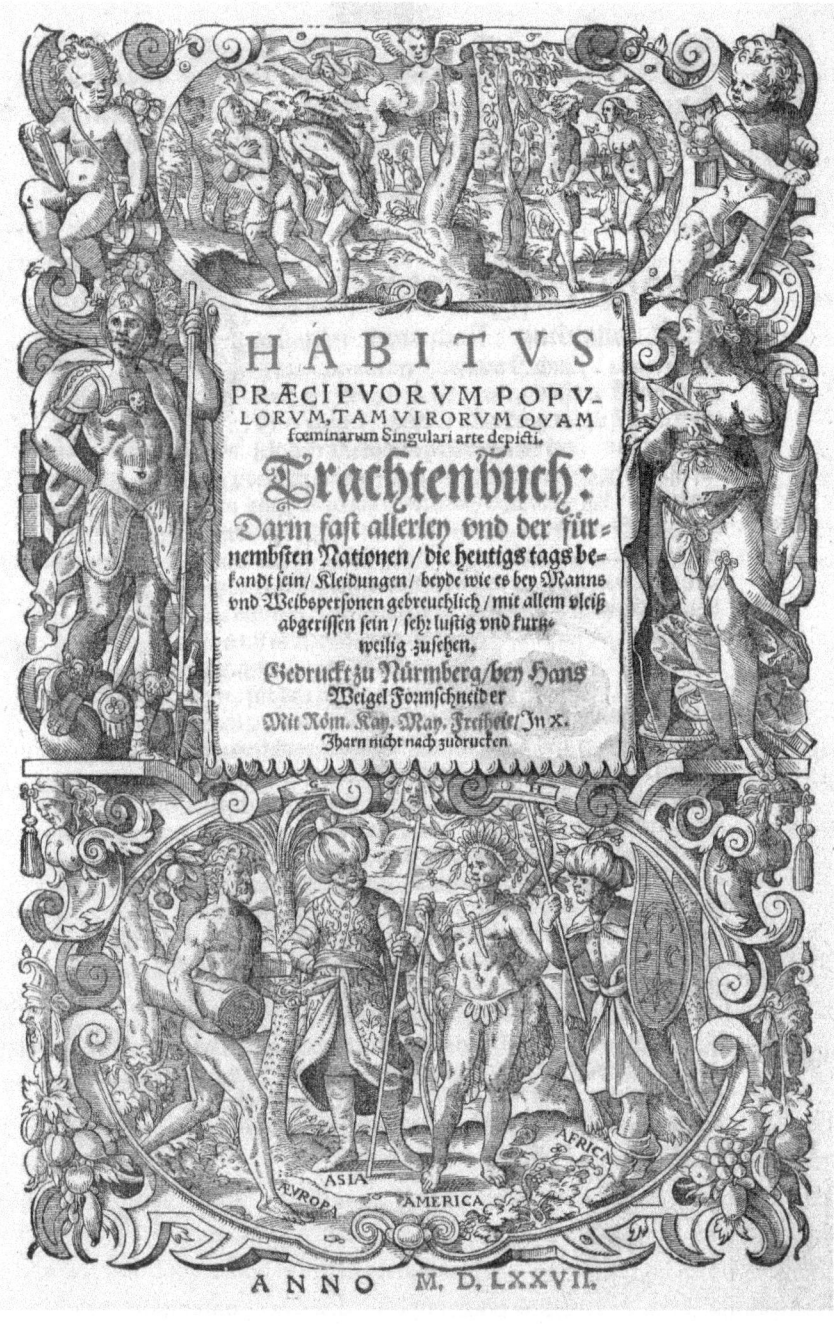

FIGURE 4.1 Frontispiece from Hans Weigel and Jost Amman, *Habitus praecipuorum populorum, tam virorum quam foeminarum singulari arte depicti* (Nuremberg, 1577), RB 66643. Huntington Library, San Marino, California.

the genre. First, as Thomas Cummins has already suggested, many of the poses adopted by figures in the *Nueva corónica* parallel the format in costume books. Specifically, Cummins highlights the mode in which single individuals are posed at the center of a page that is largely devoid of background details, often situated at the apex of a modest hill.[7] Second, costume books always contain full-page illustrations of single figures and often these are contained on every other page (most often the recto). Such an abundance of space devoted to illustrations is particularly rare in early modern books, and the *Nueva corónica* appears to emulate this general compositional pattern. Finally, as shall become clear in the remainder of this chapter, both the images and the text of the *Nueva corónica* replicate a variety of themes that are commonplace in costume books. The genre has frequently been categorized as a form of early modern ethnography that employed fashion as a means of commenting on various nations and peoples. A brief overview of some of these preoccupations—more specifically the themes of fashion and history, costume and custom, and competing representations of particular nations—will each be analyzed in relation to examples from various countries. The illustrations from these European costume books provided Guaman Poma with a model for presenting to King Philip III of Spain a history of Inca civilization and colonial Peru, one that would contain a critique of colonial authorities as well as a revisionist view of European representations of indigenous peoples.

Fashion and History: Italian Costume Books

Italian costume books, which sometimes focused on descriptions of ancient rulers from imperial Rome, are likely to have inspired Guaman Poma's illustrated accounts of Inca rulers and their accomplishments. Cummins's observations on the compositional similarities between the *Nueva corónica* and costume books largely focus on Guaman Poma's drawings of the Inca rulers and illustrations from Cesare Vecellio's *The Clothing of the Renaissance World* (1590).[8] Vecellio's work is unlike many other examples for two principal reasons. First, it contains extensive prose commentary whereas most costume books contain brief verse descriptions. Second, Vecellio's book not only discusses contemporary fashions; it also contains descriptions of what the denizens of the Roman Empire wore in the past. This type of historical inquiry, which in the Italian book is made possible by consulting classical Roman statues, is similarly at work in the *Nueva corónica*. Not only do Guaman Poma's illustrations follow a similar pattern, but the attention to detail in his prose descriptions of the tunics of Inca rulers can be seen to parallel the Italian costume book's fascination with fashion as a mode of revealing history. For example, Vecellio describes the "clothing of a Roman noblewoman two hundred years ago" in this manner: "These gentlewomen, then, wore a silk undergown, entirely of brocade and without a bodice. They pinned a mantle to their head and let it fall to the ground trailing a long way behind them, and it was decorated with a border in *porpora* or *giacinto*. These women of early Rome also often wore a tunic with a mantle, in *porpora* or *giacinto* or gold, with very precious trimmings."[9] Guaman Poma's description of the twelfth Inca queen, or *coya*, similarly focuses on particular details such as color and the patterned border (*tocapo*) of her shawl (*lliclla*) and skirt (*acsu*): "Her *lliclla* was light blue and dark green in the middle. Her *acsu* was green with *tocapo* below."[10] In both texts, the authors provide detailed descriptions of cut, materials, adornment, and pattern in addition to color. As with the Andean author's manuscript, sixteenth-century costume books did not usually contain any colored illustrations, although wealthier book-buyers could purchase or commission hand-painted editions in which the black-and-white depictions of fashion were marvelously brought to life by filling in the appropriate shades. Since the standard editions lack colored illustrations, Vecellio's volume frequently includes descriptions of colors in the accompanying prose, and these detailed depictions could aid the reader's imagination as well as serve as instructions for artists to embellish the black-and-white sketches with colored paint.

Vecellio frequently comments on the historical sources for his descriptions of fashion during the Roman Empire, largely referencing classical statues depicting Roman dress. However, it is somewhat unclear what sources the Andean author employed for his historical re-creation of Inca dress. Since scholars have largely disputed the existence of a pre-Hispanic tradition of Inca portraiture, it is unlikely that Guaman Poma would have had access to artistic representations of the Inca rulers and *coyas* that were made before the colonial period.[11] It similarly would have been improbable for Guaman Poma to have access to the material remains of what all twelve Inca rulers and their coyas had worn many centuries ago, making it more likely that he would have relied on colonial or European representations of Inca tunics. In examining Guaman Poma's drawings of Inca clothing, the anthropologist Tom Zuidema asserts that his visual and pictorial catalog of royal tunics largely conforms to the few surviving examples, although they do so in a very generic manner.[12] These confluences are explained by pointing to the existence of a material record of the past and an oral tradition preserving the codes of Inca dress. While this falls within the realm of possibility, Guaman Poma's representations of the twelve Inca rulers and coyas is primarily based on European models.[13]

Since Guaman Poma vividly describes the colors of the royal tunics, an element that was not present in most printed costume books, hand-painted manuscripts or colonial paintings might have also been a potential source.[14] Nevertheless, the likely influence of nonprint genres in his section detailing the clothing worn by Inca rulers and coyas does not negate the importance of the model provided by costume books. Zuidema's analysis of Guaman Poma's drawings cites one particular tunic in the *Nueva corónica* that is something of an aberration because it does not conform to patterns in surviving examples of Inca textiles.[15] As he observes, this curlicue design also appears on the robes of Church authorities throughout the *Nueva corónica* (see figure 4.2). He interprets this coincidence as an indication of Guaman Poma's symbolic association between Church authorities in Rome and the Inca leaders in Cuzco.[16] Whether or not this is true, the artistic similarity is most likely due to the Andean author's intent to approximate the sumptuous European fabrics of the colonial present and not the textile patterns of the Inca past.

Similar curlicue designs are replicated on clothing that appears in Vecellio's book as a form of representing damask or other costly patterned fabrics (see figure 4.3). Guaman Poma's representation of this pattern on Inca tunics communicates its association with European royalty during the colonial period. His adoption of this technique of illustration along with the general composition of the portraits and his textual commentary all point to his contact with the European genre. The native author's mode of depicting the royal line of Inca rulers and coyas within his manuscript is not the only confluence between the *Nueva corónica* and costume books. Guaman Poma's critique of Catholic clergymen as well as his desire to provide a comprehensive catalog of native Andeans are also analogous to the thematic concerns expressed in other European examples of the genre.

Costume and Custom: French and German Costume Books

While Vecellio's costume book is something of an anomaly because of its historical content, a distinguishing characteristic of some German and French costume books is that they often include illustrations of the clothing worn by clergymen accompanied by anti-Catholic rhetoric. These unflattering descrip-

FIGURE 4.2 "Inca tunic" from Felipe Guaman Poma de Ayala, *Nueva corónica y buen gobierno* (Paris: Institut d'ethnologie, 1936).

tions of members of the clergy, which parallel Guaman Poma's negative depictions of colonial Peruvian clergymen, are clearly a manifestation of Reformation propaganda.[17] Specifically in relation to the genre of the costume book, however, these anti-Catholic descriptions reflect the notion that costume could be associated with particular customs and could consequently illustrate who should be considered civilized and who should be classified as barbaric.[18] As Ann Rosalind Jones details, the French term *habit* (habit) often referred to behavior as well as modes of dress so that inevitably the commentary on a monk's habit (clothing) touched upon his comportment as well.[19] In their criticism of religious

FIGURE 4.3 "Venetian robes" from Cesare Vecellio, *De gli habiti antichi, et moderni di diverse parti del mondo libri due* (Venice, 1590), RB 144274. Huntington Library, San Marino, California.

figures, costume books often invoke the notion of a habit being a "disguise" in that a sacred garment hides the corrupt individual beneath it. The French costume book *A Collection of the Various Styles of Clothing Which Are Presently Worn in Countries of Europe, Asia, Africa and the Savage Islands* (Paris, 1562) often emphasizes the sumptuousness of the clothes worn by Catholic clergy as a means of underlining their lack of virtue. As with the following verse description of "the canon," clergymen are often criticized for a lack of humility and for eschewing the vow of poverty: "Not only is the monk fat and vigorous, / (He is) well fed, comfortably bedded, well dressed. / But the rich canon is thus content, / Adorned with clothes and not with virtue."[20] Guaman Poma similarly critiques the falseness of clergymen in the descriptions that accompany his drawings of them. In one instance, he provides a depiction of a well-dressed priest and comments:

> The aforementioned parish priests in riches . . . walk about dressed entirely in silk with their fine clothes and a cap like a soldier and a ruffian or a tavern keeper when they should be dressed as poor people, as priests of Jesus Christ. Since Jesus Christ did not walk about in silk nor did he wear a cap, instead in one unchanging robe he went about teaching us in this world. You should go forth like that, father.[21]

This critical description of priests dressed in silk is preceded by an illustration of a well-dressed priest who is carefully clutching a pair of gloves, an expensive accessory during the time period that was often pictured in costume book illustrations of richly dressed aristocratic men. Guaman Poma's criticism of the priests' robes is part of his broader message in this rather condemnatory section that emphasizes that ecclesiastical authorities fail to embrace the virtues of poverty and humility. Instead, according to Guaman Poma, the majority of the priests in colonial Peru are arrogant and greedy individuals who only seek to advance their position by taking advantage of native Andeans.

As in the French volume *A Collection of the Various Styles of Clothing*, German costume books also sometimes contained anti-Catholic discourse in the pages devoted to clergymen. A small number of the illustrations from these books address the wayward nature of the Spanish clergy. The 1577 volume *Habitus praecipuorum populorum, tam virorum quam foeminarum singulari arte depicti* shows a young boy holding the robe of a Spanish priest as if it were the train of royalty.[22] This book also goes one step further than the French example by replicating Guaman Poma's repeated complaints about the sexual transgressions of clergymen. In one particular image in the German costume book, a figure described as the priest's concubine is shown with hands outstretched, as if she were begging for money, while a child hangs at her skirt (see figure 4.4). These negative representations, which relate specifically to priests who are labeled as being from Spain, differ from the French illustrations of clergymen in that the pictures themselves provide evidence of wayward actions. Whereas the

FIGURE 4.4 "Spanish Priest's Concubine" (Plate CLX) from Hans Weigel and Jost Amman, *Habitvs praecipvorvm popvlorvm, tam virorum quam foeminarum singulari arte depicti* (Nuremberg, 1577), RB 66643. Huntington Library, San Marino, California.

depictions in *A Collection of the Various Styles of Clothing* merely show individual religious figures modeling their robes, the illustrations in *Habitus praecipuorum populorum* go beyond the often-repeated idea that ecclesiastical authorities wear inappropriate clothes or use their robes to hide their transgressions. These images are more explicit in their suggestion of purported misdeeds or, as in the case of the concubine "priest's woman" with her child, provide pictorial evidence of sexual transgressions. While these German illustrations are still rather tame in comparison to some of Guaman Poma's drawings, they reflect a larger tradition of anti-Catholic printing that existed in early modern Europe.[23] Although it is generally believed that such printing would have fallen victim to the ire of the Spanish Inquisition and would have been banned from entering the Spanish American colonies, perhaps more anti-Catholic imagery than previously imagined did find its way into colonial Peru. In Germany, negative images of clergymen frequently appeared in broadsides used as propaganda against the Catholic Church. In fact, images of drunk, gluttonous, and lecherous Catholic clergymen were ubiquitous in a wide variety of anticlerical print matter.[24]

Guaman Poma's rather shocking and negative depictions of clergymen can partly be explained as part of a widespread print tradition of anti-Catholic propaganda. Costume books provided the Andean author with both a textual and visual model of how to advance a scathing critique of a powerful sector of colonial Peruvian society. In order to offer King Philip III his controversial assessment of the members of religious orders that had been entrusted with the conversion of native Andeans, Guaman Poma would present his negative appraisal of these clergymen by showing how they repeatedly hide behind "saintly" robes in order to perpetuate a variety of misdeeds. The unchristian nature of their behavior is also emphasized pictorially by virtue of the fact that most of their indigenous victims are depicted as faithful Catholics. In many of the drawings of native Andeans in the *Nueva corónica*, the indigenous peoples are shown grasping rosaries or with their hands clasped in prayer. Guaman Poma very prudently presents to King Philip III a damaging indictment of Spanish clergymen as harmful agents of colonialism. This picture of barbarity stands in sharp contrast to his sympathetic portrait of the Indians of the Viceroyalty of Peru as helpless Christian victims. In this way the Andean author's manuscript participates in a common trope of early modern costume books in that it seeks to display the perceived refinement and civilization of particular nations/cultures while simultaneously categorizing others as savage or uncivilized.

Revising Representations: Costume Books in the Low Countries

The costume book's importance in establishing the dichotomy of civilization/barbarity is seen in terms of religion but also, more broadly, in relation to a center/periphery divide. In general, the place where the costume book was printed is considered the normative center and principal focus of the book. However, when the costume book addresses faraway regions considered peripheral, the accompanying text and images usually become more critical. For this reason, costume books printed in the Low Countries—which were a later development—often copy directly from existing European ones but sometimes revise representations of local people. For example, the Flemish costume book *Omnium fere gentium nostraeque aetatis nationum habitus et effigies*, which was printed in Antwerp in 1572, modifies some of the text from the French costume book.[25] Printed during the Dutch revolt against Spanish rule, the changes also appear to respond to Spanish representations of the Flemish as impious because of the destruction of many sacred Catholic images in the course of the rebellion. The original French version documents that Flemish men were only famous for their short robes: "If you want to know about the clothes of a Flemish man, / His short robe and also his manner, / You will by this portrait, / To change his style of clothes is not his worry."[26] While the version printed in Antwerp retained the French image and poem, it added a lengthy Latin "translation" written in a more serious tone that stresses the integrity of the men of Flanders: "The Flemish man is good and generous to the needy / Unequal in conquering and pious."[27] As a response to Spanish hegemony in the Low Countries, this Flemish costume book attempts to revise depictions of local people.

This mode of contesting existing ethnographic representations brings to mind Mary Louise Pratt's categorization of the *Nueva corónica* as an "autoethnographic" text. As Pratt explains, an autoethnographic text is one "in which people undertake to describe themselves in ways that engage with representations others have of them. Thus if ethnographic texts are those in which European metropolitan subjects represent to themselves their others (usually their conquered others), autoethnographic texts are representations that the so-defined others construct in response to or in dialogue with those texts."[28]

While Guaman Poma might have been unfamiliar with the political context of the publication of the Flemish costume book, both he and the Flemish authors constructed autoethnographic texts in response to other European representations. If the Andean author was familiar with some of the more widely circulating costume books, he might have wanted to augment their descriptions of indigenous peoples or revise negative or inaccurate portrayals of Peruvians.[29] For example, both the French costume book *A Collection of the Various Styles of Clothing* and the Flemish "translation" of the volume include a grotesque image of the "Standing Ape of Peru," along with the following verse description: "Near Peru one can in effect see that / God gave the ape such a form, / Dressed in rattan, leaning on a walking stick, / Standing upright is something similar to a man" (see figure 4.5).[30] This derogatory representation of Peruvians as animals, as well as the frequent recounting of the indigenous peoples' lack of clothing, are two common tropes adopted by costume books to inscribe the native inhabitants of the Americas into the category of barbarity. As Bronwen Wilson notes in her study of Venetian costume books, European figures are depicted with somewhat generic facial features while people from more distant locales are sometimes distinguished by marks of "otherness," and these figures are usually not as sumptuously dressed as their European counterparts.[31]

Guaman Poma appears to respond to the either incomplete or negative portrayals of Andeans in European costume books by including a vast catalog that displays the varied clothes of both historical Inca figures and colonial Peruvians. In addition to his sequence of twelve Inca rulers and coyas, Guaman Poma documents a variety of occupations as well as regional differences between the four *suyos* (quarters) of the Inca Empire. This extensive panorama, which begins with the Inca elite and then expands to include other classes of people, parallels the costume book's more comprehensive portrayal of a European social hierarchy that usually commences with kings and nobles and concludes by showcasing the lower social strata and regional differences, such as city and country dress. While most costume books include only a handful of representations of the indigenous peoples of the Americas, Guaman Poma provides an exhaustive portrait of the denizens of the Inca Empire before the arrival of the Spaniards and also includes a comprehensive picture of native Andeans living in colonial Peru. The manuscript's depiction of the complex and efficient social hierarchy that existed before the arrival of the Spaniards serves to emphasize the disruptive nature of colonial rule. At the same time, Guaman Poma's drawings of colonial indigenous subjects highlight continuities with the pre-Hispanic past. For example, the description of elite indigenous women living in colonial Peru emphasizes that they wore a shawl (*lliclla*) and skirt (*acsu*) like the coyas of the Inca Empire.[32] In the accompanying drawing, the colonial indigenous woman

FIGURE 4.5 "Standing Ape of Peru" from François Deserps, *Recueil de la diversité des habits qui sont de present en usage* (Paris, 1567), RB 495919. Huntington Library, San Marino, California.

also wears a skirt with the characteristic checkerboard patterned border (*tocapo*) but unlike her pre-Hispanic counterpart she now holds a rosary as a sign of her acceptance of the Catholic faith.[33] In truth, Guaman Poma is less apt to describe the clothes of indigenous men, although their vestments are captured in his drawings. This gendered difference could reflect his knowledge of a subgenre of the costume book known as the book of trades (*ständebuch*) that focused exclusively on depicting a range of occupations held by men.[34] As in the book of trades genre, Guaman Poma's manuscript provides images of indigenous men engaged in a variety of professions and his textual commentary centers on the types of work that they perform. This comprehensive picture of indigenous productivity along with the manuscript's display of a complex social hierarchy serves to communicate the advanced nature of Andean civilization. While many early modern European books commonly characterized Native Americans as naked and uncivilized, Guaman Poma contests this form of representation. In sharp contrast to this limited view of Amerindians, the *Nueva corónica* employs the parade of European subjects from costume books as a model for composing a more complete picture of Andean civilization.

Guaman Poma and Early Modern Print Culture

The similarities that exist between European costume books and the *Nueva corónica* not only suggest Guaman Poma's ability to access books that do not usually appear on lists of works that were circulating in the colonies; they also make apparent his ability to adopt many of the conventions of European costume books in order to create a uniquely Peruvian chronicle. His manuscript, a compendium of knowledge about both the pre-Hispanic Andean world and colonial Peru, can be categorized within the European tradition of lavishly illustrated catalogs of information. Costume books provided graphic models for the informational drawings contained in his manuscript and also contributed an appropriate format for organizing the textual and pictorial information. European costume books are also likely sources for the variety of modes in which Guaman Poma presents this information and the various functions that his complementary drawings serve. In addition to employing commentary on costume as a means of providing historical information about the Inca rulers and coyas, Guaman Poma appropriates the model provided by the costume book in order to critique colonial authorities and revise existing negative representations of indigenous peoples. Many of the sixteenth-century illustrated compendiums of knowledge, such as the costume book *A Collection of the Various Styles of Clothing* or Gonzalo Fernández de Oviedo's *Historia general y natural de las Indias* (1535–57), were dedicated to monarchs and provided information about the New World.[35] Guaman Poma similarly dedicates his manuscript to Philip III and attempts to provide the King of Spain with a catalog of information about the Viceroyalty of Peru.

Since the first costume books printed in Spanish appeared well after the composition of his manuscript, one final question relates to how Guaman Poma was able to comprehend foreign books.[36] It is possible that, as with the type of library access suggested by Murra, he was able to carry out research in a well-stocked monastic library and was perhaps aided by the translations of a clergyman. In this sense, as with Murra's suggestion that Guaman Poma was granted permission to enter the library of Cristóbal de Albornoz, the indigenous author was given the keys to the world of print by a member of the lettered elite. This conceptualization of a hierarchy of power, in which a colonial *letrado* controls the extent to which Amerindians access the realm of power and knowledge that is largely manifest through literacy and printing, brings to mind Ángel Rama's conception of the *ciudad letrada*, or "lettered city."[37] Recently, however, Joanne Rappaport and Tom Cummins's volume *Beyond the Lettered City: Indigenous Literacies in the Andes* questions the idea of the virtual exclusion of Amerindians from the lettered city and provides a broader picture of colonial literacies by more fully exploring indigenous interactions with lettered culture. Although Rappaport and Cummins primarily emphasize indigenous participation in manuscript culture, the illustrations and textual references in Guaman Poma's manuscript suggest that some native Andeans during the colonial period had frequent interactions with books and other print matter.[38]

If Guaman Poma was inspired by European costume books, volumes that were written in languages he could not comprehend and not printed for an indigenous readership, it is possible that he encountered individual volumes that were glossed in Spanish. Notation and commentary in the margins of foreign books was a frequent practice, and Guaman Poma could have purchased such works from used-book sellers.[39] Equally plausible, as was the case with many genres of early modern literature, the often comic verses from costume books were possibly read out loud and explained to a listening public that could also marvel at the entertaining illustrations.[40] The sheer number of drawings in Guaman Poma's *Nueva corónica* in addition to the broad range of his artistic repertoire suggest a familiarity with the conventions of print illustration as well as frequent practice in the composition of line drawings, a skill that he could have acquired in a workshop or studio dedicated to engraving.[41] Perhaps there were more printing presses in colonial Peru than previously imagined and Guaman Poma gained experience by helping produce engraved illustrations in an unsanctioned workshop, one that was stocked with a broad selection of illustrated books that could aid in the training of novice artists.[42] In short, speculation on the ways in which Guaman Poma encountered the genre of the costume book can lead us to conclude that his library was possibly a monastic cell, or a knapsack, or a chair by the hearth of a tavern, or an indigenous workshop, or some combination of all of the above. In any case, while the specificity of place is difficult to determine, we can assume that Guaman Poma had the ability to gain access to collections of books. The vast repertoire of print matter that appears to have been incorporated into the *Nueva corónica* not only suggests a wide range of titles that he must have consulted; it also hints at a broad range of spaces and places in which an indigenous writer was able to interact with European books.

Notes

Publication of this chapter was funded in part by the University of Northern Colorado Fund for Faculty Publication.

1. Murra, "Guaman Poma's Sources." Guaman Poma's *El primer nueva corónica y buen gobierno* came to the attention of Andean scholars in 1908, when Richard Pietschmann announced his discovery of the work in the collection of the Royal Library of Copenhagen. The 1,189-page manuscript, which contains almost four hundred drawings, chronicles Andean history from the origins of the Inca Empire to the establishment of colonial society. Rolena Adorno, who has studied the autograph manuscript most extensively, has proposed that it was most likely completed in 1615, although it was emended in 1616. Adorno, *New Studies of the Autograph Manuscript*, 7.
2. Murra, "Guaman Poma's Sources," 60–61.
3. Murra, "Guaman Poma's Sources," 61.
4. The oral tradition and the Andean knotted strings known as *khipus* also influenced the structure and content of the manuscript. For more on this indigenous form of textuality in relation to Guaman Poma, see the following studies of khipus: Brokaw, "Khipu Numeracy and Alphabetic Literacy in the Andes"; Rasmussen, *Queequeg's Coffin*; and Solomon and Niño-Murcia, *The Lettered Mountain*.
5. Murra, "Guaman Poma's Sources," 60. Murra points to Adorno, *Guaman Poma*; and López-Baralt, *Icono y conquista*.

6. Bailey, "Ambivalent Identities," 203. Bailey's comment, however, should be contextualized as a call for art historians to more fully explore the arts of Latin America. As an art historian, he laments that Guaman Poma's drawings (like *casta* paintings) have received a great deal of scholarly attention whereas a myriad of works of colonial Latin American art and architecture have been completely ignored.
7. Cummins, "The Images in Murúa's *Historia General del Pirú*," 151.
8. This is the title of the recent English translation of Vecellio's *De gli habiti antichi, et moderni di diverse parti del mondo libri due*.
9. Vecellio, *The Clothing of the Renaissance World*, 79. According to editors Rosenthal and Jones, *porpora* is a bright red or purple dye from the *Purpura* mollusk (*The Clothing of the Renaissance World*, 589) and *giacinto* is a purplish blue color (587).
10. Guaman Poma de Ayala, *The First New Chronicle and Good Government*, 111.
11. There are references in colonial chronicles to a pre-Hispanic tradition of Inca painting on walls or boards, but there are no extant examples. López-Baralt, *Icono y conquista*, 100–104. Furthermore, Cummins argues convincingly against the claim of Catherine Julien (and others) that the portraits commissioned by viceroy Toledo (the "lienzos de Toledo") were modeled after pre-Hispanic Inca portraits that preserved images of the royal line of Inca rulers and coyas. Cummins, "The Images in Murúa's *Historia General del Pirú*," 173n51; Julien, *Reading Inca History*, 56–59. Cummins explains that the portraits of Inca rulers and coyas in the Galvin manuscript, the Getty manuscript, and the *Nueva corónica* are all based on "an established European template." Cummins, "The Images in Murúa's *Historia General del Pirú*," 150.
12. Zuidema, "Guaman Poma and the Art of Empire."
13. See Cummins, "The Images in Murúa's *Historia General del Pirú*," 171n16.
14. Two other Andean manuscripts containing colored illustrations of the Inca rulers and queens (the Getty manuscript and the Galvin manuscript) also include artwork that has been attributed to Guaman Poma. See Juan M. Ossio's comparison of the two manuscripts with the drawings in the *Nueva corónica*. Ossio, "Inca Kings, Queens, Captains, and Tocapus."
15. Zuidema, "Guaman Poma and the Art of Empire," 190.
16. Zuidema, "Guaman Poma and the Art of Empire," 190.
17. As Adorno details, not all of Guaman Poma's depictions of clergymen are negative. His portrayal of the Jesuits is more positive and most likely relates to their more tolerant attitude toward indigenous cultures in missionary efforts to proselytize. Adorno, "Las otras fuentes de Guaman Poma," 150–51.
18. Ulrike Ilg discusses the parallel between discussions of local "costume" and "custom" in examples of the genre. Ilg, "The Cultural Significance of Costume Books in Sixteenth-Century Europe," 43–47.
19. Jones, "Habits, Holdings, Heterologies."
20. Deserps, *A Collection of the Various Styles of Clothing*, 76.
21. All translations are mine unless otherwise indicated. In the final sentence of the quote, Guaman Poma employs the informal *vos*, "Ací aués de andar, padre," which

implies a lack of reverence. Guaman Poma de Ayala, *El primer nueva corónica y buen gobierno*, 549.

22. Weigel and Amman, *Habitus praecipuorum populorum*, 154.
23. See Guaman Poma's numerous depictions of clergymen physically abusing native Andeans or his drawing of a muleteer on his way to Lima with a group of mestizo children who are described as the offspring of priests. Guaman Poma de Ayala, *El primer nueva corónica y buen gobierno*, 535, 543, 545, 551, 554, 574, 594, 609, 611, 612.
24. See Scribner, *For the Sake of the Simple Folk*, 37–58.
25. Van den Rade, *Omnium fere gentium nostraeque*. I discuss some of these revisions in more detail in another article: Thomas, "Fashion and Nationalism."
26. Deserps, *A Collection of the Various Styles of Clothing*, 72. The short comical description is typical of the poems in this costume book, which was written for King Henry IV of France when he was a child. The sometimes nonsensical verses can also be interpreted as a product of the author's desire to find an appropriate rhyme in composing each poem.
27. Van den Rade, *Omnium fere gentium nostraeque*, 48v.
28. Pratt, "Arts of the Contact Zone," 35.
29. Most sixteenth-century costume books include only a handful of images of scantily clad Native Americans from Brazil, Florida, Mexico, and Virginia. As Cummins notes, Vecellio added illustrations of fully dressed Incas in the expanded edition of his costume book (1598). Cummins, "The Images in Murúa's *Historia General del Pirú*," 151. Nevertheless, Vecellio includes only five representations of Inca costume: a Peruvian man, a Cuzco nobleman, two Inca soldiers, and a Peruvian woman. Vecellio, *The Clothing of the Renaissance World*, 554–58.
30. Deserps, *A Collection of the Various Styles of Clothing*, 86.
31. In addition to highlighting their dissimilar clothing and cultural practices, the body markings, facial hair, and articulated profiles of non-Europeans were often showcased to underline difference. Wilson, "Reproducing the Contours of Venetian Identity."
32. Guaman Poma de Ayala, *El primer nueva corónica y buen gobierno*, 707.
33. Guaman Poma de Ayala, *El primer nueva corónica y buen gobierno*, 706.
34. Costume books sometimes include pictures of a few occupations (such as "fisherwoman" or "farmer"). Books of trade focus exclusively on male professions and, in contrast to the blank backgrounds that are employed in costume books, often feature elaborate and detailed renditions of the environments in which these figures work. See Garzoni, *La piazza universale di tutte le professioni del mondo*; Lehmann-Haupt, *The Book of Trades in the Iconography of Social Typology*; and Rabb, *A Sixteenth-Century Book of Trades*.
35. Portions of Gonzalo Fernández de Oviedo's rather lengthy illustrated manuscript were published in three separate editions (1535, 1547, and 1557), the last of which included one book from part 2. The entire three-part work would not be published until the nineteenth century. See Myers, *Fernández de Oviedo's Chronicle of America*.

36. The first printed costume book in Spanish might be the volume authored by Juan de la Cruz Cano y Olmedilla, *Colección de trajes de España, tanto antiguos como modernos* (1777).
37. John Charles Chasteen defines these terms in the introduction to his translation of Rama's work: "a nexus of lettered culture, state power, and urban location that Angel Rama calls *la ciudad letrada*, the lettered city. The brokers of this relationship were a group of men called *letrados*—a 'lettered' elite closely associated with the institutions of state and invariably urban in orientation." Rama, *The Lettered City*, vii.
38. Rappaport and Cummins offer a variety of examples to illustrate how native Andeans employed manuscript culture to represent themselves and their claims to authority, from the map and legal documents produced by Guaman Poma in response to a land dispute to native petitions for coats of arms. Rappaport and Cummins, *Beyond the Lettered City*, 174–88.
39. In colonial Peru, a thriving used-book market existed in association with the sale of secondhand books by traders as well as the liquidation of goods left by the deceased. González Sánchez, *New World Literacy*, 143–84.
40. See Frenk, *Entre la voz y el silencio*.
41. Guaman Poma's skill in drawing could have been gained through making engravings, since the process is somewhat analogous. The engraver usually employs a burin to incise lines into a metal plate. The corresponding line drawing becomes a printed image when the metal grooves are filled with ink and pressed onto paper. This is in opposition to woodcut illustrations, in which carving into a woodblock produces negative space and the remaining raised surfaces transfer the ink onto paper. See Bohen and Imhof, *Christopher Plantin and Engraved Book Illustrations in Sixteenth-Century Europe*.
42. Traditional scholarship has highlighted the existence of a small number of presses in sixteenth- and seventeenth-century Peru, most of which were primarily associated with the production of books to aid in the process of evangelizing indigenous populations. See Thompson, *Printing in Colonial Spanish America*, 34–44; and Torre Revello, *Orígenes de la imprenta en España*, 104–12. Nevertheless, there are some indications of alternative presses that were employed for other purposes. Kathryn Burns documents the existence of a Cuzco notary who owned plates for printing decks of playing cards. Burns, *Into the Archive*, 53. Cummins points to a surviving copper plate depicting an Inca confession as evidence of local printing. Cummins, "The Indulgent Image," 222–25.

Works Cited

Adorno, Rolena. *Guaman Poma: Writing and Resistance in Colonial Peru*. Austin: University of Texas Press, 1980.

———. "Las otras fuentes de Guaman Poma: Sus lecturas castellanas." *Histórica* 2, no. 2 (1978): 137–58.

———. *New Studies of the Autograph Manuscript of Felipe Guaman Poma de Ayala's "Nueva corónica y buen gobierno."* Copenhagen: Museum Tusculanum Press, 2003.

Bailey, Gauvin Alexander. "Ambivalent Identities: Catholicism, the Arts, and Religious Foundations in Spanish America." *Latin American Research Review* 48, no. 1 (2013): 191–204.

Bohen, Karen L., and Dirk Imhof. *Christopher Plantin and Engraved Book Illustrations in Sixteenth-Century Europe.* Cambridge: Cambridge University Press, 2008.

Brokaw, Galen. "Khipu Numeracy and Alphabetic Literacy in the Andes: Felipe Guaman Poma de Ayala's *Nueva corónica y buen gobierno.*" *Colonial Latin American Review* 11, no. 2 (2002): 275–303.

Burns, Kathryn. *Into the Archive: Writing and Power in Colonial Peru.* Durham, N.C.: Duke University Press, 2010.

Cruz Cano y Olmedilla, Juan de la. *Colección de trajes de España, tanto antiguos como modernos.* Madrid: Casa de M. Copin, 1777.

Cummins, Thomas B. F. "The Images in Murúa's Historia General del Pirú: An Art Historical Study." In *The Getty Murúa: Essays on the Making of Martín de Murúa's "Historia General del Piru,"* edited by Thomas Cummins and Barbara Anderson, 147–73. Los Angeles: Getty Research Institute, 2008.

———. "The Indulgent Image: Prints in the New World." In *Contested Visions in the Spanish Colonial World*, edited by Ilona Katzew, 203–25. New Haven, Conn.: Yale University Press, 2011.

Deserps, François. *A Collection of the Various Styles of Clothing Which Are Presently Worn in Countries of Europe, Asia, Africa and the Savage Islands.* Edited and translated by Sara Shannon. 1562. Reprint, Minneapolis: University of Minnesota Press, 2001.

———. *Recueil de la diversité des habits qui sont de present en usage.* Paris: Richard Breton, 1567.

Fernández de Oviedo y Valdés, Gonzalo. *Historia general y natural de las Indias.* Edited by José Amador. 4 vols. Madrid: Imprenta de la Real Academia de la Historia, 1851–55.

Frenk, Margit. *Entre la voz y el silencio: La lectura en tiempos de Cervantes.* Alcalá de Henares: Centro de Estudios Cervantinos, 1997.

Garzoni, Tomaso. *La piazza universale di tutte le professioni del mondo.* Venice: Giovanni Battista Somascho, 1585.

González Sánchez, Carlos Alberto. *New World Literacy: Writing and Culture Across the Atlantic, 1500–1700.* Lewisburg, Penn.: Bucknell University Press, 2011.

Guaman Poma de Ayala, Felipe. *El primer nueva corónica y buen gobierno.* Edited by John V. Murra and Rolena Adorno. Mexico City: Siglo Veintiuno Editores, 1980.

———. *The First New Chronicle and Good Government.* Edited and translated by Roland Hamilton. Austin: University of Texas Press, 2009.

———. *Nueva corónica y buen gobierno.* Edited by Paul Rivet. Paris: Institut d'ethnologie, 1936.

Ilg, Ulrike. "The Cultural Significance of Costume Books in Sixteenth-Century Europe." In *Clothing Culture, 1350–1650*, edited by Catherine Richardson, 29–47. Burlington, Vt.: Ashgate, 2004.

Jones, Ann Rosalind. "Habits, Holdings, Heterologies: Populations in Print in a 1562 Costume Book." *Yale French Studies*, no. 110 (2006): 92–121.

Julien, Catherine. *Reading Inca History*. Iowa City: University of Iowa Press, 2000.

Lehmann-Haupt, Hellmut. *The Book of Trades in the Iconography of Social Typology*. Boston: Trustees of the Public Library of the City of Boston, 1976.

López-Baralt, Mercedes. *Icono y conquista: Guaman Poma de Ayala*. Madrid: Hiperión, 1988.

Murra, John. "Guaman Poma's Sources." In *Guaman Poma de Ayala: The Colonial Art of an Andean Author*, edited by Mercedes López-Baralt, 60–66. New York: Americas Society.

Myers, Kathleen Ann. *Fernández de Oviedo's Chronicle of America: A New History for a New World*. Austin: University of Texas Press, 2007.

Ossio, Juan M. "Inca Kings, Queens, Captains, and Tocapus in the Manuscripts of Martín de Murúa and Guaman Poma." In *Unlocking the Doors to the Worlds of Guaman Poma and His "Nueva corónica,"* edited by Rolena Adorno and Ivan Boserup, 291–330. Copenhagen: Museum Tusculanum Press, 2015.

Pratt, Mary Louise. "Arts of the Contact Zone." *Profession* (1991): 33–40.

Rabb, Theodore K., ed. and trans. *A Sixteenth-Century Book of Trades: Das Ständebuch*. Palo Alto, Calif.: Society for the Promotion of Science and Scholarship, 2009.

Rama, Angel. *The Lettered City*. Edited and translated by John Charles Chasteen. Durham, N.C.: Duke University Press, 1996.

Rappaport, Joanne, and Tom Cummins. *Beyond the Lettered City: Indigenous Literacies in the Andes*. Durham, N.C.: Duke University Press, 2012.

Rasmussen, Birgit Brander. *Queequeg's Coffin: Indigenous Literacies and Early American Literature*. Durham, N.C.: Duke University Press, 2012.

Salomon, Frank, and Mercedes Niño-Murcia. *The Lettered Mountain: A Peruvian Village's Way with Writing*. Durham, N.C.: Duke University Press, 2011.

Scribner, Robert W. *For the Sake of the Simple Folk: Popular Propaganda for the German Reformation*. Cambridge: Cambridge University Press, 1981.

Thomas, George Antony. "Fashion and Nationalism: Political Critique in Early Modern Costume Books." *Laberinto Journal* 7 (2014): 8–26.

Thompson, Lawrence S. *Printing in Colonial Spanish America*. Hamden, Conn.: Shoestring Press, 1962.

Torre Revello, José. *Orígenes de la imprenta en España y su desarrollo en América Española*. Buenos Aires: Institución Cultural Española, 1940.

van den Rade, Gilles. *Omnium fere gentium nostraeque aetatis nationum habitus et effigies*. Antwerp: Jean Bellero, 1572.

Vecellio, Cesare. *The Clothing of the Renaissance World: Europe, Asia, Africa, the Americas*. Edited and translated by Margaret F. Rosenthal and Ann Rosalind Jones. New York: Thames and Hudson, 2008.

———. *De gli habiti antichi, et moderni di diverse parti del mondo libri due*. Venice: Damian Zenaro, 1590.

———. *Habiti antichi et moderni di tutto il mondo; di nuova accresciuti di multe figure.* Venice: Gio. Bernardo Sessa, 1598.

Weigel, Hans, and Jost Amman. *Habitus praecipuorum populorum, tam virorum quam foeminarum singulari arte depicti.* Nuremburg, 1577.

Wilson, Bronwen. "Reproducing the Contours of Venetian Identity in Sixteenth-Century Costume Books." *Studies in Iconography* 25 (2004): 221–74.

Zuidema, Tom. "Guaman Poma and the Art of Empire: Toward an Iconography of Inca Royal Dress." In *Transatlantic Encounters: Europeans and Andeans in the Sixteenth Century,* edited by Kenneth J. Andrien and Rolena Adorno, 151–202. Berkeley: University of California Press, 1991.

5

Rioplatense Sound, Text, and Transmission in the Early Era of Sonic Reproducibility

SAM CARTER

EIGHT DOGS SIT BEFORE A GRAMOPHONE on the May 28, 1904, cover of *Caras y Caretas*, the Buenos Aires weekly whose color artwork, abundant advertising, and extensive cultural coverage all contributed to its uniquely mediating presence among various social classes in a burgeoning metropolis during the first decades of the twentieth century (see figure 5.1).[1] The title of the illustration—"La 'voz del amo'" (The "master's voice")—alludes to the Victor Talking Machine Company slogan "His Master's Voice" used alongside a trademark that became recognizable worldwide after its introduction in England in 1900: Nipper, the fox terrier occasionally misidentified as the "talking dog."[2] Like their British counterpart, however, these variously anthropomorphized Argentine canines, some sporting collars with names of provinces, listen rather than speak. Absent is the hand that abandoned the *rebenque*, or whip, lying beside the dogs in favor of a different instrument of persuasion—namely, the crank responsible for rotating the disc under the needle and thus producing the sound waves that have been miraculously transcribed into an incomplete yet legible script: "lcorta."[3] Referring to then-senator, soon-to-be vice president, and future president José Figueroa Alcorta, the cover visually and vividly addresses issues of electoral influence by invoking the power of a machine capable of sonic playback.

A reference to a quarter-century-old technology would be unremarkable if it did not participate in a prominent depiction of political machinations that

FIGURE 5.1 Cover of *Caras y Caretas*, May 28, 1904.

mirrored the magazine's own ability to articulate a set of beliefs in the hands and homes of readers.[4] Print, which required the special skill of literacy, had been broadcasting information long before sound reproduction technologies, and the *Caras y Caretas* portrayal underlines how a device capable of writing and later reading a script indecipherable by humans might ultimately occupy a similar position.[5] Like the stylus that "engraves and later traces the phonographic groove,"[6] the comparison between print and phonograph worked in both directions as publications sought the perceived influence of a device attempting to attain print's popularity.

Three weeks later, in the June 18, 1904, issue, the *Caras y Caretas* cover concerning sonic reproducibility was itself reproduced at quarter scale as part of a full-page advertisement for the Cassels & Co. store (see figure 5.2). Four stanzas of rhyming verse eulogizing the gramophone accompany the image of the carefully listening canines, as do brief reports on Pope Pius X's decision to reinstitute Gregorian chant by distributing recordings of a Vatican Mass and Czar Nicholas II's delivery of a rousing speech to troops on the front lines while the monarch maintained a comfortable distance from the theater of war. Proclaiming that "absorto está el mundo en oír el Gramofón" (the world is engrossed in hearing the gramophone), the advertisement offers these examples as a demonstration of how the device unsettled previously well-established relations between sound and text: in both St. Peter's and St. Petersburg, it was now clear that no text could capture the nuances available in a reproduction of a particular vocal technique or voice. The shrewd combination of visual and rhetorical strategies suggested that the new technology exceeded the capacities of the medium in which it was advertised.[7]

Both the *Caras y Caretas* cover and the Cassels & Co. copy record some of the tensions between reproduced sound and printed text that form the focus of the present chapter. Drawing in part on the methodology of Friedrich Kittler, who characterizes his *Gramophone, Film, Typewriter* as a compilation of passages demonstrating "how the novelty of technological media inscribe[s] itself into the old paper of books," I examine how the phonograph's "fantásticos zig-zags de la palabra" (fantastic zig-zags of the word), to quote a nineteenth-century commentator's memorable phrase, complicate the relationship between sound and text in the Río de la Plata region.[8] Following Lisa Gitelman, who argues that the rise of technologies both sonic and otherwise helped consolidate notions of print and print culture in the United States, I attend to the contingent aspects of a similar process in a period marked at one end by José

LA VOZ DEL GRAM-O-FÓN

"La media palabra,
  la voz del amo es!
"Que claro enuncia
  el nombre Cordobés"
Y todos los oyentes
  conocen ya el son;
La voz del amo solo,
  en la voz del Gramofón.

Así en la política,
  en artes y ciencias,
El Gramofón inspira
  las altas influencias.
Escuchad, oh! mortales
  la voz de su bocina,
Pues que en todas partes
  El Gramofón domina.

En ranchos tan humildes,
  en palacios reales,
En casas de familia,
  y en los hospitales;
Los ricos y los pobres;
  los grandes de la tierra,
Escuchan las estrofas
  que el Gramofón encierra.

Absorto está el mundo
  en oír el Gramofón
Pues la voz de su bocina
  es la voz de un patrón.

ÚLTIMAS NOTICIAS SOBRE EL GRAM-O-FÓN

ROMA, 12 de MAYO 1904. — S. S. el Papa Pío X, ha ordenado se restablezca el canto llano Gregoriano, en todas las iglesias católicas del orbe. En consecuencia y con el propósito de dar á conocer la edición correcta de esta música sagrada, se ha resuelto utilizar el GRAMOFÓN (el único); y la Compañía del Gramofón ha recibido encargo de reproducir la música completa de la Missa solemne celebrada en la catedral de S. Pedro, el 11 de Abril último, á fin de que los discos sean distribuidos á todas las iglesias del mundo. La reproducción se hará bajo la dirección del Maestro Perosi.

SAN PETERSBURGO, MAYO 2, 1904. — El Czar, deseando dirijir una arenga patriótica á sus soldados, — ha resuelto sea reproducida en discos de GRAMOFÓN (el único), aún de ser enviado al teatro de la guerra, para ser oído por el ejército en los campamentos.

Á ADQUIRIR PUES UN GRAM-O-FÓN
El entretenimiento más útil y más instructivo del siglo vigésimo
Es un conservatorio de música en casa

De las máquinas parlantes
Hay enorme batallón,
Una turba de farsantes
Más un solo GRAMOFÓN.

Gran colección de discos nuevos

Marca "ANGELITO"   Marca "PERRO"

AGENTES AUTORIZADOS **Cassels & Co.**
FLORIDA, 43
En breve se inaugurará LA NUEVA Y CÓMODA SALA DE AUDICIÓN

FIGURE 5.2 Cassels & Co. advertisement, 1904.

Hernández's writing of *Martín Fierro* in the 1870s and at the other by the activity of avant-garde *martínfierristas* fifty years later.[9] Excavating cultural material to read the record of the phonograph's arrival in the Río de la Plata makes it possible to uncover conceptions about the role of text in a period when the eventual uses of sound reproduction technologies were far from clear. In much the same way, treating the device's later association with music not as inevitable consequence but rather as the end of a process of culturally negotiated uses allows for a more nuanced understanding of sound, text, and the transmission of both. As the following analyzed works demonstrate, questions regarding the difference between original and copy and even the very act of recording itself were reformulated as sound technologies exercised an understudied influence on a number of figures variously involved with the written word.

Although neither Edouard Scott, inventor of the phonautograph, nor Charles Cros, the poet who submitted plans for what would have been a functional phonograph to the Academie des Sciences in Paris eight months before Thomas Edison constructed a working model, had roots in the Río de la Plata region, Argentina nevertheless still participated in the prehistory of the phonograph since it was Guillermo Parody who in 1871 was the first to adapt Isaac Pitman's 1845 *Manual of Phonography, or Writing by Sound* for use with Spanish. Linguist Edward Hincks had coined the term "phonography" to describe hieroglyphs that were "representations of sounds," but Pitman's shorthand system popularized it before Edison's invention overshadowed these other uses.[10] If measured solely by the claims they inspired, the distance between man- and machine-made recordings was negligible. Seven years before Edison famously highlighted his phonograph's ability to capture and permanently retain "all manner of sound-waves heretofore designated as 'fugitive,'" Parody made a surprisingly similar remark: "Qué hombre estudioso no habrá . . . que no haya muchas veces deseado poseer el arte de poder estampar en el papel, con la misma rapidez que se presentan, los pensamientos fugitivos?" (What learned man could there be . . . who has not many times wished to possess the art of printing fugitive thoughts onto paper, with the same quickness with which they present themselves?).[11] Different phonographic discourses coincide as Parody's emphasis on an immediacy that results from mediation diminishes the distinction between writing sounds and writing thoughts.

In 1872, one year after Parody's tachygraphic treatise appeared in Buenos Aires, the publication of the first part of José Hernández's gaucho epic *Martín Fierro* marked a culminating moment in a genre familiar with capturing not only fugitives and delinquents but also speech.[12] Hernández in fact characterized his work in quasi-phonographic terms in a letter that same year, suggesting that "cuantos conozcan con propiedad el original, podrán juzgar si hay o no semejanza en la copia" (those who properly know the original will be able to judge whether there is a similarity in the copy).[13] Yet when returning to this distinction in 1879 in the preface for *La vuelta de Martín Fierro*, he no longer leaves these judgments to the reader: "Sólo diré que no se debe perder de vista al juzgar los defectos del libro, que es copia fiel de un original que los tiene" (I will only say that one must not forget when judging the defects of the book that it is the faithful copy of an original that has them).[14] The advertisement of high fidelity has changed: Hernández's fictional recording is now so exact that even the errors remain. The presence of seemingly false notes, in other words, guarantees a certain fictive truth, and it was precisely by claiming to provide such careful reproductions that literary texts like Hernández's demonstrated an alertness to possible conversion back into sound that did not exist in the efficient transcriptions produced by Parody's system.[15]

The first phonograph demonstrations in 1878 thus occurred in a context where the possibilities the device represented would resonate widely.[16] In 1881, for instance, the phonograph becomes the object of discussion in the Argentine legislature when one representative, noticing differences between what has been said and its written record, states the obvious: "Yo, que no poseo las propiedades del fonógrafo, no tengo la facilidad de conservar el sonido. . . . Si alguno de mis colegas tiene las propiedades eléctricas del fonógrafo, tanto mejor para él! yo solamente veo lo que está escrito" (Lacking the qualities of a phonograph, I do not have the capacity to conserve sound. . . . If one of my colleagues has the electrical properties of the phonograph, so much the better for him! I see only what is written).[17] These inadequacies of writing with respect to capturing speech in this sensitive legal context resembled its deficiencies related to conveying vocality.[18] The latter surfaced when the fidelity of the record was called into question once more forty years later: "No es el término, es el tono y el ademán con que lo dijo el señor diputado; tono que no puede quedar en el Diario de Sesiones para las generaciones del porvenir, porque el Diario de Sesiones no es fonógrafo" (It is not the word but the tone and the gesture with which the deputy said it; a tone that cannot remain in the record of the sessions for future generations, because the record is not a phonograph).[19] This representative repeats so that the congressional register might actually *record*: the lack of a phonograph demands periphrasis, which renders the incompleteness of text even more apparent.

The device's successful reproductions could, however, turn it into a term of disparagement. Outside of a legislative context, a writer in the February 23, 1879, issue of the Uruguayan satirical magazine *El Negro Timoteo* took aim at journalists "á quienes he calificado de *fonógrafos* del Gobernador, y desearía que el término se generalizara porque es propio y merecido" (whom I have labeled *phonographs* of the Governor, and I would hope the term becomes widespread because it is appropriate and deserved).[20] His hopes were met: in 1896 one representative refers to a newspaper "que con justicia es reputado como el fonógrafo del ministerio de hacienda" (that is justifiably reputed to be the phonograph of the tax ministry).[21] Although print's precedence might have suggested it would control the reception of the phonograph, the latter instead emerged as a viable metaphor for the mindlessness that could arise when the former was subject to political interests.[22]

As a perfect example of these confluences of print and political power that partly defined the *letrado*, the Argentine doctor, diplomat, and writer Eduardo Wilde visited an exhibition of Edison's machines in Brooklyn and described the experience in one of his letters to the Buenos Aires newspaper *La Prensa*. Echoing Edison's reference to fugitive sounds, he writes, "El fonógrafo detiene la vida y perpetúa los fujitivos momentos; con él ya no hay pasado para la palabra hablada" (The phonograph stops life and perpetuates fugitive moments; with it there is no longer any past for the spoken word).[23] This disappearance of a past that was previously the province of print creates a nascent media ecology in which "el fonógrafo es el complemento de la imprenta. Esta, por medio de los libros perpetúa el pensamiento humano; aquél con sus delicadas impresiones conserva los sonidos para darles vida en cualquier momento del más remoto futuro" (the phonograph is the complement of printing. The latter, through books, perpetuates human thought; the former with its delicate impressions conserves sounds to give them life at any moment in the most remote future).[24] As he rehearses a typical association of phonography with the preservation and reanimation of the past, Wilde recognizes the playback capacity print so crucially lacks.[25] Even if it could reproduce text, print could never resurrect traces of the writing body in quite the same way as the phonograph.[26]

During a trip to Bayreuth in 1896 for the annual festival celebrating the works of composer Richard Wagner, the phonograph prompts Wilde to reach unexpected conclusions regarding the relationship between sounds and the methods of writing used to represent them: "Cuando podamos sistematizar las marcas de los sonidos en el fonógrafo la escritura i la taquigrafia dejaran de copiar silabas i palabras; escribiremos con signos hoi no conocidos" (When we are able to systematize the marks of sounds in the phonograph, writing and tachygraphy will cease to copy syllables and words; we will write with signs unknown today).[27] He considers the device an improvement on earlier attempts to capture sound in visual form since it would allow for a system of writing that was less arbitrary and more directly tied to the production of sound waves.[28] But the phonograph, in Wilde's view, will lead to more than just a revolution in writing; it also poses the possibility of changing language itself: "Cuando ya eso sea habitual i antiguo, la música hará respecto al lenguaje lo que el fonógrafo respecto a la escritura. Entonces no *hablaremos* ya, *fonaremos*, es decir cantaremos dentro de los límites de pocas notas; la fonación será el lenguaje único, el idioma de todas las naciones" (Later, when that is old habit, music will do for language what the phonograph did for writing. Then we will no longer *speak*, we will *phoneticize*, that is to say we will sing within the limits of a few notes; the phoneticization will be the only language, the language of all nations).[29] The ultimate feasibility of this proposal matters less than the fact that it is the phonograph standing at the beginning of this radical reconsideration of both language and text.

Another piece exploring a fanciful premise brings the phonograph's relationship to print into sharper focus by including a slightly older sound reproduction technology: the telephone. "Diálogo entre el teléfono y el fonógrafo" (Dialogue between the telephone and the phonograph), a humorous piece first published in Montevideo's *La revista moderna* in May 1900, transcribes a conversation between these "aparatos rivales" (rival apparatuses).[30] The telephone derides the phonograph as a "lorito francés, / que repite todo el día / lo que oyó al amanecer, / con esa voz de falsete" (little French parrot / that repeats all day / what it heard at dawn / in that falsetto voice).[31] Yet, as the phonograph retorts, longevity outweighs quality: "Yo guardo la voz de todos, / y no sé si lo hago bien; / pero puedo asegurarle / que esto me coloca cien / codos por encima suyo" (I store the voice of all / and I don't know if I do it well / but I can assure you / that this puts me head / and shoulders above you).[32] Storage, in other words, seems more valuable than transmission, yet one would do well to distinguish between instantaneous and delayed transmission since phonograph recordings could travel both temporally and spatially whereas telephones only permitted immediate reproduction across space. Print and phonography were therefore more closely aligned with each other than with telephony, and even those elements of print culture that fulfilled arguably telephonic functions like letters quickly found phonographic counterparts. In an advertisement from 1900, for instance, María receives a cylinder from Arturo, who finally declares his love. As his absent voice proclaims, "Hago al grafófono intérprete mío y mensajero de mi amor ilimitado" (I make the graphophone my interpreter and the messenger of my boundless love), which precipitates María's unexpected embrace of the mechanic messenger that, unlike the telephone, does leave a trace (see figure 5.3).

If recordings could render distance insignificant, making death somehow less devastating also seemed attainable. In "Las voces dormidas" (The dormant voices), a four-part piece that began appearing in January 1910 in the Montevideo magazine *La Semana*, a young man decides to commemorate his birthday by inviting his guests to join him in recording a cylinder. Those who wax poetic include his mother and father, whose subsequent deaths lead to a consideration of what exactly the device retained.[33] As the narrator explains in another echo of Edison's remark on seizing fugitive sounds, "allí estaban aprisionadas aquellas voces: palabras, vibración de pensamientos, de emociones, que la muerte no había podido llevarse; extraña supervivencia física, sensible, de lo que es más intensamente vida; la palabra" (those voices were imprisoned there: words, vibrant thoughts, emotions, that death had not been able to carry off with it; strange physical survival, sensitive, of what is most intensely life: speech).[34] Speech is so vital that it produces an excess that resists death; its capture, however, cannot entirely escape ties to writing, as in the repetitive reference to "aquel tubillo de cera que las voces ya extinguidas para siempre habían escrito con viviente escritura de vibraciones" (that little wax tube that those voices, now extinguished forever, had written with the living writing of vibrations).[35] "Living writing" encapsulates the sense that phonography's reproductions had imbued text with a sense of quietus.

Later that same year, Buenos Aires' *El Hogar* published "El vértigo de la vida" (The vertigo of life), a one-act comedy that features a phonograph operated offstage and speculates about the future of 1930, when print nears extinction. The media objects inducing the titular vertigo, which include letters and newspapers that circulate only as phonograph cylinders, both distract Mr. Fromont from helping his daughter, Cristina, find a suitable husband and fluster Paul, a poet who has come to Fromont in order to confess his feelings for Cristina. Irritated, Paul decides to leave Cristina a letter before departing Fromont's office, but the secretary, appalled anyone still writes, suggests an alternative: "Pase usted al escritorio vecino donde usted encontrará fonógrafos excelentes. . . . Dictará

LA DECLARACION

1

«Un cilindro de Arturo; al fin tendré noticias de él»

4

intermedio le declaro, le juro que yo la amo, sí, con toda la pasión de mi corazón ardiente, que

2

A ver si declara por fin! Muero de curiosidad!»

5

no puedo vivir ya sin ti! Sí, María, mi adorada, mi vida, mi todo, yo la idolatro, y si quieres hacer de mí el más feliz de los mortales, ven á mis brazos, así

3

«¡Señorita María! Perdone que me atreva imprimir en este cilindro todo mi sentir, mi pensamiento y mis deseos, pero mi corazón rebosa y no me puedo contener!... Hago al grafófono intérprete mío y mensajero de mi amor ilimitado, y por su

6

que pueda posar sobre tus labios de coral, el primer beso de amor.»

NOTA — Todos los novios (y los que no lo son) deben munirse de un Grafófono en la casa de

San Martín 368 — **F. R. GUPPY Y C^{IA}** — Buenos Aires

GRANDES REBAJAS DE PRECIOS PARA NAVIDAD Y AÑO NUEVO—CATÁLOGOS GRATIS CONSULTEN NUESTRO AVISO EN EL PRÓXIMO NÚMERO

FIGURE 5.3 F. R. Guppy y Compañía advertisement, 1900.

usted á un cilindro su carta" (Go to the neighboring office where you will find excellent phonographs. . . . You will dictate your letter onto a cylinder).[36] As a result of the illegibility of phonographic grooves, Paul's cylinder accidentally gets mixed in with those of two potential suitors, who, in Cristina's estimation, exhibit no appealing qualities. In an echo of the graphophone advertisement, however, she realizes what they lacked when Paul's cylinder is unexpectedly placed on the phonograph. In it he explains his fears of being forced to put down the pen—just as he had to when composing this phonograph letter—now that Cristina, his muse, is due to be married, but the wax reveals he still possesses a way with words. Working with the same materials, the poet nevertheless finds new power in the voice as a means of delivery.

Like Paul, later writers would confront the distinctly new possibilities posed by the phonograph and other sound reproduction technologies such as the radio. A short note on the first page of the May 17, 1925, issue of the literary journal *Martín Fierro* describes a series of poetry recitals on the radio in which, over the course of four installments, Oliverio Girondo, Norah Lange, Leopoldo Marechal, Jorge Luis Borges, and others would send their verses across the skies. The effect on these poets must have been considerable: a few weeks later another note informed readers that "un grupo de conocidos escritores se ha presentado a la jefatura de Policía solicitando permiso para organizar una 'Revista Oral' que se desarrollará semanalmente en la calle, en público" (a group of well-known writers presented itself at Police Headquarters seeking permission to organize an 'Oral Magazine' that will be carried out in the streets, in public).[37] Radio had facilitated a new method of distributing poetry that in turn led to the questioning of a familiar form's dependence on print. Many of those who read their work on the air would now participate in the *Revista Oral* that was ultimately "published" Saturday nights in the spring of 1926 in the Royal Keller café, where a gramophone recording announced the table of contents before contributors read their pieces aloud. Just as critics have framed *Revista Oral* as "una especie de audición radiofónica" (a type of radio show) or even as a "versión parlante de *Martín Fierro*" (talking version of *Martín Fierro*), various print publications produced content for the new medium and some radio programs developed a magazine-like format.[38] What both the radio readings and the *Revista Oral* revealed, however, was a desire for poetry that went beyond the page and presented the possibility of encountering new publics.

Amid the increasing popularity of radio, Eduardo González Lanuza, who had been involved with the radio recitals and helped found the *Revista Oral*, reflected on the state of the soundscape and penned an "Apología del fonógrafo"

(Defense of the phonograph) in the November 15, 1927, issue of *Martín Fierro*. More attuned to the uses of sound technologies than many of his contemporaries, he argues that the phonograph "tiene para la música, la misma importancia fundamental que tuvo para la literatura la imprenta" (has for music the same fundamental importance that printing had for literature) and identifies print's limitations with respect to sound:

> La representación escrita de las palabras, es traducible de inmediato, puesto que disponemos en todo momento del órgano adecuado para ello mientras que la escritura de los sonidos musicales, es un procedimiento que en el mejor de los casos, solo nos da el fantasma de la composición, pero no nos permite vislumbrar su cuerpo, ni menos aún su alma.
>
> [The written representation of words is immediately translatable since we always possess the adequate organ for it, whereas the writing of musical sounds is a procedure that, in the best of cases, gives us only the ghost of the composition, but it does not allow us to make out its body, even less so its soul.]³⁹

If the phonograph had previously been understood to produce ghosts by storing the voices of the dead that print could not capture, González Lanuza now proposes an inversion: by means of inscription the former avoided the hollow transcriptions of the latter. Even in this markedly musical context, explaining these particularities of phonography requires a turn to print—one that reverberates in another of his works.

An opening section of González Lanuza's 1932 collection, *Treinta i tantos poemas*, includes a poem dedicated to audition, that "pórtico de la entrada sin salida" (entrance without exit),⁴⁰ which sets the stage for González Lanuza's "Poem to be recorded on a phonograph disc" (Poema para ser grabado en un disco de fonógrafo). The proposed process of remediation is designed to amplify the particularities of each medium since, if one were to record the poem as instructed, playback would consist of little more than an explanation of what defines the device. Text, in other words, can talk about itself, but the talking machine cannot articulate its unique features without some assistance. The poem therefore begins by invoking the now-familiar defeat of mortality—"Sabes que acaso te está hablando un muerto?" (Did you know that perhaps a dead person is speaking to you?)—before further addressing the specificity of the medium. "Eco callado soi que resucito" (I am a silent echo that I resurrect), the voice explains, adding that "frájil cera guarda / esta inmortalidad que estás oyendo" (fragile wax stores / this immortality you're hearing).⁴¹ A subtle acknowledgment of print's durability appears in this contrast between "fragile" and "immortality," but phonography's elastic temporality with respect to past and present returns as the poem concludes: "vendrá una mano i volaré de nuevo: / diré otra vez lo que te estoi diciendo" (a hand will come and I will fly again: / I will say once more what I'm saying to you).⁴² By offering a plan for the indexical recording of the decisive differences between written word and record groove, the text insists on its own incompleteness.

This poet whose pieces could perform a kind of media theory would later turn to radio and its relationship to text. Although "Radiotelefonia," a short 1932 poem, takes radio broadcasting as its subject, it was only later that González Lanuza more extensively explored the medium, beginning with a 1937 issue of the literary journal *Sur* in which he reflected on its cultural potential in "¿Habrá que suprimir la radio?" (Will it be necessary to abolish the radio?): "La radio, máxima difusora, máxima facilitadora posible de la cultura, es también su mayor enemiga" (Radio, supreme transmitter, supreme facilitator of culture, is also its greatest enemy).⁴³ Such a position might seem surprising given his prior experience with the medium, but it becomes more understandable when one considers the way its transmissions differ from storage technologies like phonography or print: "Lo escrito sobre el papel o el lienzo, perdura y puede penetrar en el corazón de los hombres; pero lo afirmado, no ya en el aire, sino en ese aire del aire que es el éter, es imponderable como él, y con la misma rapidez con que se transmite, muere" (What's written on paper or canvas lives on and can penetrate the hearts of men; but what's declared, not in the air but in that air of the air that is the ether, is just as imponderable, and dies as quickly as it is transmitted).⁴⁴ By broadcasting sound, radio can distinguish itself from the similarly instantaneous reproductions of telephony, yet it still fails to provide the possibility of reflection born of repetition found in print and phonography.

Published in *Sur* in December 1944, González Lanuza's "Poema para ser leído por radio" (Poem to be read on the radio) quickly echoes his earlier concerns about disappearance as the speaker bemoans the fact that "mis trémulas palabras se me mueren a mi alrededor" (around me die my trembling words).⁴⁵ This poem for radio, which would in any case do little to preserve the speaker's words, confronts the nature of a medium characterized by a technical resemblance between transmitter and receiver: "me acerco a este pequeño círculo mágicamente imantado . . . a este íntimo oído por muchedumbres multiplicado" (I approach this small magically magnetized circle . . . this intimate ear multiplied many times over).[46] These figurations of the near-simultaneity and similarity of radio speaking and listening soon yield to an exclusive focus on the speaker. "Este mismo poema desde aquí ya no es mío" (This very poem is no longer mine), the voice explains before alluding to its own similar status: "Mi voz, mi voz, mi voz ya de mí liberada" (My voice, my voice, my voice now liberated from me).[47] Extending the reach of the voice but maintaining its ephemerality, radio evokes questions of authorship and possession that neither phonography nor print could ever address in quite the same way, and González Lanuza, recognizing the potential for a possible counterpoint to his earlier phonograph poem, both examines radio and exploits its differences from text for poetic effect.[48]

To trace the trajectory of these works by a single writer is to follow some of the patterns that surfaced in the reception of sound reproduction technologies in the Río de la Plata from the first phonograph exhibitions at the end of the 1870s to the beginning of the widespread influence of radio in the 1920s. Much like the *prismas* in the title of his first poetry collection, González Lanuza refracts through text not only sound reproduction technologies themselves but also the ever-developing popular conceptions of them. As he echoed others from the region in his fascination, he too insisted on placing word- and wave-based reproductions alongside each other in poems and essays that thoroughly demonstrate how reflecting on the phonograph or radio forces a reconsideration of text with respect to sound and the practices of recording and transmission more generally. Just as examining the roles of textual objects helps us appreciate the contexts into which sound reproduction technologies first emerged, evaluating how later works defined themselves either with or against the phonograph and other technologies including tape and radio enriches our conception of textuality. In other words, if the *Caras y Caretas* canine cover depicted one way the gramophone might be understood, it also voiced crucial questions about print's own alleged mastery or "monopoly on the storage of serial data" as man's best friend suggested text need not be his only companion.[49]

Notes

1. Adriana Bergero, for instance, emphasizes the magazine's role "as an intermediary between middle-class and proletarian readers." Bergero, *Intersecting Tango*, 27. Beginning with 15,000 copies per issue in 1898 and reaching 110,700 by 1910, the considerable growth in circulation was matched by a comprehensiveness in content. Sylvia Saítta describes the magazine as "uno de los ámbitos en los cuales se enlazaron elementos provenientes del circuito restringido de la cultura alta con la

cultura del consumo y los géneros populares" (one of the areas in which elements of the restricted circle of the elite were connected with the culture of consumption and popular genres). Saítta, "Balconeando el Rosario de Santa Fe desde Buenos Aires," 185. All translations are mine unless otherwise indicated.

2. In issues both before and after the one featuring this canine cover, advertisements for sound-reproduction technologies regularly appeared, including two instances of a Victor Talking Machine advertisement with "His Master's Voice" untranslated as well as others with the typical Spanish translation, "la voz de su amo." Readers were therefore not unfamiliar with a marketing campaign that had now inspired a cover. Illustrations like this one often reflected the history of the device: Francis Barraud's original painting of Nipper was titled *Dog looking at and listening to a phonograph*, yet once the London Gramophone Company (Victor's British counterpart) purchased it the cylinder phonograph had to be converted into a disc gramophone. As John Picker notes, "The alteration in the painting foreshadowed the impending shift in technology during the ensuing decade, when the device that had inspired active, personal engagement with recording became eclipsed by the commercially dominant playback-only gramophone." Picker, *Victorian Soundscapes*, 142.

3. The caption reads "la media palabra" (the slightest hint). A caricature of Figueroa Alcorta later in the same issue provides an explanation: "La 'media palabra,' Roca, dijo entre la expectación de muchos interesados é hizo al vicepresidente. Lo que obligó á Villanueva á gritar con gran razón:—¡Hombre! ¡Parece mentira que triunfe más fácilmente éste con media palabra, que yo con medio millón!" (Amid the excitement of the many interested, Roca gave the slightest hint and selected the vice president, which forced Villanueva to justifiably shout: What! It's incredible that he triumphs more easily with barely a word than I do with half a million). This cover therefore represents the influence of President Julio Roca in the election of a future vice president.

4. Adolfo Prieto highlights how reading practices varied according to the material being consumed: with magazines, "el acto de lectura marcadamente individualista del diario tendía a convertirse en un acto de lectura familiar o de grupo" (the markedly individual act of reading the newspaper tended to become an act of reading as a family or as a group). Prieto, *El discurso criollista en la formación de la Argentina moderna*, 41. In other words, families would resemble the canine cover when gathered to listen to the magazine.

5. As Raymond Williams reminds us, "The unique factor of broadcasting—first in sound, then even more clearly in television—has been that its communication is accessible to normal social development; it requires no specific training which brings people within the orbit of public authority." Williams, *Television*, 135.

6. Kittler, *Gramophone, Film, Typewriter*, 33.

7. The advertisement offers a further example of phonography assuming the role of print since the stories about the pope and the czar would have normally appeared in a segment of the magazine responsible for highlighting curiosities from around the world. In a 1909 installment of the section "Apuntes y Recortes" (Notes and

snippets), for example, readers learned of a Stuttgart schoolteacher attempting to bring gramophones into the classroom; later that year the same section commented on a Canadian railway's use of a phonograph to announce arrivals and departures.

8. Kittler, *Gramophone, Film, Typewriter*, xl; Castro, "La música," 257.
9. Lisa Gitelman, *Paper Knowledge*, 11. Elsewhere, Gitelman points out that "Edison identified his phonograph as a textual device, primarily for taking dictation. With this mandate, the invention emerged from Edison's laboratory into and amid a cluster of mutually defining literary practices, texts, and technologies." Gitelman, *Scripts, Grooves, and Writing Machines*, 1. Jonathan Sterne has stressed the importance of carefully attending to context because "the functions of these new technologies shifted as they moved across cultural contexts and as they were embedded in different kinds of cultural practices, including the use of other sound-reproduction technologies." Sterne, *The Audible Past*, 192.
10. Butler, *The Ancient Phonograph*, 11.
11. Edison, "The Phonograph and Its Future," 32; Parody, *Manual de fonografía española*, 1. By posing another rhetorical question—"A cuántos poetas no habrá sucedido olvidar una idea feliz, mientras han principiado a estamparla en papel?" (How many poets have not had the experience of forgetting a fortuitous idea while beginning to write it down?)—Parody also anticipated what José Martí later identified as the phonograph's utility for poets: "En las altas horas de la noche . . . el poeta, que no puede perder tiempo en buscar fósforos, sacude a las sabanas fogosas, palpa en la oscuridad el fonógrafo que tiene a su cabecera, habla por la trompeta al rollo que recoge sus imágenes" (In the late hours of the night . . . the poet, who cannot waste time looking for matches, shakes off the burning sheets, feels in the darkness for the phonograph he has at his head, speaks through the trumpet to the roll that collects his images). Qtd. in Price, *The Object of the Atlantic*, 67.
12. As Josefina Ludmer has argued, "The distinctive trait of the genre is the appropriation, in verse, of the gaucho's oral register"; she elaborates that "the gauchesque poets wrote as if it were a gaucho speaking or singing in his own words, style, and tone." Ludmer, "The Gaucho Genre," 609.
13. Hernández, *Martín Fierro*, 5.
14. Hernández, *Martín Fierro*, 261.
15. The practice of reading *Martín Fierro* aloud in *pulperías* made the work familiar to many before the turn of the twentieth century. Ana María Ochoa Gautier has written about Colombian poet Candelario Obeso's attempts to achieve a similar effect in 1877 when bringing the sounds of speech in his native region to the urban setting of Bogotá: "His phonography is one of transcription rather than inscription in that it seeks to carefully document through a highly acousticized orthography, the sounds he heard, knew, and pronounced onto the page." Ochoa Gautier, *Aurality*, 105.
16. For more on newspaper reports of the first public demonstrations of phonographs in Buenos Aires, which took place in December 1878, see Lucci, "Noticias sobre el fonógrafo en Buenos Aires," 6–7.

17. *Diario de sesiones de la cámara de diputados año 1881*, 3:325.
18. Butler reminds us that the Greek root *phōnē* in phonograph can mean voice as well as the human capacity for speech and explains that the emphasis on speech in early phonograph patents "reveals that Edison and his contemporaries saw the phonograph not as the *first* technology to record and play the voice, but simply as a much *better* one than ordinary writing." Butler, *The Ancient Phonograph*, 55.
19. *Diario de sesiones de la cámara de diputados año 1918*, 2:110.
20. Timoteo [pseud.], "Apertura de las Honorables Cámaras," 62.
21. *Diario de sesiones de la cámara de diputados año 1896*, 480.
22. Not all references to newspapers as phonographs were negative: some adopted the name of the device as their own, as did *El Fonógrafo Hebraico*, a Hebrew-language periodical in Buenos Aires, and *El Fonógrafo* in Navarro. If the *Caras y Caretas* canine cover had depicted political influence and susceptibility through the gramophone, the naming of these newspapers instead drew on the phonograph's ability to testify "in an indexical voice." Rothenbuhler and Durham Peters, "Defining Phonography," 258.
23. Wilde, *Viajes y observaciones*, 2:101.
24. Wilde, *Viajes y observaciones*, 2:101.
25. Sterne has studied the parallels between phonography and preservation: "Recording was the product of a culture that had learned to can and to embalm, to preserve the bodies of the dead so that they could continue to perform a social function after life. The nineteenth century's momentous battle against decay offered a way to explain sound recording. The ethos of preservation described *and prescribed* the cultural and technical possibilities of sound recording." Sterne, *The Audible Past*, 292.
26. Rothenbuhler and Durham Peters suggest that "phonography offers something like handwriting, with its tracing of the quirks of the author's body, rather than typewriting, which effaces such crucial contingencies." Rothenbuhler and Durham Peters, "Defining," 259.
27. Wilde, *Por mares i por tierras*, 187.
28. Even its inventor had difficulties deciphering the phonograph's script: Edison's attempt to compare two recordings of the letter "a" proved disastrous (Gitelman, *Scripts, Grooves, and Writing Machines*, 132).
29. Wilde, *Por mares i por tierras*, 187.
30. It was republished in January 1909 in *El Fogón*, also based in Montevideo. The earlier version included the following note: "Escrito expresamente para el fonógrafo de mi querido amigo el doctor Víctor Pérez Petit" (Written expressly for the phonograph of my dear friend Dr. Víctor Pérez Petit). Martínez Vigil, "Diálogo entre el teléfono y el fonógrafo." Whether it constitutes a simple dedication or instructions for a conversation to be recorded and later replayed on his friend's phonograph remains unclear; in either case, the reproduced nature of the conversation (and the fact that the piece itself was reproduced) align it more closely with the phonograph than the telephone.

31. Martínez Vigil, "Diálogo entre el teléfono y el fonógrafo."
32. Martínez Vigil, "Diálogo entre el teléfono y el fonógrafo."
33. Cros captured this sentiment in a poem titled "Inscription": "I wanted beloved voices / To be a fortune which one keeps forever." Qtd. in Kittler, *Discourse Networks 1800/1900*, 231.
34. Gimenez Pastor, "Las voces dormidas."
35. Gimenez Pastor, "Las voces dormidas."
36. "El vértigo de la vida,"
37. "Noticias literarias." The April 11, 1926, issue of *Última hora* reported that "DESDE ANOCHE BUENOS AIRES CUENTA CON UNA NUEVA REVISTA QUE SE IMPRIME EN EL AIRE" (since last night Buenos Aires has a new magazine printed in the air) and cited the following editorial statement: "Los impresores de la *Revista Oral* hacemos constar editorialmente, que según es lógico en una revista escrita en el aire, venimos, pues, a llenar un vacío" (The printers of *Revista Oral* affirm editorially that, as is logical for a magazine written in the air, we come to fill a void). Qtd. in Gasió, *El viento de las circunstancias*, 256–57.
38. Requeni, *Cronicón de las peñas de Buenos Aires*, 100; Gasió, *El viento de las circunstancias*, 16. Christine Ehrick studies Silvia Guerrico's *Cartel Sonoro* alongside *Sur*. Ehrick, *Radio and the Gendered Soundscape*, 44–46.
39. González Lanzua, "Apología del fonógrafo."
40. González Lanuza, *Treinta i tantos poemas*, 13.
41. González Lanuza, *Treinta i tantos poemas*, 41.
42. González Lanuza, *Treinta i tantos poemas*, 42.
43. González Lanuza, "¿Habrá que suprimir la radio?," 106.
44. González Lanuza, "¿Habrá que suprimir la radio?," 106.
45. González Lanuza, "Poema para ser leído por radio," 25.
46. González Lanuza, "Poema para ser leído por radio," 27.
47. González Lanuza, "Poema para ser leído por radio," 27.
48. We might characterize González Lanuza's poem as both radiophonic and radiogenic. Rubén Gallo summarizes French theorist André Coeuroy's distinction between radiophonic and radiogenic works when discussing Maples Arce and other avant-garde Mexican poets involved with the radio: "Radiophonic works—like the mechanographic poems about the typewriter—treat radio as a subject, but their structure and language remain untouched by the medium. Radiogenic works, in contrast, are written for broadcast, and their style, structure, and even length are shaped by the possibilities and limitations of the radio." Gallo, *Mexican Modernity*, 157.
49. Kittler, *Discourse Networks 1800/1900*, 245.

Works Cited

Bergero, Adriana. *Intersecting Tango*. Translated by Richard Young. Pittsburgh: University of Pittsburgh Press, 2008.

Butler, Shane. *The Ancient Phonograph*. New York: Zone Books, 2015.

Castro, D. Gonzalo de. "La música." *Revista contemporánea* 467 (1895): 252–58. http://hdl.handle.net/2027/uc1.a0002996825.

Diario de sesiones de la cámara de diputados año 1881. Vol. 3. Buenos Aires: Imprenta y Librería de Mayo, 1882. http://hdl.handle.net/2027/hvd.hwbu6f?urlappend=%3Bseq=8.

Diario de sesiones de la cámara de diputados año 1896. Buenos Aires: Compañía Sud-Americana de billetes de banco, 1897. http://hdl.handle.net/2027/uc1.b2889588.

Diario de sesiones de la cámara de diputados año 1918. Vol. 2. Buenos Aires: Talleres Gráficos Argentinos de L. J. Rosso y Compañía, 1918. http://hdl.handle.net/2027/uc1.b2889618?urlappend=%3Bseq=9.

Edison, Thomas Alva. "The Phonograph and Its Future." In *Music, Sound, and Technology in America*, edited by Timothy D. Taylor, Mark Katz, and Tony Grajeda, 29–37. Durham, N.C.: Duke University Press, 2012. Originally published in *North American Review* 126 (1878): 530–36.

Ehrick, Christine. *Radio and the Gendered Soundscape*. New York: Cambridge University Press, 2015.

"El vértigo de la vida." *El Hogar*, September 15, 1910. http://hdl.handle.net/2027/uiuo.ark:/13960/t5k95px57?urlappend=%3Bseq=857.

Gallo, Rubén. *Mexican Modernity*. Cambridge. Mass.: MIT Press, 2005.

Gasió, Guillermo. *El viento de las circunstancias*. Buenos Aires: Teseo, 2011.

Gimenez Pastor, Arturo. "Las voces dormidas." *La Semana*, February 5, 1910. http://hdl.handle.net/2027/uiuo.ark:/13960/t0rr5fz7d?urlappend=%3Bseq=186.

Gitelman, Lisa. *Paper Knowledge*. Durham, N.C.: Duke University Press, 2014.

———. *Scripts, Grooves, and Writing Machines*. Stanford, Calif.: Stanford University Press, 1999.

González Lanuza, Eduardo. "Apología del fonógrafo." *Martín Fierro*, November 15, 1927.

———. "¿Habrá que suprimir la radio?" *Sur*, April 1937.

———. "Poema para ser leído por radio." *Sur*, December 1944.

———. *Prismas*. Buenos Aires: J. Samet, 1924.

———. *Treinta i tantos poemas*. Buenos Aires: Talleres gráficos argentinos L. J. Rosso, 1932.

Hernández, José. *Martín Fierro*. Edited by Élida Lois and Ángel Núñez. 1872. Reprint, Nanterre: Allca XX, Université Paris X, 2001.

Kittler, Friedrich. *Discourse Networks 1800/1900*. Translated by Michael Metteer with Chris Cullens. Stanford, Calif.: Stanford University Press, 1990.

———. *Gramophone, Film, Typewriter*. Translated by Geoffrey Winthrop-Young and Michael Wutz. Stanford, Calif.: Stanford University Press, 1999.

Lucci, Héctor. "Noticias sobre el fonógrafo en Buenos Aires." *Club de tango* 52 (2002): 6–7.

Ludmer, Josefina. "The Gaucho Genre." In *The Cambridge History of Latin American Literature*, edited by Roberto González Echevarría and Enrique Pupo-Walker, 608–31. Cambridge: Cambridge University Press, 1996.

Martínez Vigil, Carlos. "Diálogo entre el teléfono y el fonógrafo." *La revista moderna*, May 20, 1900. http://hdl.handle.net/2027/ucl.31158013035786?urlappend=%3Bseq=193.

"Noticias literarias." *Martín Fierro*, June 26, 1925.

Ochoa Gautier, Ana María. *Aurality*. Durham, N.C.: Duke University Press, 2014.

Parody, Guillermo. *Manual de fonografía española*. Buenos Aires: Imprenta del orden, 1871. http://hdl.handle.net/2027/ucl.b2794867.

Picker, John. *Victorian Soundscapes*. New York: Oxford University Press, 2003.

Price, Rachel. *The Object of the Atlantic*. Evanston, Ill.: Northwestern University Press, 2014.

Prieto, Adolfo. *El discurso criollista en la formación de la Argentina moderna*. Buenos Aires: Editorial Sudamericana, 1989.

Requeni, Antonio. *Cronicón de las peñas de Buenos Aires*. Avellaneda, Argentina: Fundación Banco de Boston, 1984.

Rothenbuhler, Eric W., and John Durham Peters. "Defining Phonography: An Experiment in Theory." *Musical Quarterly* 81 (1997): 242–64.

Saítta, Sylvia. "Balconeando el Rosario de Santa Fe desde Buenos Aires." *Prohistoria* 21 (2014): 183–99.

Sterne, Jonathan. *The Audible Past*. Durham, N.C.: Duke University Press, 2003.

Timoteo [pseud.]. "Apertura de las Honorables Cámaras." *El Negro Timoteo*, February 23, 1879. http://hdl.handle.net/2027/txu.059173018090948?urlappend=%3Bseq=67.

Wilde, Eduardo. *Por mares i por tierras*. Buenos Aires: Imprenta, Litografía y Encuadernación e Jacobo Peuser, 1899. http://hdl.handle.net/2027/txu.059173023295699.

———. *Viajes y observaciones*. Vol. 2. Buenos Aires: Imprenta de Martín Biedma, 1892. http://hdl.handle.net/2027/nc01.ark:/13960/t9v13790f.

Williams, Raymond. *Television*. New York: Routledge, 2003.

6

The Postcard Poetics of Nicanor Parra's *Artefactos*

REBECCA KOSICK

IN 1972 CHILEAN POET NICANOR PARRA published his latest collection of poetry: a cardboard box containing 242 postcards, titled *Artefactos* (Artifacts). At the time, Parra was well known in Chile for having made an enormous and then-controversial splash in the country's literary scene with his *Poemas y antipoemas* (*Poems and Antipoems*), published almost two decades earlier in 1954. As Chile's famous antipoet, Parra had already forwarded an irreverent, aggressively down-to-earth approach to poetry in the 1954 collection, but the *Artefactos* took Parra's challenge to the norms of poetic production and distribution considerably further. These postcards continued to employ the colloquial, humorous, and at times vulgar language characteristic of the antipoems, but they also incorporated drawings by artist Guillermo Tejeda and, most radically, left behind the codex structure of pages bound together into a single volume. Loose and nonsequential, each postcard's face shows either a drawing alongside a text written by Parra or a facsimile of text written in the poet's own hand. The words themselves are often few, and take the style of slogans, brief ironic commentaries, and what José Miguel Ibáñez Langlois refers to as "poetic jokes."[1] The back of each card (see figure 6.1) looks exactly as a postcard would be expected to look, with horizontal lines where the address would be written, an outline of a square in the upper-right corner where the stamp would go, and blank space on the left side for a message yet to be recorded. In

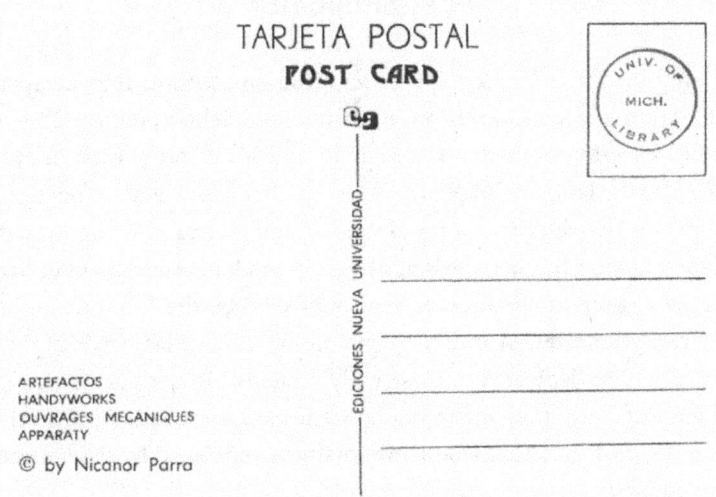

FIGURE 6.1 Nicanor Parra, reverse of *Artefactos*, 1972. © Herederos de Nicanor Parra, 1972.

the top, centered, are the words "TARJETA POSTAL," and just below them, in a smaller but darker font, their English translation, "POST CARD." In two languages, these cards announce that they do not just look like it—they really are postcards.

The postcard as we know it today, with an image on its face, first began circulating in Chile in the late nineteenth century, but it was in the twentieth century that it became an important form of correspondence. As a document, it was closely associated with "the everyday, the lived experience of common people" and, unlike other documents that more typically constitute the artifacts of history, postcards represent casual records of interpersonal exchange.[2] As Karen S. Van Hooft points out, when adapted into poetry, the postcard grants each poem "more individuality than if it were included in a bound volume," giving the poems "something of the personalized, intimate quality of a written communication between friends."[3] Parra's use of this form is provocative in light of his well-known preference for poetry that closes the gaps between everyday language, life, and art. And this chapter will argue that the postcard functions for the *Artefactos* not just as a poetic provocation or an experimental alternative to the codex but as a material realization of Parra's poetics.

Post-antipoetry

Scholarship on the collection *Artefactos* often emphasizes that it represents a continuation and concentration of Parra's established poetics. This would include his rejection of poetry as a high art and his incorporation of everyday language into the language of poetry. Among other features of his poetics, these things are also characteristic of the *Artefactos*, and several texts that would later be included among the postcards appeared in more conventional publications first. In 1967 some of these texts were published by the Venezuelan journal *Imagen*. Two years later, an anthology put out by Casa de las Américas in Cuba included a section dedicated to these early versions.[4] In both cases, these *Artefactos* were text only. They incorporated no images and made no material reference to the postcards that would eventually be published by the Universidad Católica de Chile.

In addition to their prior appearances as not-postcards, the *Artefactos* have also been compared to Parra's earlier antipoetry. The *Artefactos* maintain many of the features characteristic of poems that appeared in earlier collections such as *Poemas y antipoemas* but the *Artefactos* are notably shorter and less discursive. Both writing in 1974, Van Hooft and Marlene Gottlieb identify the increasing brevity of Parra's poetry in the years between the more narrative *Poemas y antipoemas* and the *Artefactos*, whose primary text frequently consisted of only a handful of words. In addition to the *Artefactos*' early appearances without images, the collection borrows from and reconfigures lines from elsewhere in Parra's oeuvre, re-presenting fragments of longer works as new, shorter wholes.[5] Early accounts of the *Artefactos* emphasize the ways in which this collection, despite its unconventional form, grows from the poet's work not as a counter to prior practice but as a diverse new complement to it. In using image and text in the service of an ever-more-succinct antipoetry, Parra is able to build on the poetic trajectory he established decades before.

One way this happens is via the *Artefactos*' incorporation of images. Parra had used multimedia methods previously, for example in the *Quebrantahuesos* (Osprey, 1952), a collaboration Parra participated in with Enrique Lihn and Alejandro Jodorowsky, among others. *Quebrantahuesos* consisted of collages of newspaper clippings that were publicly displayed as broadsides in Santiago. Later in his career, Parra continued to make use of found and borrowed materials in other ways. In the discursive antipoems, for example, the found consisted of the kinds of language the poet would overhear in the public sphere. This language was then filtered through the poet on its way to becoming poetry, or antipoetry. Presaging the *Artefactos*' later incorporation of political speech and slogans, "El peregrino" (from *Poemas y antipoemas*) begins, for example:

> *Atención, señoras y señores, un momento de atención:*
> *Volved un instante la cabeza hacia este lado de la república,*
> *Olvidad por una noche vuestros asuntos personales,*
> *El placer y el dolor pueden aguardar a la puerta:*
> *Una voz se oye desde este lado de la república.*
> *¡Atención, señoras y señores! ¡un momento de atención!*

> *[Your attention, ladies and gentlemen, your attention for one moment:*
> *Turn your heads for a second to this part of the republic,*
> *Forget for one night your personal affairs,*
> *Pleasure and pain can wait at the door:*
> *There's a voice from this part of the republic.*
> *Your attention, ladies and gentlemen! Your attention for one moment!]*[6]

In this opening stanza, Parra borrows from familiar forms of public address. The poetic voice speaks directly to readers but, in an ironic twist for a poem, asks them to forget the personal, pleasure, and pain. These things are common poetic meditations but are here subverted to an emphasis on the rhetoric of political pronouncement. While the poem does go on to address the speaker's personal affairs, including pleasure and pain, this first stanza establishes a poetics in which Parra borrows language typically found in other domains and asserts its place in poetry.

In conversation with Leonidas Morales, Parra notes that this found approach to poetics extends to the *Artefactos*, which he envisions as "prefab poems" rather than his own "creations."[7] In the *Artefactos*, Parra continues to borrow phrases and linguistic registers from non-poetic speech. In this, he maintains a degree of authorial control, acting as the medium by which found language comes to be poetic language. That said, the *Artefactos* introduce new strategies for prefabrication and provide new opportunities for eroding the poet's role as sole creator or mediator of what will become the poem. Unlike in the antipoems, Parra was only ever partially responsible for the content of the postcards that, together, made up the *Artefactos*. He supplied the texts, but Tejeda's drawings were done without any oversight whatsoever from Parra. The brief remarks that accompany the postcards, written by editor Cristián Santa María, describe how "all the artist had were Parra's texts. He received no directions and never met the poet until after the project had finished."[8] The *Artefactos* thus represent an even greater incorporation of the found or prefab in that their very construction builds on a de facto relinquishment of authorial control over the creative process. This is one way in which the *Artefactos*, while continuing from prior practice, do represent a significant break from established poetic conventions, both Parra's and others'.

The *Artefactos* cede control to other real and potential collaborators to such a degree that they fundamentally reconfigure the modes by which poetry communicates, reconstituting both writerly and readerly subjectivity such that readers *are* writers and writers are all of us. This becomes evident to readers by way of the collection's overt invitation to write, address, and mail these postcards, and is constantly thematized throughout the available text and images, which emphasize a polyphony of speakers, poetic and not. In this, the *Artefactos* do extend the antipoetic project that Parra describes in his famous poem "Manifiesto" (Manifesto), as one in which "los poetas bajaron del Olimpo" (the poets have come down from Olympus).[9] But, as postcards, they are able to materially realize this goal for the first time, disrupting the divisions between art and life in ways that remained out of reach for the codex-bound poetics that came before.

Post-book

As a result, the *Artefactos* challenge the relationship between poetry and the history of the book in the late twentieth century. Poetry has always been, and remains, a language-based art that need not necessarily manifest in print, or in the form of a codex. It can be—and many poetry enthusiasts argue that it must be—recited. In the twentieth century, though, its primary means of circulation was the book, even in cases where poetry's sonority was highly prized. Parra, for example, remarks that "Neruda's poetry, and *modernismo* in general, is acoustic, sonorous, it enters through the ear."[10] Though this might seem paradoxical, even poems like these—ones that exploit the lyric's traditional relationship with song and sound—materialized as printed text, bound and delivered via the codex. On the other hand, Parra claims that, in the case of the *Artefactos*, poetry "enters through the eye."[11] This happens thanks to their incorporation of images, the brevity of their textual components, and the visuality of the textual components themselves. The cards employ an enormous variety of fonts and font sizes, display text in visually inventive ways, and combine printed with handwritten text. As such, these postcards are something to be seen and displayed, artifacts in and of themselves, rather than the material means of delivery for a form that demands to be recited. That said, the challenge the *Artefactos* make to the book is even greater than a shift from sonority to visuality. The collection rejects the codex entirely. Its construction as a box of postcards suggests poetry can circulate differently, and more widely, when it undoes its binding. While a collection of loose cards could still conceptually be thought of as a book, as Gottlieb points out, the collection has a built-in "self-destruct" feature because "when all of the cards have been mailed, the 'book' disappears."[12]

The disappearance of the book in the contemporary moment is most often associated with the rise of digital media. It has become clear by now that the arrival of digital texts does not necessarily mean the era of the book has ended. Even so, the digital landscape has profoundly impacted print culture, and most discussions about the disappearance of the book surround the move from paper to ebooks and other electronic media.[13] While this path does apply to a great many examples, the *Artefactos* demonstrate another kind of poetic excursion from the codex. The collection remains intimately engaged with another common material home for text—the postcard—which is neither a book nor a digital alternative or adaptation of one. Electronic media is often painted as offering a radical departure from the constraints of print media. This is often true, but at the same time, many digital books overtly display their ties to the codex that preceded them. Ebooks, for example, often mimic the material construction of the printed book, including by incorporating a cover, a fixed sequence of pages, and even, at times, digitally reproducing the sound and look of a page being flipped. Rather than a cover and binding, the *Artefactos* are held together in a box, just as any set of postcards would be. They have no fixed sequence, and they need not stay together as a set at all. In fact, with one side of each card yet to be composed, leaving the set behind is what allows the *Artefactos* to realize their final form. As such, the codex appears in the collection only as the immaterial trace of the form not chosen, the norm against which the postcards pronounce their poetics.

As I have indicated, this approach allows Parra to realize certain tenets of antipoetry. The postcards bring poetry down from its rarefied position as an elite form and enable an increased proximity between poetic and everyday language. The *Artefactos* manage both of these feats and overcome a divide still in place in earlier manifestations of antipoetry, which, however much it bucked the norms of what ought to go into a poem, was still poetry and perceived as such. This was due both to its binding to poetry's then-established material support (the codex) and by way of its incorporation of traditional poetic forms and features. As René de Costa describes, "though it reads like prose, [antipoetry] is perceived as poetry thanks to a balance between the fluid syntax of the narrative and the regular rhythm of the phrasing," which employs "perfectly measured quartets in *endecasílabo* that are linked by rhyme."[14]

The *Artefactos* are poetry, too, but they are also actually postcards. Many of the texts on these cards are in endecasílabo as well, but instead of materializing in the pages of a book, these verses are able to circulate in the world as any other postcard would. They can be perceived as poetry, or (importantly) not. As such, they manage to materialize the coincidence of poetry and not-poetry, something that is a bit trickier for antipoems, which remain bound to the book. In her introduction to *Antipoems: How to Look Better & Feel Great*, translator Liz Werner points out that "Parra does not only write antipoems, as the title of *Poemas y antipoemas* clearly tells us."[15] She suggests that, in thinking about "antipoetry," "antimatter" is a useful metaphor: "Viewed through the lens of antimatter, antipoetry mirrors poetry, not as its adversary but as its perfect complement; it is not by nature negative, but negative where poetry is positive and vice versa."[16] The antipoetic project, then, is always about poetry itself—mirroring it, opposing it, challenging it—and it is fitting that it would make its material home the codex. The *Artefactos*, on the other hand, are both *about* the relationship between poetry and not-poetry and a material constitution of that relationship itself.

Post-Huidobro

In constituting that relationship, the *Artefactos* represent a further realization of antipoetry's aims and share its antagonisms with the poets of Chile's recent past. Of these, Vicente Huidobro bore the brunt of antipoetry's critique. From his early practices in "creationism" to his later vanguard experimentations, Huidobro favored poetic language that specifically marked its difference from the language of everyday speech. As he wrote in "Arte Poetica" (Ars poetica), "el poeta es un pequeño Dios" (The poet is a little god) charged with creating a new and distinct world for poetry.[17] The theory Huidobro deemed "creationism," as he describes, "is a general aesthetic theory that [he] began to elaborate around

1912."[18] According to him, "The creationist poem is comprised of created images, created situations, created concepts,"[19] which manifest poetically as surprising images invented for the poem alone that do not (and should not) correspond to the natural world. An example he gives is the phrase "square horizon," the title of his 1917 collection *Horizon carré*. The phrase is creationist to Huidobro specifically because a square horizon is not something that could occur in the natural world—it belongs to, and helps create, the world of the poem alone.

Later, though no longer explicitly "creationist," his vanguard writing shared this interest in seeking a distinctly poetic language. This is something taken to its perhaps furthest degree at the end of 1931's *Altazor*. A long poem in seven cantos, its final lines consist of what translator Eliot Weinberger, in his introduction to the book, calls "a language of pure sound."[20]

Lalalí
Io ia
i i i o
Ai a i ai a i i i i o ia[21]

These lines are unlikely to be considered everyday speech. They are certainly rarefied and distinct from the conversational uses of language Parra advocated. Despite this, I would say that for *Altazor*, which depicts the interstellar fall of the lyrical "I" of the same name, it is also not entirely unimaginable that this "pure sound" would, in fact, sound quite a lot like the kinds of noises a falling person might make on the way down.

Parra's rejection of Huidbro is a long-standing given in accounts of antipoetry, but their difference is not as absolute as the prevailing narrative suggests, and is sometimes overstated. As Niall Binns points out, the two poets overlap in a number of ways. Among their shared concerns are an "intent to transform ossified language" and a dedication to poetic engagement with "the latest technological advances."[22] What's more, twentysome years before *Poemas y antipoemas*, Canto IV of *Altazor* included the line "aquí yace Vicente antipoeta y mago" (here lies Vicente antipoet and magician).[23] For the purposes of this chapter, it is also important to stress that both poets integrated visual materials into their poetry, though in notably different spheres. Huidobro, for example, exhibited his painted poems in Paris, whereas Parra's *Artefactos*, as postcards, suggest more modest and interpersonal means of making themselves visible in the world. In this way, though the two poets share interests and methods, Parra's poetics do oppose the kind of division between poetic and natural worlds that Huidobro, especially during his creationist period, insisted on.

Rather than there being two sets of language, one that belongs to poetry and one that belongs to the world outside it, for Parra's antipoetry, poetic language should sound like language that is overheard on the street, circulating in political or commercial slogans, or spoken among friends and strangers. This remains true even though, in his codex-bound collections, Parra makes this case *with* poetry. In his poem "Manifiesto," Parra specifically calls out Huidobro by condemning "la poesía de pequeño dios" (the poetry of a little god),[24] but Parra also writes in endecasílabo. He does this at the same time as he critiques the role of poet as a magical or special figure.

Que el poeta no es un alquimista
El poeta es un hombre como todos

[A poet is no alchemist
A poet is a man like all men][25]

This might seem like a contradiction, but to return to the metaphor of antimatter, antipoetry *was* poetry, even as it was anti. And, even in endecasílabo, Parra plainly makes the case against a poetry that would seek to separate itself from other kinds of speech and speakers.

That said, the codex, in some manners, limits this poetry's potential to circulate in the ways nonpoetic speech or text does. Though *Poemas y antipoemas* made a huge splash, and Parra's antipoetics, in general, sought to broaden the potential audience for poetry, the book's means of circulation suggest a readership that would be likely to coincide quite substantially, if not entirely, with the typical readers of poetry. The *Artefactos*, on the other hand, actively seek ways out of this bind, by bringing plain, accessible speech into what had become, prior to antipoetry's intervention, the domain of precious or rare "poetical" language, and inviting poetry out from between the pages of a book. Made not just to look like postcards but to actually be postcards, these poems significantly reorient the possible modes by which poetry can circulate in the domain of everyday life. Combining their postcard form with antipoetry's already established program of closing the gaps between poetry and everyday life and speech allows the *Artefactos* new material avenues for making good on the promises of Parra's poetics.

Post-politics

The artefacto in figure 6.2 is characteristic of the ways the collection combines Parra's antipoetic program with resources that help materialize its message. The words spelled out, "todo es poesía menos la poesía" (everything is poetry except poetry), amount to a pared-down, straightforward rendering of antipoetry's paradoxical message. Poetry is still on the table, this artefacto announces, but it will not consist of "poetry" this time. Read in context with his "Manifiesto," it becomes clear that the poetry excepted by this artefacto is "la poesía de gafas obscuras / La poesía de capa y espada / La poesía de sombrero alón" (The poetry of dark glasses / The poetry of the cape and sword / The poetry of the plumed hat).[26] These lines all reject a poetry divorced from the contemporary moment, one marked by romantic, anachronistic images like capes and swords whose ability even to see the world in front of it is obscured by dark glasses.

While this intertextual definition would not necessarily be at hand for every reader of this artefacto, it is also not necessary for the successful communication of its message. Readers of this card are free to come up with their own definitions of poetry, which, whether Huidobro's rarefied language, the clichéd swans of modernismo, or European poems learned in school, are all likely to share

FIGURE 6.2 Nicanor Parra, "Todo es poesía menos la poesía," *Artefactos*, 1972. © Herederos de Nicanor Parra, 1972.

considerable distance from the language of readers' lived experiences. On the other hand, the images that appear visually in this artefacto function as ready examples for what might count as poetry, now. Their randomness proposes, as the words do, that poetry really could be anything, from bicycle wheels, to handcuffs, to pencil sharpeners. There are also some notable things missing—for example, there is nothing here that marks poetry as belonging to the privileged classes. On the contrary, the appearance of the butler figure in the *T* of "TODO" suggests that poetry is constituted by the serv*er* rather than the served. While the Victorian-looking lady faces that contribute to the *D* might make the opposite suggestion, their disembodiment also implies considerable destruction of the values of refinement and chastity associated with both this feminine type and the poetry antipoetry antagonized.

Challenges to sexual propriety are even more strongly pronounced elsewhere in the collection. Like the nudie postcards known as "postales francesas" (French postcards), the *Artefactos* are replete with sexual imagery in both their illustrations and text.[27] According to Samuel León Cáceres and his coauthors, in Chile, "the female nude found a way into the market thanks to the postcard."[28] The presence of male and female nudity in the *Artefactos* is thus both an appropriation of already circulating postcard types and a poetic provocation that challenges conservative sexual politics in both art and life. Like other of the *Artefactos*' politics, though, there are many conflicting messages to be drawn from the sexually provocative poems, many of which represent not just a shock-the-bourgeois ethos common to artistic vanguards in general but depict problematic racial and sexual politics. There are cards that uphold, for example, the sexual fetishization of mixed-race women or announce, in type set between an illustration of two legs spread open, that for poetry to live "hay / que / poseerla / y humillarla en público" (you / have / to possess "her"/ and humiliate "her" in public). Though certainly likely to upset a politics of sexual prudence, these cards do nothing to destabilize existing racial or sexual power structures.

There are cards that can be interpreted more progressively, though. The artefacto in figure 6.3, which shows a coed exposing her rear, can be translated as "freshman woman / it doesn't matter that you're / not a virgin / the movement needs you," positing that a woman's worth is not tied to the maintenance of her sexual purity, and, too, that she has value as a political actor. Of course, this card can also be interpreted in the opposite direction, coercively suggesting that a woman's worth to the movement lies precisely in the relinquishment of her sexual agency.

FIGURE 6.3 Nicanor Parra, "Compañera mechona / no importa que no / seas virgen / el movimiento te necesita," *Artefactos*, 1972. © Herederos de Nicanor Parra, 1972.

This and other kinds of political ambiguity are common to the *Artefactos* that combine sex and politics. Another card depicts two line drawings, one of two individuals shooting crude guns at each other, and a second of two nude individuals entangled in a sexual encounter. Combined with these images are captions in a simple sans-serif font that read (in English) "Fighting for peace" and "Fucking for chastity." Here, sex and politics are combined but, this time, with little specificity or connection to politics as it is practiced. An ironic denunciation of hypocrisy of all kinds, more than sex or politics in themselves, is the ultimate takeaway of this artefacto.

What Gabriel Villaroel has referred to as the *Artefactos*' "infinite irony" is on display in this example, like almost all the cards in the collection.[29] This feature has provoked some frustration on the part of its readers, especially in the domain of politics, where the *Artefactos*' irony sometimes functions to undermine clear political convictions. As many scholars have noted, the *Artefactos* do not fit neatly into any single ideological camp. For instance, one, in large letters, reads, "MAO." An image of Mao appears in the O. Beneath his name, in smaller type, is printed "Deja que abran las cien flores" (let a hundred flowers bloom), and beneath that, it reads, "—No: con 99 basta y sobra" (No: 99 is more than enough). Quoting Mao, the poem refers to the Hundred Flowers Campaign in China during which time the Communist Party encouraged (and then later forcibly discouraged) open expression among its citizens. With "'99 is more than enough'" (Parra's addition to the original quote), this *Artefacto* uses humor to reference both the opening of the regime and the violent crackdown that followed. As a result, readers might take from this a criticism of communism more generally. Other cards, though, appear to propose the opposite. For example, one says, in the poet's own writing, "Queman esa bandera chilena / Mucho mejor una hoz y un martillo" (Burn that Chilean flag / Better a hammer and sickle).

In addition, there are many artefactos where political confusion is itself the message. Included among these examples would be one that reads, in the poet's own hand, "Cuba si / Yankees tambien" (Cuba yes / Yankees too) or "L'etat c'est moi / La revolución cubana soy yo" (I am the state / I am the Cuban Revolution).[30] Both of these play with political slogans and their approximations, another common feature of the *Artefactos*' found or prefab poetics. The first inverts the slogan "Cuba yes, Yankees no" with a kind of political double speech in which both are the favored. The second employs two expressions that sound almost identical on their own. The French is a quote attributed to Louis XIV, taken to represent how the power of governance is concentrated in the monarchical leader alone. Below that, in Spanish, is a phrase that, given the context of the Cuban Revolution, would indicate an entirely different "yo" (I) to mean, as a result, that any given "I" can embody the revolution, the exact opposite of what would be possible in a monarchical form of government.

Van Hooft takes this political and subjective confusion to be evidence of Parra's role as a "compiler" more than an author of these poems, which do not just use everyday language but borrow from and tinker with language already circulating in the public sphere.[31] I take Parra's role in the *Artefactos* to be an even more radical unraveling of authorial control. Compile as he may, in formulating this process, as the postcards and their conditions of production show, Parra is just one compiler among many who actually or potentially contribute to the creation of these poems. Their visual artist, Tejeda, played at least as important a role in the compilation of the *Artefactos*. In adding images to Parra's text, he first compiled textual and visual regimes within the postcards. Within the illustrations themselves, Tejeda frequently incorporated juxtaposition and collage, strategies that are, themselves, compilations. That the postcards are meant to be—or at least, in their paratextual makeup, suggest they might be—scribbled, addressed, and mailed further underscores the potential future intervention of additional compilers. What's more, these compilers need not already have established themselves as authors (visual or textual) in order to contribute meaningfully to *Artefactos*' final "editions."

This is also why the confusion of allegiances expressed in the *Artefactos*, together, is not necessarily representative of political confusion on the part of Parra. It is true that the poet never declared his belonging to any given party, although, as Iván Carrasco Muñoz describes it, "Parra lived through the most significant, conflict-ridden, and tense political moments in the history of modern Chile."[32] Unlike many other poets at the time, Parra maintained what he has called an "open, but never sectarian leftism."[33] This is also apparent in the *Artefactos*, which are political but unpartied. The *Artefactos*' politics is one of generalized irreverence and rejection of authorities of all kinds, something Carrasco Muñoz describes as approximate to "the rebelliousness of anarchism."[34] Despite this proximity to leftist politics in general, Parra has been criticized by both the left and the right. The collaborative making of the *Artefactos* themselves, which took place just prior to the U.S.-backed military junta that installed Augusto Pinochet, was described by Tejeda as "a mark of the improvisatory and carnivalesque environment of *Allendismo* fighting with anti-*Allendismo* and vice versa."[35] Ultimately, this is in part the reason why some of the postcards do not contain Tejeda's illustrations but only reproductions of Parra's handwriting. Because of the atmosphere at the time, the young artist began to grow nervous about the "ironic provocations that Parra was making toward the left and right alike."[36]

Equally provocative is not the same as politically neutral, and Parra has insisted that his work "acts in the public sphere and is engaged with history, ideas, and problems."[37] After the coup, the military took over the Universidad Católica, and Parra recounts how when asked why the coup took place, the new chancellor, Admiral Jorge Swett, "took out a box of the *Artefactos*, placed them on the table, and said 'so that this would never happen again.'"[38] After that, the remaining stock was burned on his orders. Coinciding with this, there was a long period in which the left was extremely suspicious of Parra, after the poet accepted an invitation to have tea with First Lady Pat Nixon in the White House in 1970. Parra would later reflect that he had repaired relations with the

Left, but he would continue to describe his poetics as one that "hasn't identified with any flag." Rather, it is an "invitation to a certain type of waltz, one of relativity and indeterminacy."[39]

Taken as a whole, the *Artefactos* carve out a space for this indeterminate dance to take place, but it is the case that many of the individual *Artefactos* do address contemporary (and historical) politics, in Chile and abroad. Just as postcards deliver news from elsewhere, many of the examples are drawn from outside the Chilean context. The United States appears a number of times and usually as a target of critique, as in the artefacto that reads, "USA / donde la libertad / es una estatua" (USA / where freedom / is a statue), the ironic "Our Nixon thou art in heaven," or, as in figure 6.4, "V-Day / the North American flag / flutters triumphantly / in the middle of a polydimensional cemetery / packed with crosses, large, medium, and small." Though Parra is often painted as apolitical, the *Artefactos*, in fact, make many political statements. The card in figure 6.4, and others, for example, clearly criticizes the United States' history of violence, imperialism, and hypocrisy.

The *Artefactos* do not opt out of politics but present a range of sometimes contradictory political critiques and statements. As such, the collection maintains a kind of poetic commons in which critique itself is a poetic practice. In this space, voices other than Parra's are enabled to play significant roles in the authoring of their own utterances—poetic and political. This comes about as much as a result of the cards' diverse political expressions as of their material construction as postcards that open the opportunity that other opinions beyond the many Parra and Tejeda already compiled might be recorded in these poems.

The postcards also make it possible for this poetry to circulate in the manners that politics and political speech do—on fliers, in the mail, in public and interpersonal exchanges of all kinds. Parra has commented on the inspiration he drew from the political graffiti students would scratch onto bathroom stalls. The artefacto that reads, in English, "Death has no future" was lifted wholesale from one such example. Werner also describes how the *Artefactos* were "inspired by the contagious art of advertising," and Parra remarks to Morales that the advertising slogan "Did you Maclean your teeth today?" is a perfect example of an artefacto.[40] Advertising shares a name with "propaganda" in Spanish and, like its political counterpart, makes use of the kind of sloganeering and text/image integration the *Artefactos* also employ. As Roman Jakobson famously pointed out in his reading of "I like Ike," political slogans rely on the poetic function.[41] Commercial ones do too, as Parra points out. And the *Artefactos*' frequent use of succinct, slogan-style phrasing highlights this already extant convergence of

FIGURE 6.4 Nicanor Parra, "V-Day / La bandera norteamericano / flamea triunfante / en medio de un cementerio polidimensional / abarrotado de cruces grandes, medianas y chicas," *Artefactos*, 1972. © Herederos de Nicanor Parra, 1972.

propagandistic and poetic speech and then deliberately blurs the lines between the two. According to the *Artefactos*, poetry is everything and everywhere, and can be written by anyone. What's more, it might already be in your mail, on your billboards, or graffitied on your bathroom stalls.

Post-author

A convergence of multiple voices is also an end result of many of the *Artefactos*. Though the United States figures as an antagonist in a number of the poems, many of the *Artefactos* are written in English, or combine English and

Spanish. This is perhaps best on display in one that reads, "Spanglish / Cierren la windowa / que parece que / va a reinar." This card blends the two languages in the mode of Spanglish and can be read as "Close the window / it seems like / it's going to rain." Its joke hinges on the words "windowa" and "reinar." "Windowa" is not a word in Spanish but a calque of the English word "window" ("ventana" in Spanish). "Reinar," on the other hand, is a word in Spanish but is a cognate of the English "to reign" and not its homophone "to rain" ("llover" in Spanish).

"Spanglish" differs from the U.S.-antagonizing artefactos, which, for the most part, address state-level politics and the hypocritical national myths the United States tells itself and others. Alternately, the "Spanglish" artefacto represents a more organic encounter between South and North America, and the speakers of Spanish and English. This postcard "travels" in both directions. In this way, it represents the journeys of countless immigrants, particularly into North America, and the impact, in both directions, of their multilingual encounter. This artefacto also puts into practice Parra's investment in the poetry of everyday language. As "Spanglish" shows, this is not just a matter of poetry's inclusion of topics and themes previously considered unpoetic but a matter of showing how language itself is responsive to the contexts of its speakers, and of providing an opportunity for poetry to demonstrate this responsiveness too.

This artefacto also reiterates the ways in which the *Artefactos*, taken as a whole, work against the privileging of a single, authorial "I." Just as a multitude of political stances are expressed in the collection, a multiplicity of voices are enabled, or invited, to compose these poems. As postcards, the *Artefactos* always start out unfinished. They are always awaiting another writer who will add another message to the backside of each card. Their rejections of propriety and antagonizing of both right and left, together, are part of a more generalized rejection of authority, which extends even to their author.

In figure 6.5, Albert Einstein represents the rejected authority. This poem reads, "The world is what it is / and not what a son of a bitch named Einstein / says it is." This artefacto takes Einstein's authority down a peg (or several) first, by calling him a son of a bitch, and second, by refusing to give him the final word on what the world is. It also implies that the authority to make this kind of determination might reside in any (or none) of us, radically leveling the playing field for all potential authorities. Because Parra was also a physicist, the rejection staged by this poem returns to the poet's own author-ity. In the *Artefactos*, poetry is what it is, and not even what Parra might say it is.

FIGURE 6.5 Nicanor Parra, "El mundo es lo que es / y no lo que un hjio de puta llamado Einstein / dice que es," *Artefactos*, 1972. © Herederos de Nicanor Parra, 1972.

Parra was not the first to reject the authority of a single, stable, and assured author-figure. Roland Barthes's "Death of the Author" came out in 1967 and Michel Foucault delivered his lecture "What Is an Author?" in 1969. In addition to the poststructuralist undoing of traditional notions of authorship, twentieth-century poetic vanguards throughout the Americas rejected the lyrical "I" that had previously provided the poem with the appearance of a unified authorial or speaking voice. In the *Artefactos*, this rejection splits the author into many distinct subjectivities, all equally getting their say. The poetic rejection the *Artefactos* stage of an authoritative form is coupled with a rejection of extrapoetic authorities of all kinds. Though this collection does not ultimately dismantle every aspect of authority or social privilege, in or outside poetry, what might be said to its credit is that the *Artefactos* authorize a combination of contradictory perspectives, which prevent, as a matter of course, the dominance of any single one.

This is made especially possible thanks to their construction as postcards, a feature that enables this collection of poetry to find heretofore unavailable opportunities. Set loose from the codex, the *Artefactos*' heteroglossia is not just a feature of their diverse content but a material fact. The already multiple authors—Parra and Tejeda—share in the making of these poems with countless other authors, including all speakers, sloganeers, copywriters, and bathroom stall scrawlers whose language Parra borrows, adapts, and claims for poetry. They also include all the inferred and potential authors who might fill in the backs of each of these postcards, finally finishing the job Parra, Tejeda, and their other invisible collaborators began. Figure 6.6 thematizes this gesture, with text that reads, "Hello / Hello / let it be known that it's not me who's speaking." This text replaces the head of the figure pictured, such that the very voice of the not-speaker has no mouth from which to proceed. It comes as already available language, emerging from an only partially embodied speaker.

Because readers are invited to fill in the back of the postcards, the *Artefactos*' first readers are also their potential writers. Villaroel argues that "dialogue with

FIGURE 6.6 Nicanor Parra, "Alo / Alo / conste que yo / no soy el que habla," *Artefactos*, 1972. © Herederos de Nicanor Parra, 1972.

the reader is fundamental" for the *Artefactos*, and that the reader is the one who "interprets and unfolds their potential."[42] While the role of interpreter belongs to the reader in most conditions of reading, and certainly in the reading of poetry, Villaroel underscores the way the collection's constant ironizing leaves the reader with an unusually high degree of interpretation yet to be done. Dialogue with the reader is also something the *Artefactos* stage literally. With filled front faces and blank backs, each card is a conversation opened but not yet finished, and the reader's job is not just to interpret what's on the front of the card but to compose its reverse. In this way, the postcards further enable the antipoetic aim of including nonpoetic speech and writing in poetry. They make use of commonly circulating and found language, and they invite nonpoets to partake of their authorship as much as, or more than, their already multiple authors.

The *Artefactos* thus profoundly shift the reading experience from a model in which the reader is the receiver of the author's message to a model in which the reader is able to actively participate as another such author. The result of this radical remodeling of the reading experience is a fundamental leveling of the two roles. Everyone is able to partake in the making of poetry. In the *Artefactos*, the poets do not need to come down from Olympus; they were never up there to begin with.

This also means that the poems are able to incorporate not-poetry in an even more expansive way than they might if they were bound to the codex. Whatever aspirations Parra might have in borrowing and adapting precirculating language, the Duchampian gesture of then calling these texts poetry (or antipoetry) inevitably reinstates some of the old hierarchies. In the author's newly reanimated hands, what was once not-poetry now is, and not everyone has the power to incite this transformation. While it is true that the same thing can be said of the *Artefactos*, their construction as postcards is a way of overcoming this challenge, of first inviting nonpoets to contribute to the text of these cards, and second, as a way of including their language wholesale. The *Artefactos* thus insist on the potential contributions of other speakers and writers and, as postcards, make it possible for the reader and the writer to come, literally, together. Correspondence from nonpoet writers is able to circulate with poetry and poetry is able to circulate alongside this correspondence as part of the postcard. For the *Artefactos*, the postcard is not just an alternative to the book but one that specifically makes the alternative possibilities Parra seeks for poetry materially possible. It melds the everyday with the poetic to such a degree that poetic language goes beyond approximating the language heard and seen in everyday life to ultimately embody that language itself.

Notes

I am grateful to Nicanor Parra and the Agencia Literaria Carmen Balcells for permission to reproduce images of the *Artefactos*.

1. Ibáñez Langlois, *Para leer a Parra*, 73. All translations are mine unless otherwise indicated.
2. Cáceres et al., *Historia de la postal en Chile*, 11.
3. Van Hooft, "The 'Artefactos' of Nicanor Parra," 68.
4. Binns and Echevarría, "Sobre *Artefactos*," 981; Parra, *Poemas*.
5. Van Hooft, "The 'Artefactos' of Nicanor Parra," 69–70. Gottlieb likens the *Artefactos* to concrete poetry, which was, in the early 1970s, just coming to the end of its midcentury heyday in Latin America, especially Brazil. The *Artefactos*, though, "don't depend on the arrangement of letters on the page alone," as she sees it, but incorporate the visual as "another dimension that the poet adds to the poem" in the way that, "on television, the image reinforces and concretizes what the speaker says." Gottlieb, "Del antipoema al artefacto al . . . ," 33.
6. Parra, "El peregrino," in *Antipoems: New and Selected*, 4–5, translation by W. S. Merwin.
7. Quoted in Parra, *Obras completas & algo +*, 991. This is also a critique of Vicente Huidobro, known for advocating an approach to poetry he called "creationism."
8. Santa María, Preface, n.p. These remarks appear in a glossy booklet made of a single folded sheet of paper, printed front and back. The booklet was packaged in the box along with the individual postcards and is the closest the set comes to the codex, with a cover image of Parra, interior commentary by Santa María, and a back cover bearing the collection's copyright information.
9. Parra, "Manifiesto," in *Emergency Poems*, 118–19.
10. Piña, *Conversaciones con la poesía chilena*, 35; also quoted in Parra, *Obras completas & algo +*, 997. Starting in the late nineteenth century, Latin American modernismo does not directly correspond to North American "modernism," which dates to the interwar period in the twentieth century.
11. Piña, *Conversaciones con la poesía chilena*, 35; also quoted in Parra, *Obras completas & algo +*, 997.
12. Gottlieb, "La evolución de la antipoesía."
13. See, for example, chapter 10 in this volume (Edward King).
14. De Costa, "Para una poética de la (anti) poesía," 8. *Endecasílabo* is a poetic form consisting of eleven syllables per line that traces its origins to Greek and Roman poetry, notably that of Catullus. In the Middle Ages, the form was adopted into Spanish from Italian and used in the *poesía culta* (learned or cultured poetry) of the time. Parra's adoption of the form emphasizes firm ties with poetic tradition, despite, and alongside, the rupture he wished to initiate.
15. Parra, *Antipoems: How to Look Better & Feel Great*, x.
16. Parra, *Antipoems: How to Look Better & Feel Great*, x. Antimatter is also an apt metaphor for Parra, a trained physicist who, in addition to his long career as a poet, taught physics for half a century.

17. Huidobro, "Arte Poetica," in *The Selected Poetry of Vicente Huidobro*, 2–3; translation by David M. Guss.
18. Huidobro, *Manifestos Manifest*, 40.
19. Huidobro, *Manifestos Manifest*, 45.
20. Huidobro, *Altazor*, xi.
21. Huidobro, *Altazor*, 150.
22. Binns, "Herencias antipoéticas," 143.
23. Huidobro, *Altazor*, 94.
24. Parra, "Manifiesto," in *Emergency Poems*, 118.
25. Parra, "A poet is no . . . ," in *Emergency Poems*, 112–13.
26. Parra, "A poet is no . . . ," 114–15.
27. The term "postales francesas" was used because France produced many of these postcards in the early days of their circulation in the late nineteenth and early twentieth centuries.
28. Cáceres et al., *Historia de la postal en Chile*, 20.
29. Villaroel, "Ironía y descentramiento," 115.
30. Neither "si" nor "tambien" are written with accent marks on this *Artefacto*. Adding further confusion to the postcard's message, it can thus also be read as "Cuba if / Yankees too."
31. Van Hooft, "The 'Artefactos' of Nicanor Parra," 70.
32. Muñoz, "La antipoesía," 96.
33. Piña, *Conversaciones con la poesía chilena*, 117.
34. Muñoz, "La antipoesía," 97.
35. Quoted in Parra, *Obras completas & algo +*, 985.
36. Quoted in Parra, *Obras completas & algo +*, 985.
37. Piña, *Conversaciones con la poesía chilena*, 49.
38. Piña, *Conversaciones con la poesía chilena*, 50.
39. Piña, *Conversaciones con la poesía chilena*, 50.
40. Parra, *Antipoems: How to Look Better & Feel Great*, xi; quoted in Parra, *Obras completas & algo +*, 992.
41. Jakobson, "Linguistics and Poetics," 357.
42. Villaroel, "Ironía y descentramiento," 117.

Works Cited

Binns, Niall. "Herencias antipoéticas: Vicente Huidobro y Nicanor Parra." *Nuevo Texto Crítico* 9, no. 18 (1996): 139–52.

Binns, Niall, and Ignacio Echevarría. "Sobre *Artefactos*." In *Obras completas & algo +*, by Nicanor Parra, edited by Niall Binns and Ignacio Echevarría, 981–98. Barcelona: Círculo de Lectores, 2006.

Cáceres, Samuel León, Fernando Vergara Benítez, Katya Padilla Macías, and Atilio Bustos González. *Historia de la postal En Chile*. Valparaíso, Chile: Pontificia Universidad Católica de Valparaíso, 2007.

Carrasco Muñoz, Iván. "La antipoesía: Manifestación política heterogénea." *Atenea* 510 (2014): 95–109.
de Costa, René. "Para una poética de la (anti) poesía." *Revista Chilena de Literatura* 32 (November 1988): 7–29.
Gottlieb, Marlene. "Del antipoema al artefacto al . . . : La trayectoria poética de Nicanor Parra." *Hispamérica* 2, no. 6 (1974): 21–38.
———. "La evolución de la antipoesía: Un siglo, un milenio más tarde." *Ciberletras* 21 (2009). http://www.lehman.edu/faculty/guinazu/ciberletras/v21/gottlieb.htm.
Huidobro, Vicente. *Altazor*. Translated by Eliot Weinberger. 1931. Reprint, Middleton, Conn.: Wesleyan University Press, 2003.
———. *Horizon carré*. Paris: n.p., 1917.
———. *Manifestos Manifest*. Translated by Gilbert Alter-Gilbert. Los Angeles: Green Integer, 1999.
———. *The Selected Poetry of Vicente Huidobro*. Edited by David M. Guess. Translated by David M. Guess et al. New York: New Directions, 1981.
Ibáñez Langlois, José Miguel. *Para leer a Parra*. Santiago: Aguilar Chilena de Ediciones S.A., 2003.
Jakobson, Roman. "Linguistics and Poetics." In *Style in Language*, edited by Thomas Albert Sebeok, 350–77. Cambridge, Mass.: MIT Press, 1960.
Parra, Nicanor. *Antipoems: How to Look Better & Feel Great*. Translated by Liz Werner. New York: New Directions, 2004.
———. *Antipoems: New and Selected*. Translated by Lawrence Ferlinghetti et al. New York: New Directions, 1985.
———. *Artefactos*. Santiago: Ediciones Nueva Universidad, Universidad Católica de Chile, 1972.
———. *Emergency Poems*. Translated by Miller Williams. New York: New Directions, 1972.
———. *Obras completas & algo +*. Edited by Niall Binns and Ignacio Echevarría. Barcelona: Círculo de Lectores, 2006.
———. *Poemas*. Havana: Casa de las Américas, 1969.
———. *Poemas y antipoemas*. Santiago: Nascimento, 1954.
Piña, Juan Andres. *Conversaciones con la poesía chilena*. Santiago: Pehuén Editores, 1990.
Santa María, Cristián. Preface to *Artefactos*, by Nicanor Parra, n.p. Santiago: Universidad Católica de Chile, 1972.
Van Hooft, Karen S. "The 'Artefactos' of Nicanor Parra: The Explosion of the Antipoem." *Bilingual Review/La Revista Bilingüe* 1, no. 1 (1974): 67–80.
Villaroel, Gabriel. "Ironía y descentramiento en los *Artefactos* de Nicanor Parra y Guillermo Tejeda." *Hallazgos* 11, no. 21 (2014): 111–22.

7

Reading Images

Art, Aesthetics, and the Imagery of the Future in Argentine Science Fiction

SILVIA KURLAT ARES

IN 1850, AS ARGENTINA WAS debating what its modernization process would look like, Domingo Faustino Sarmiento (1811–88), wanting to solve the controversial issue of the seat of Argentina's federal administration, imagined the foundation and development of a city built on an island with all the technological advantages and novelties science and engineering could offer at the time. The country's future president dreamed of a city whose civilizing power would be anchored and disseminated by canals, roads, docks, steamers, and telegraphs: these were the material conditions for a new social contract. Argirópolis, the imaginary city's name, was both a political program and the first fully articulated utopian narrative representation of the urban space in Argentina. As such, the essay where Sarmiento articulated his project became a foundational book that deployed all the possible meanings and values of civilization and state institutions, from industry and commerce to education and lawfulness. The essay also established the way in which future generations would create metaphors from which to imagine representations of past, present, and future cities, their inhabitants, and the ideologies they brought forward. If the Pampas were the locus of barbarism, cities were not only civilizing machines but stages and devices to explain the national ethos and to deploy ideological programs.[1] This dichotomy (civilization/barbarism) informed Argentine ideological discussions for over 150 years. Although literature and essay were for the most part of the nineteenth and twentieth centuries the preferred vehicles to narrate the intimate relationship between political programs and urban experiences, images of the city also contributed to these meditations. From the distant strike seen through the window in the painting *Sin pan y sin trabajo* (1894) by Ernesto de la Cárcova (1866–1927) to photography that spoke optimistically about modern technologies in magazines like *Caras y Caretas* (1898–1941), and the variegated spaces of Antonio Segui's painting (1934) *Techos con gente* (2010), visual representations of the city seem to forever be in a complex dialogue with both Sarmiento's original proposal and its critique.

Cities appear everywhere in Argentine art, either as subjects or as backgrounds, and are of particular importance in science fiction comics and graphic novels. Here, as it was in Sarmiento's essays, cities are the mise en scène of diverse projects' ideological underpinning. Yet, we need to ask, what is the representational standard of visual images of cities in Argentine science fiction if there is one? How and with what visual vocabularies are cities depicted? What are these city images portraying and what are they trying to show? In the pages that follow I will address these questions by centering my attention on the images of cities and ruins that appear in *Slot-Barr* (1977) by Ricardo Barreiro (1949–99) and Francisco Solano López (1928–2011) and the industrial city that appears in *Reparador de sueños* (2012) by Matías Santellán (1981–) and Serafín (1976–). These two graphic novels bookend a meditation on the role of the city as the locus of Argentine political and national state projects: one as a visual narrative of the end of an imperfect modernization era; the other as a visual narrative of the city within the globalization process. The first is an example of the reworking of realism, whereas the second, while showcasing a universe on the borderline of the Gothic aesthetic, is an example of the transformation and uses of neorealism. And in both cases, aesthetic choices both underpin and disrupt the narrative, bringing to the fore the graphic novels' ideological contradictions. Although it can be argued that my choice is arbitrary, these two comics offer an interesting arc of ideological visions representative of Argentine politics over the last fifty years in their portrayal of a variety of images of increasingly technologized cities in a changing world.[2] Both graphic novels provide visual dystopian spaces that draw on different sources in order to build their own distressed, ambivalent view of a modernity in flux. Yet these operations not only reflect how Argentine science fiction has evolved and changed its own relationship with different art forms and aesthetics but also reveal how different media and vocabularies have merged into a common redefined cultural agenda as Argentine uneven modernity came to a close by the end of the seventies and in the years that followed.

The Language of Images: Aesthetics and Ideological Programs

Since the Dada period, aesthetic lines have become increasingly blurred and the distinction between art forms and media, between high and low areas of cultural production, and also between the perception of centers and peripheries seem to have splintered to the point of almost nonexistent concepts. In the case of Argentine science fiction images (pictures, illustrations, covers, comics), this porosity scaffolds a naturalist aesthetic that operates with the instruments of pop surrealism; with the languages of pop and op arts but with the rigor of realism and cubism. These complex operations can be found both in the production of high and low arts, even if the former does not always identify itself with science fiction, and even if the latter is still struggling to find legitimacy in the cultural field. Visual imaginaries at both ends of the spectrum share a common view of the disjunction between modernity's potential and utopian visions, between realism and nonrepresentational forms of art, between cultural experience and technological gadgetry. One can trace the promise and anguish of these binary alternatives in all sorts of artifacts as some recent exhibition catalogs attest: the visual language necessary to make what was to come seeable, operated from an ample range of traditions and aesthetics that allowed for the emergence of what is now often called art of anticipation or prospective art.[3] It is, in many respects, a visual universe that places its myths in an unstable not-yet time, where social and technological imagination build a desirable vision of the collective or at least parts of it. This perspective draws a line connecting surrealist artist Raquel Forner's (1902–88) many astronauts with aesthetic projects such as *La ciudad hidroespacial* (1971) by abstract visual artist Gyula Kosice (Hungary, 1924–Argentina, 2016) and the famed *Juanito Laguna y la aeronave* (1978) by new realist painter Antonio Berni (1905–81). But this path also travels through the many book covers, magazine illustrations, and graphic novels that populated Argentine futuristic imagination during the twentieth century. The same ambivalences about technology and hopeful aspirations about society's future appear in a wide range of images, from the 1956 *Más Allá* magazine cover by C. Cruz that showed a half-done puzzle of an orbiting station hovering over Earth, to the surrealist book covers of Domingo Ferreira (Uruguay, 1940) for the original Minotauro collection that showed a dark technological future depicted with Victorian nostalgia, or to the searing, expressionist visual vocabulary of Fati (alias of Luis Scafati, 1947) for the *Péndulo* science fiction magazine in the eighties and nineties.[4]

It can be said that Argentine science fiction imagery built its relationship with art and literature anew by reworking the country's visual traditions. However, magazine and book illustrations frequently offered a very different aesthetic take than the one in graphic novels and comics. On the one hand, science fiction artists often claimed for themselves (and cultivated) an otherwise weak gothic tradition that owed much of its vocabulary to surrealism.[5] Starting in the fifties, surrealism seemed to be the predominant visual choice in book and magazine covers as exemplified by the *Fantaciencia* (1956–57) book collection of the Jacobo Muchnick Press, or, later on, by Oscar Chichoni's (1957) famous covers for magazines like *Péndulo* and *Fierro*.[6] Yet the uses and transformations of the surrealist vocabulary did not always percolate into comics and graphic novels.[7] Although comics borrowed some of their images from surrealism (as in the case of *El Sueñero* [1985] by Enrique Breccia [1919–93]), their sources were often aligned with expressionist aesthetics, which provided the framework for a raw, radicalized view on politics. Such is the case for draftsmen like Enrique Alcatena (1957–), whose aesthetics have strong ties with the oneiric and dense universes of creators akin to Phillip Druillet (France, 1944–). Alcatena's complex aesthetic not only allowed for the development of a visual imagery that delves into fantasy and the fantastic but also provided the opportunity for a complex dialogue with graphic arts and international trends within comics.

On the other hand, since the late fifties, science fiction graphic novels turned to new forms of realism, albeit a realism that had abandoned explicit forms of documentation in favor of ideologically charged readings and representations of the real. The second version of the famed *Eternauta* (1969) scripted by Héctor G. Oesterheld (1919–78?) and drawn by Breccia is a good example of the blending of radical politics and radical aesthetics. It is a graphic novel whose visual narrative operates within realism but where all key political scenes are highlighted by expressionist images that break into the space of the plates. Although none of what I have described were entirely new operations (since their origins can be traced back to the nineteenth century), the instruments and vocabularies of modernism supported and amplified the ideological and political complexity of a visual language that sometimes underpinned and sometimes disrupted the narratives it was supposed to "simply" bring into vision.

Argentina had a long tradition of realistic comics, heavily documented with historical maps, photography, and ethnographic research that changed substantially during the sixties, due partly to the politicization of the cultural field, and partly to the renewal of visual vocabularies in the arts.[8] The transformation of realism into something that was both speaking to, and betraying, the imagery of the real underlines the ideological tensions that appear in many Argentine comics since then. In an interview, legendary draftsman Solano López said:

> Pongo mis recursos técnicos al servicio de la narración de la historia. Me convierto en un servidor. Como podría haber sido, salvando las distancias, Goya o Rembrandt, o alguno de esos grandes pintores que ponían su oficio para hacer un retrato del Papa, o de su madre o de su amante o de algún personaje de la época. Y estaban representando algo objetivo pero al mismo tiempo estaban creando una obra de arte, y de una profundidad difícil de expresar con palabras. Quise hacer algo parecido, pero no ya para estar colgado de la pared sino ser un objeto que llegue a miles de personas, y parece que, en algunos casos la pegué cerca.[9]

> [I put my technical resources into the service of narrating stories. I become a server. As it might have been, relatively speaking, with Goya or Rembrandt, or any of those great painters who applied their craft to making a portrait of the Pope, or their mother or lover or a character of the time. And they were representing something objective but at the same time they were creating a work of art, with a depth difficult to express in words. I wanted to do something similar, but not to be hung on a wall but instead to be an object that could reach thousands of people, and it seems that in some cases I came close.]

Realism was not only a work of art's visual vocabulary but also the vehicle to express the urgency of the historical moment and the language that would guarantee that a political message would reach thousands. The stories that comics told and showed were ideologically anchored and purposefully crafted to underline their own political programs. Realism became a radicalized political tool, but it was now contaminated by surrealist utopian visions and expressionist angst. Solano López's point of view was shared by many comic creators and illustrators as well as by key midcentury artistic movements such as the Espartaco group (1959–68), whose militant stake and radical engagement with ideology served as one of the models for the engaged intellectual able to marry aesthetics and politics by bringing art to the masses.[10] Comics were viewed as one of the ideal mediums to make this project feasible, which identify them as loci where politics, ideology, consumerism, and new forms of productivity could be discussed and tested. Realism (and forms of realism increasingly tainted by the imagery of neorealism borrowed from French and Italian movies as well as aesthetic trends that were otherwise incompatible with them) became the visual language to attempt this complex dialogue.[11]

The apparently mix-matched aesthetic visual vocabulary used to depict cities and to narrate the urban experience in part mirrored how Buenos Aires itself had developed in the previous fifty years. Beatriz Sarlo has pointed out that

> the originality of Buenos Aires lies in the individual elements that form a mixture, captured, transformed, and deformed by a huge system of translation. Buenos Aires is a translation from many languages and urban texts in conflict, a translation that bears the distortions of the American space and social reality.[12]

In the same way, comics and graphic novels appropriated and translated a multitude of aesthetic movements to their own ends. In doing so, they created the vocabulary to talk about the city as the motor of political and ideological programs, from both the utopian and the dystopian points of view. Realism provides the instruments to reproduce the city grid, the modernist buildings, and the vanishing elements of the small town. Modernist aesthetics would provide the imagery of the cities' rapid changes, the juxtaposition of temporal elements, the ever-presence/absence of nature, and the cues of a transforming sociability. Mixture and translation (visual and aesthetic) were the first representational standards of cities in conflict.

Longings of Futures Past

The intricate relationship between literature and science fiction illustrations, or the strong iconographic bind that allows graphic novels' sequential series to become utterable, cannot be understood solely as a problem of representation. Nor are these images semiotically organized outside major questions the Argentine cultural field as a whole had been considering in one way or another for more than one hundred years. Imagined spaces convey a myriad of cultural and social cues, in particular when they project onto themselves questions about the nature of the state, desirable social subjects, and the conditions for a feasible, new social contract. These issues have underlined how political agendas envision the future and are at the core of the country's foundational national project that was first discussed by Sarmiento. Yet, in political speeches and essays, Argentina was never the country at hand but the country to be, a sort of mirage in the political discourse. Argentina was going to come to fruition once immigrants became full citizens, or once blue-collar workers became fully integrated into the economic machine and the labor force was controlled by the state, or once democracy was fully respected or restored, or once the regional economy became stable, or once something happened that would bring into reality promises inscribed in a now-betrayed, ever-blurry romanticized past. Despite their fuzzy logic, such assertions had some rooting in the very concrete, liberal national state project that first coalesced in the mid-nineteenth century, and that would be contested by conservatives and populists alike (albeit for very different reasons) throughout the twentieth century. The images of cities and ruins (and of their inhabitants) I am going to investigate here are not images of the past or the future but the imagined present of these debates, for ruinous cities cannot simply be translated as the failure of the liberal project, even when such reading is partially possible. As critic and philosopher Andreas Huyssen once said, "Real ruins of different kinds function as screens on which modernity projects its asynchronous temporalities and its fear of and obsession with the passing of time."[13]

Contrary to the well-organized, luminous spaces described by Sarmiento, or even to the sleek visual representations that accompanied many fanzines in either their paper or electronic format, Argentine science fiction imagery published in graphic novels and professional magazines often showed postapocalyptic universes whose city structures had corroded to their bare bones.[14] These spaces are the settings of dystopian narratives that also offered a highly contrasting view to the more optimistic future often presented in the visual art of many canonical artists.[15] Notably, this dark point of view echoed literature's perspective. Dystopian novels written since the late sixties in Argentina showcased chaotic social and political worlds. Novels like *Diario de la guerra del cerdo* (1969) by Adolfo Bioy Casares (1914–99), *A la sombra de los bárbaros* (1977) by Eduardo Goligorsky (1931–), or, more recently, Rafael Pinedo's (1954–2006) trilogy with *Plop* (2002), *Frío* (2004), and *Subte* (2006, but published posthumously in 2011), narrate societies past the point of disarray and about to collapse or already undone. The urban spaces where these novels take place are likewise declining, dilapidated architectural environments if they still exist at all.

Dystopias set in urban ruins are not a novelty in science fiction narrative or visual arts. Ruins offer ways of looking; propose physical, aesthetic, and political journeys; and harbor diverse projections of our own sense of sociability and public space. Since the late 1950s, with the publication of the first version of the graphic novel *El Eternauta* (1957–60) by Oesterheld and Solano López, Argentine science fiction has produced an intensely recognizable corpus of graphic novels and comics staged in a ruined or destroyed Buenos Aires and other urban spaces. Even comics whose storylines are not located in Buenos Aires, as in the case of *Gilgamesh, el inmortal* (1969–75) by Lucho Olivera (1942–2005) or *Nueva York, Año Cero* (1984) by Barreiro and Juan Zanotto (1935–2005), still reflect on the role of the city and its social fabric as the main engine of civilization, transforming its decay (both physical and social) into a metaphor for ideological meditations. If real cities are the locus of social and political conflict, the imagined cities of dystopian Argentine science fiction are a reflection of what could happen to those spaces and its inhabitants: with and against Sarmiento, the (future) city is the stage where history unfolds its darkest possibilities. Such is the case for comics and graphic novels as diverse as *Bárbara* (1979) by Barreiro and Zanotto; the already mentioned *Slot-Barr*; *Basura* (1984) by Carlos Trillo (1943–2011) and Juan Giménez (1943–); *El mundo subterráneo* (1991) by Barreiro and Alcatena; *Ciudad* (1991) again by Barreiro, this time with Giménez; or *Borderline* (1996) by Trillo and Eduardo Risso (1959–).[16] As the next pages will show, even though the ruins depicted in these visual narratives cannot be affiliated a priori with any given ideological project, they all share some common core perspectives on the uses of technology, progress, and sociability. For all of them, as was the case with Sarmiento, the city is a device to deploy ideological programs within the cultural field and thus, their imageries are not only proposing or evaluating but also fighting the pristine mirage of the liberal Argirópolis. Hence, the spaces where those notions are projected are contesting the original liberal project and providing a certain ideological understanding of history in reverse.

The Argentine City in Context

In 2003, in the new edition of his famous 1964 book, *Buenos Aires, vida cotidiana y alienación seguido de Buenos Aires, ciudad en crisis*, philosopher Juan José Sebreli

(1930–) noted the transformation of the social and urban landscape of Buenos Aires by summarizing its history in the opening pages of a new essay on the city.

> Buenos Aires quedó como testimonio de la época de esplendor, casi como una ruina histórica. Varias capas arqueológicas se superponen: la más antigua se remonta a la década del ochenta, cuando la gran aldea se transformó en gran ciudad. . . . La infraestructura, los servicios públicos, los medios de transporte, las plazas y parques, la costanera sur, el rediseño del centro, los grandes edificios, monumentos e instituciones culturales y artísticas, así como obras de embellecimiento, procedían de los tiempos de la república conservadora.[17]

> [Buenos Aires was a testimony to its own golden age, almost a historical ruin. In it, several archaeological layers overlap: the oldest one dates back to the eighteen eighties, when the great village became a big city. . . . [Major city works such as] infrastructure, utilities, transportation, plazas and parks, the southern water front, the redesign of downtown, large buildings, as well as monuments and cultural and artistic institutions and beautification works all came from the times of the conservative republic.]

Since then, the city that once was called the "capital of the empire that never existed" by André Malraux has lived through a number of crises that have eroded its understructure. Planned urbanism has been replaced by mostly unregulated, never-ending building of massive consumer ventures, garden towers, and gated neighborhoods, all of which appear in a chaotic way, and have distorted traditional forms of sociability and communication. Sebreli and other thinkers talk about the atomization of the urban space and the end of the inclusive, democratic city. Several economic crises since the mid-1970s made visible not only a process of insularization but also the emergence of multiple edges of new developments, both poor and rich.[18] These changes created new forms of economic, cultural, and social exchanges that, in a way, were either anticipated or depicted early on in the science fiction graphic novels I have previously mentioned. In the case of illustrations, these changes became the point of departure to imagine and project complex and dark visions of the future. Again, Chichoni's universe is a good example of this visual approach. A master of what he calls "narrative illustration," his poetic, rusty, and heavily material universes are a mise en scène of worlds already undone, already decaying. His is a future built upon the traces of old civilizations' richness and sophistication, which seem to evoke better times.

Chichoni's artwork is at the crossroads between realism and surrealism, between classicism and postmodernity. In a way, these illustrations reorganize the terms in which art returns to representationality after the 1960s, for these images provide us with the "reality" of our experience of the passing of time in a globalized world as much as with fleeting images of the impact of politics on everyday life. His monsters (either cyborgs or exo-animals) make utterable the transformation of the classic liberal subject as much as of the transformation of city as the engine of civilizing projects. And these spaces give materiality to what-would-be, anchoring future histories. Hence, his aesthetics exemplify how visual artifacts organize their narrations on top of the real archaeological layers left from lack of investment, drawing their imaginary spaces with the hypertrophied perspective of a fait accompli, and making them into stage sets for all sorts of dystopian meditations. As an example, we can turn to Chichoni's cover for *Minotauro* 8 from 1984. It displays something that can be the eroded, grayish-blue landscape of a fantastic city, or the portrait of five or six cyborgs walking straight into the foreground in such a way that only the heads and hats are visible. There is nothing in the cover that cues the viewer into the true nature of what he or she is seeing, but it is clear that in the image the past is forever canceled out and that whatever set these things in motion is also gone. The objects or beings have the stony quality that characterizes Chichoni's work, and we cannot say if the buildings or machines are alive or ever were. Everything in the illustration can be something else. The eyes can be glasses or broken windows. The hats are both exaggerated top hats and fuming chimneys. If this is a space, it is an archaeological skyline of the future, something that once was and that now has been abandoned and whose function is irrecoverable. If these are cyborgs, then there is nothing biological about them; they are utterly menacing beings whose identity and mission cannot be understood or explained in human terms for whatever was human about them has been lost in time. Because we cannot anchor it in our present but we can perceive it as a possible future, there is something mysterious in the image, albeit it is also removed and distant, foreign. It speaks of the future without naming it, while describing the present of 1984, with its return to an uncertain democracy and the unchecked violence and terror of the past. There are many other examples, but this cover is particularly disturbing and clearly showcases why the universes that illustrations and science fiction graphic novels build and explore are conjectures about the presentism of the (national) future.

Notably, the cities that appear in many of the graphic novels and illustrations since the mid-1950s do not have an outside or the outside is a canceled-out space. Whereas the nineteenth-century Argentine liberal project rested on the dichotomy of countryside/city, many graphic novels organize their narratives at the very core of the future or imagined city, and settle their outside in faraway places, or in barren or unreachable lands (i.e., *Nueva York, Año Cero* locates its exterior in a distant Venus that vaguely mimics 1960s Vietnam's battlefields; *El mundo subterráneo* cancels the outside by locating civilization in a cave). In some cases, either the cities themselves or some of the neighborhoods have been reclaimed by an out-of-control nature that does not reflect the Pampas natural environment but a hypostasized one. Even when storylines posit that the original decline of civilization was caused by human beings themselves, nature (unless controlled as a means of agrarian production) is represented as a menacing entity that threatens human existence. For instance, in the case of *Bárbara*, Buenos Aires (which is located in the Pampas and still has famously temperate weather) is a tropical, watery paradise, populated by crocodiles and postapocalyptic tribes that fight one another.[19] The same happens in later environments drawn by Giménez: his two versions of *Ciudad* have chapters that show tropical forests swallowing the flooded city. In resuscitating nature's sublime and somewhat indomitable character, many graphic novels backtrack on the original realist aim (that is, they renounce any possible mimetic effect in favor of something akin to a Romantic gesture), at the same time that they keep its visual vocabulary to rearticulate radical political programs.[20] Nature becomes both a liberating space from an encroaching civilization as well as a monster to be dominated and tamed at humanity's own risk. The contradiction makes painfully clear pervasive elements in the Argentine political imagination: it expresses a flawed relationship not only with the real, geographical environment but also with the symbolic one, for Argentina's national identity rested securely for more than one hundred years on the flatness of the "empty" Pampas, whose rich soil was simply ready for sowing and reaping. Transformed into a tropical forest, nature's promises had now been canceled out, and the ruined city that was to be the engine of civilization has regressed to tribal times. The realist drawings that make everything simultaneously recognizable and strange bring forward that which is known of the real and of the political, transforming it into something else. Although somewhat anomalous, floods are part of life in the region, and inundations in big cities are mostly the result of poor planning or overgrowth. Therefore, these enclosed, watery universes, with their crumbling cities and biologically distorted flora and fauna, or these distant worlds with clear, almost transparent political models, offer metaphors of the present built with a common visual vocabulary of natural disaster and crumbling civilization that addresses questions of sociability and polity.[21] If aesthetics provided the means to stage ideological issues, the choice of particular cataclysms provided a common language to express their development.

The Revolutionary and Civilization

As we have seen, representational standards in science fiction comics and illustrations rest upon contradictory aesthetic choices and political readings of the national state project's ideological elements. In the case of a graphic novel like *Slot-Barr*, the conceptualization of the city allows us to understand this operation. Originally published in 1977 and reprinted ten years later in the well-known *Skorpio* magazine, *Slot-Barr* is a collaboration between Barreiro, who often wrote science fiction comic scripts in a dark dystopic vein; Solano López, who provided the realistic main drawings; and occasionally Jorge Schiaffino, who designed some of the backgrounds.[22] Organized in thirteen chapters or episodes, the comic narrates the adventures of Slot-Barr, a rather unambitious and uneducated young man who stumbles around the galaxy performing a variety of menial jobs around six hundred years into our future. During an accident, as he is floating away in space, Slot-Barr becomes the host for Lim, a foreign organism with whom he will become symbiont. The episodes follow their travels and inner discussions as well as their takes on the societies where they work. Slot-Barr has a clearly mestizo origin, and can be described as one of those "descamisados" to whom Eva Perón (1919–52) dedicated her last public speech in 1952.[23] His portrait evokes physically and socially the lowest classes of the Argentine population. Yet the only chance for him to be successful (socially, sexually, or intellectually) is to be manipulated by the highly more intelligent and morally superior Lim. Despite his unassuming persona, when Slot-Barr merges with Lim, he becomes somewhat a representation of the Nietzchean superman in his righteousness, superhuman strength, readiness to mock social mores, and worship of youth. His arrogant view of the social environment often takes the form of sarcasm and humor.

Returning to sociopolitical issues later, for now I would like to discuss how the visual and narrative realist representation of both a subject of the working classes (Slot-Barr is at the same time an everyday blue-collar worker and his perfected, ideological projection) and the lives and suffering of the dispossessed (with their lack of employment, low wages, compulsory military draft, etc.) collides with what the comic is doing on several levels. The symbolic seizure of free will by the foreign parasite betrays a lack of confidence in the very subject the comic is attempting to foreground, and this contorted micro-relationship transfers to major issues throughout the rest of the episodes. As the comic attempts to build a project for collective revolt, it makes *Slot-Barr* into a hero-centered, historically circular narrative, where governments are able to put all political transformative ideas into the service of their own oppressive systems, and where regressively social concepts become the building blocks to return to a never-existing golden age. Alejo Steimberg has pointed out that such dislocation is possible because the structure of the narrative elements as well as the construction of Slot-Barr as a classic hero undermine all attempts at creating a coherent ideological, radical discourse.[24] While I agree with this approach, I would like to add that it is also how realism is put to work that undoes Solano López's stated will, cited earlier, to make technique work for the story.

Realism operates in a series of complex contradictions between the visual and the narrative. The realistic representation meant to deploy a radicalized project, as discussed in the previous pages, here only underlines how this hijacking symbolically reproduces (and even celebrates) the structures of power it attempts to denounce. This contradiction also taints the structure of the graphic novel as a whole. In some chapters, Slot-Barr saves some towns from economic exploitation and religious oppression by helping in their revolts ("Un planeta llamado rebelión"; "Vida y obra de Acriz y el pueblo") or by destroying a sect of priests that practice human sacrifice ("El pueblo y la bestia"), although he never stays to see the projects come to fruition. In these cases, realism serves the purpose of underlining the visio-narrative bind of the most ideologically charged chapters by making easily recognizable the ties with recent Argentine history and radicalized politics. However, these very same aesthetics underscore patriarchy and oppression by depicting women as hypersexualized beings or by showing disenfranchised people as monsters: realism operates in a sort of infinite mirrored image, becoming its own pitfall for it turns into itself in order to make visible that to which the comic is blind. For example, the novel's last episode closes with Slot-Barr raping the Queen of Laetnia as punishment for kidnapping him and other men and forcing them to participate in a sort of Roman game: there is no social or cultural change, just exercises in violence. White slave traffic is naturalized in most episodes as a matter of fact, perpetuating the icon of the willing prostitute. In one episode ("Planeta Capital"), as an advertisement ploy, a woman is apparently attacked and killed by her lover: she is not helped by anyone and when the ruse is up, no one seems to be disturbed by the violence they have witnessed. Even robots intended to provide sexual pleasure cannot be distinguished from real or vampire women that attack and menace men throughout the entire comic.

As in the case of Isaac Asimov's *Foundation* series or Frank Herbert's *Dune* original hexalogy, most of the comic's episodes are preceded by a historic future chronology that provides some context to the narration, as well as by an interview with an imaginary historian and an apocryphal entry in a galactic encyclopedia. Some chapters are also followed by other encyclopedia entries that further the reader's knowledge of this imaginary universe. These materials offer a written context to the visual narrative and situate it politically in a future, vast empire ruled by the planets Imperia, Tecnia, and Militaria, which have destroyed all alien resistance and colonized the galaxy. Not especially subtle in its political choices, the comic echoes the discourse about imperialism as it was understood in the mid-1970s, with a core technological and military power, and dependent suppliers of raw materials. *Slot-Barr* makes a startling economic division between center and periphery, between developed and underdeveloped planets, between manufactured and basic good producers, between wealth and poverty. All representations are in the service of this conceptualization of the political world, making it blind to its own paradoxes and contradictions. Some of the episodes are built around absurd elements that provide a certain humorous and satirical respite in a series marred by its own ideological pitfalls and deeply disturbing gender biases. The civilization that Solano López offers is the dream of a technified universe where the poor and destitute are depicted with the visual vocabulary and the information background of exoticism imagined by the first anthropologists of the late nineteenth century. Therefore, realist aesthetics here operate as both an instrument of social critique and conservative dreaming.

The series does not fully provide, as other comics of this period do, a political blueprint for building an ideal future society,[25] although one chapter discusses a robot-based economy at length ("Era otoño en la tierra"), and at least two of the episodes ("Un planeta llamado rebelión"; "Vida y obra de Acriz y el pueblo") narrate rebellions that are a cross between a Latin American leftist revolution and a retelling of the Gospels. These two chapters are in direct dialogue with the populist ideology that underpinned many radical leftist movements of the sixties and seventies. Yet the entire comic's ideological and political aims exist in a tension between the written bubbles and captions, the visual representation of characters and spaces they inhabit or visit, and an indictment of civilization that does not dare to return to barbarism: while it is clear that all forms of highly advanced civilization are to be distrusted or condemned, the novel does not go so far as to destroy it all in an atomic holocaust (like the *Eternauta II*) in order to create a political tabula rasa. An overall reading of *Slot-Barr* provides the geography of a universe that opposes a triad of images in conflict: against the highly sleek technological environments of space crafts and cities stand ruined, destroyed societies and small, agrarian or communal towns that evoke nineteenth-century sociability and economic development. The graphic novel inscribes itself in a tense space: it is an antimodernist stance that dreams and fears the future and acritically yearns for the sociability and economics of the past. I argue that this triangulation (of which this comic is a paradigmatic example) became both the representational standard of Argentine graphic novels and the visual degree zero of Argentine science fiction imagery since the fifties. As a result of the juxtaposition and adjacency of different forms of written materials in the case of the illustrations, as well as because of the iconic binding between images and text in the case of comics, ideological conflicts emerged with a more raw, urgent presence: the written and visual vocabularies sometimes collide with unexpected results.

The episode that visually organizes the ideology of the entire series is the sixth chapter, "Era otoño en la tierra" (It was fall on Earth). It opens with a brief narrative history of the planet in which readers are informed that Earth is barely populated by ten thousand "normal" people and three million mutants. The "normals," all named after famous characters, artists, or philosophers, control Earth's economy. I am not going to discuss here the idealization of a leisure economy that leaves out destitute subjects because of their monstrosity and because those subjects are deemed outside the possibility of social control. However, such a society exists (and it is deployed in the graphic universe) despite the entry in the galactic encyclopedia that precedes Slot-Barr's adventure, where the narrator makes a point differentiating the past of the story (our present) as a time of radical change and of emergence of a "humanist philosophy" free of the master-slave dichotomy.[26] These blatant contradictions are at the core of Barreiro's script and they are the scaffolding of the ideological universe of *Slot-Barr*. Solano López's drawings, for all their intensity, fully partake in this perspective. Spaces drawn in the comic provide a visual ideological backdrop that both participates in Argentina's political and artistic traditions and reinforces the political contradictions of the comic.

The geographical backdrops of this chapter are the colonies of the Earth survivors and what is left of Paris. The episode opens with a sleek view of the spaceport where Slot-Barr arrives: machines are clean, the environment is civilized and planned, the gardens and parks that Slot-Barr sees have been carefully landscaped; the land is self-managed by specialized robots that take care of all the work. The opening of the story, almost four entire plates, visualizes the promise of the "humanist philosophy" that serves as the chapter's epigraph. At the end of the fourth plate, however, readers realize that this idyllic universe is a self-enclosed bubble, surrounded by a vast emptiness populated by monsters. This is not the outside of civilization located in the Pampas by the engineers of the national project of the nineteenth century. Nor is it the empty locus of a future civilization of farmers, hence a clean, "virginal" space to be conquered and domesticated and put to good use. The emptiness that Slot-Barr is about to encounter is the literal outside of civilization, a copy of hell whose inhabitants have ceased to be subjects a long time ago either to regress to a nonhuman condition or to assume such a radical form of otherness as to become incarnations of evil. Indeed, one of the monsters portrayed in the first vignette of the sixth plate (the first close-up of the mutants) is a quotation from a malevolent "Manos" from the *Eternauta*, a cruel alien from Oesterheld's 1957 invading force. The same vignette piles up meanings without words by showcasing those monsters in two planes. In the foreground, four portraits show us not simply ugly characters but increasingly animalistic and deranged faces, the last one a man frozen in a mute, desperate scream. In the background of the vignette, small black ink silhouettes reminiscent of paper cuts depict several scenes of their lives: these scenes reinforce the link between otherness and savagery as hallmarks of the outside of civilization. The images at the fore and at the back reinforce the discourse about the brutality and violence of this otherness that, as one of the characters states, cannot be controlled. The entire episode seems to be built around the idea that uncontrolled nature seethes in uncontrolled spaces. Hence, when the characters travel to what used to be Paris, the city has been obliterated, and the images of its ruins emerge against images of the clean, bright lines of the civilized spaces of Earth. A completely unrecognizable, demolished Paris is presented to the readers in six sharply contrasting black-and-white vignettes, with small generic landscapes that do not show any of the iconographic buildings of the city. Mutants attack the characters, who will fail in their mission to find a famed book in the abandoned library. So, here realism operates by erasing any possible cultural allusion in favor of a clear underlining of the ideological reading. The barren images of an obliterated Paris are symmetric to the sleek Imperia and its social mores, which, despite being described in a rather sardonic tone, provide a weak moralist tale about city life. It could be said that these choices sustain the visual and narrative economy of the comic's architecture. However, I am inclined to think that these images are intended as an ideological cautionary tale that betrays its own premises: in a book that praises populist uprisings, blue-collar workers only succeed if they are controlled by foreign beings or are condemned to a life of abject barbarism; by the same token in the most advanced society in history, Slot-Barr's love interest will die of cancer; aging women of faraway societies in several episodes are metaphorical and literal vampires over which male dominance and violence is always acceptable; nature incarnates its own dangerous chimeras, which can only be tamed by death; and revolution is intended to move history not forward but backward, to the comfortable little houses of 1950s suburbia, where the intellectuals of the comic take their last stand.

Thirty-five years later, the first winner of Premio Ñ de Historieta, the standalone culture section of the newspaper *Clarín*, will return to the issue of the city from a rather different perspective. Originally defined as a negative utopian narration, *Reparador de sueños* by Santellán and Serafín tells the story of Cacho, a dream repairman, in the imaginary city of Polenia.[27] In Polenia's universe, sleep and dream are carefully controlled by the state. Individuals sleep connected to machines and "natural sleep" is forbidden. The intimate relationship between technology and power is depicted in the hexagonal, repetitive design of the urban plant that makes it look like a flat hive, where houses are called cells, and where social control has acquired the quality of an invasive social policy that literally takes over the bodies of citizens. Dominated by a triumvirate of engineers, the city seems more a vast mechanical machine than the sleek dream of urban planners. Private and public spaces are drawn in clear contrast, with the first organized with soft lines in recognizable and familial spaces, and with the second presented as a dark, alien environment drawn in stark, straight lines. As in the case of *Slot-Barr*, this is a universe of clear-cut choices, and the black-and-white drawing rarely offers any form of chiaroscuro or shadowing, creating characters that are very close to a sort of expressionist universe without actually veering into it. Also, like in the previously analyzed comic, Cacho belongs to the lower classes of his own society, and he is also depicted as a mestizo without any particular heroic or political will, although he is not as physically fit as Slot-Barr. Cacho will be called into action when his love interest, Elizabeth, is kidnapped and disappears. In order to find her, he starts working for the government, and eventually triggers a revolt when people realize that they have literally been robbed of their dreams; a major difference with Barreiro's work is that here politics are the result of individual necessities and of the individual's search for his own well-being. Collective practices emerge as an unwanted or unexpected result.

Although the spaces proposed by Santellán and Serafín are not recognizable as any individual city, the images quote *Metrópolis* (1927), directed by Fritz Lang, and the morose climates of movies like *Blade Runner* (1982), directed by Ridley Scott. It is the oppressive, constant presence of all forms of social and cultural control that makes this graphic novel particularly poignant. Because of its veiled references to Argentine history in the seventies (with its dictatorship, repression, disappeared, etc.) and its recognizable winks to intimate, everyday barrio life, the visual universe of this graphic novel exists in the difficult boundary between realism and surrealism.

Quotations from the surrealist movement open every single one of the chapters of this graphic novel, from men trapped in the gears of invisible machines to disarmed and boxed mannequins or far-fetched tools. These images serve as both epigraph and chapter cover, and their theme repeats itself in the interior of the chapters. If these images remind us of the fragility of the human body as we enter the hexagonal universe of Polenia, they also bring to mind armored spaces. Polenia is a city where dreams and desires (as they represent human frailty) have been eliminated by a system in search of extreme (fascist) forms of self-protection. *Reparador de sueños* is thus a meditation on the fear of individual assimilation into a system (any system) and on the transformation of community and collective identities in the era of globalization. What is at stake here is the elimination of difference. The triumvirate (composed of two men and a woman with disquieting emotionless features) bring forward issues of common morality (people who dream about love and art disappear) and common good (the perfect organization of the city brings happiness), which are put to the test. When Elizabeth is taken by the state, the imperative of the triumvirate is to improve on what they understand as common good and morals. When Cacho infiltrates the government to rescue her, he is operating from the perspective of his individual needs. Their views of the political and moral worlds are on a collision course. Yet, interestingly enough, Cacho's revolt will only bring him a Pyrrhic victory: the prisoners of the city will bring the government down, the techno-military order will tumble down, but he will not be able to save Elizabeth.

In contrast with Slot-Barr's increasing heroics and intense political awakening, Cacho goes through several complex identity transformations. The simple mechanic will become a reluctant rebel. His mutation is also staged in the parallel transformation of his environments. The simple man lives in simple, neighborly, familial spaces that he will eventually call a lost paradise.[28] The man in love and in search of vengeance will then become a highly qualified blue-collar worker at the dream factory, and it is this man who will bring down the government once he discovers why they took Elizabeth. In all these passages, the environment also changes: the more ingrained Cacho becomes in the factory (and hence, in the system), the sleeker and more technified the spaces become. Yet the destruction of the city's political engine does not restore the past or its pastoral spaces. Contrary to what happens in *Slot-Barr*, where every single turn of the historical wheel made the whole system return to its own beginning, here the future seems completely uncertain and impossible to grasp. The city does not guarantee the future to come; nor does it provide a blueprint for political action outside immediate personal freedoms. Even though both graphic novels take very different approaches to politics, they both share a certain level of technophobia as accelerated processes of modernization and globalization threaten old forms of sociability.

At the start of this chapter, I asked if there was a representational standard of visual images of cities in Argentine science fiction and what such a standard might represent. I believe that it is not simply an issue of the ruined cities that is at stake but the cities in their environment and historicity. Visual representations of spaces bring forward a material conceptualization of utopian or dystopian imagination. As Portolano said,

> Without naming it "utopia," rhetorical theorists have consistently referred to an imagined, often idealized aspect of place as a part of ethos, the artistic rhetorical proof that is drawn from an audience's collective character. In a corresponding vein, rhetorical practices are inherent in what utopian theorists Herbert Marcuse and Ernst Bloch have called the "utopian impulse." For these writers . . . utopia is treated as a function of human social thought and communication. . . . "Utopia" is not an impossible political dream or a philosophical ideal but, rather, any kind of symbolic expression of hope for a better world, whether in a concrete future or

in fictional or spiritual realms, and no matter if that expression is considered in a positive or negative light.[29]

Following this line of reasoning, we can say that the reworking of different aesthetics and programs allowed Argentine science fiction to re-create its own political and ideological myths. The visual imagery that appears in the two examples that I have analyzed in the previous pages shows how images can articulate ideological worlds in ways that make explicit that which is not said in the discourse and is yet present in its horizon. Here, the idealization of utopian discourse collides with the imagery that attempts to support, making the "symbolic expression of hope for a better world" a complicated equation whether intentional or not. At their core, utopias also reveal our anxieties about the future. Images make those anxieties transparent.

Notes

1. Sarmiento discussed the urban/rural-civilization/barbarism dichotomy in two long essays: *Argirópolis*, which I broadly discussed earlier and *Facundo: Civilization and Barbarism* (1845). While the former is an argument in favor of complex legal and institutional projects based in the urban space, the second is an exploration of Argentine culture and its ideological choices between the legacy of its colonial, savage past located in the Pampas and the promise of future economic development modeled by European industrialized cities. This book would be the cornerstone of the liberal nation-state building project in years to come. As Argentina emerged from its postindependence civil wars, *Facundo* became a sort of ideological blueprint in the construction of a civilized, modern nation. During the country's modernization process, starting with Sarmiento's own presidency in 1868, many of the policies implemented followed the spirit of these as well as other essays of Sarmiento's generation.
2. Here I am using the word "interesting" in a luhmanian sense. For Niklas Luhman, a work of art is "interesting" as it speaks by exploring "new semantic stabilities" within an evolving cultural archive. Luhman, *Art as a Social System*, 223–43. This operation, however, can only happen as works of art compare their own meanings with each other when confronting their own processes for describing society.
3. Alonso, *El futuro ya no es lo que era*; Battistozzi, *La ciudad*; Montross et al., *Past Futures*.
4. Covers sometimes were, as in the case of *Más Allá*, accompanied by an interior caption. Here, either the draftsman or the editor explained that the puzzle was incomplete because humanity needed to still work on this collective, historical project. *Más Allá* 3, no. 36 (1956), published by Abril Press in Buenos Aires. The Minotauro book collection and press was the brainchild of Paco Porrúa (1922–2014) and was

originally edited in Argentina from 1955 to 1977. After Porrúa moved back to Spain, he continued working on Minotauro until he sold the press to Planeta in 2001. Nowadays, Minotauro Ediciones resides in Barcelona and continues publishing science fiction, albeit including Spanish and Latin American writers in its roster. It has also diversified its portfolio to include fantasy, the fantastic, and horror collections.

5. In a 2012 essay, Graciela Speranza argues that surrealism has proved to be particularly resilient beyond essentialist definitions of magical realism and modernist practices of the fifties and sixties. News of surrealism's demise had been greatly exaggerated and rarely takes into account its strong presence in science fiction visual imagery. Although Speranza does not work with this production, she analyzes the existence of a "clandestine surrealism" that has always survived in the margins of the cultural field. Speranza, "Wanderers."

6. Although Chichoni is famous for his magazine covers such as *Urania*, *Péndulo*, *Fierro*, *Metal Hurlant*, and so on, some of his already aged environments can be seen in a number of video games as well as in movies such as *Restauration* (1995), in which he worked in the art department unit under the direction of another Argentine, Eugenio Zanetti. Chichoni later worked on *Pacific Rim* (2013) and *Crimson Peak* (2015), lending them similar atmospheres. He has also left his mark in a number of other movies directed by Peter Jackson and Alfonso del Toro.

7. Although I analyze the role of surrealism in science fiction in my forthcoming book, *La ilusión persitente*, here I would like to point out how the covers of magazines such as *La revista de ciencia ficción y fantasía*, *Péndulo*, or even *Sinergía* have contributed to a very recognizable visual universe that departs from previous pulp imageries.

8. This was a process that transformed the entire cultural field, as aesthetic choices also implied increasingly more radicalized positions. Confrontations between realistic and fantastic writers, between figurative and nonfigurative painters, and so forth became increasingly more polarized over the next fifteen years.

9. Freidenberg, "Imágenes con vida humana." All translations are mine unless otherwise indicated.

10. In its manifesto in 1959, the group said: "El arte es el libertador por excelencia y las multitudes se reconocen en él, y su alma colectiva descarga en él sus más profundas tensiones al recobrar por intermedio las energías y las esperanzas. De ahí que para nosotros el arte sea una insustituible arma de combate, el instrumento precioso por medio del cual el artista se integra con la sociedad y la refleja, no pasiva sino activamente, no como un espejo sino como modelador" (Art is a liberator par excellence. Because of this, multitudes recognize themselves in art. Their collective soul unloads their deepest tensions in art so to recover their energies and hopes through interactions with it. Hence for us art is an irreplaceable combat weapon, the precious instrument by which the artist integrates with society and reflects it, not passively but actively, not as a mirror but as a guide). Cippolini, *Manifiestos argentinos*, 287. This formative role, closely intertwined with political realism, was the aesthetic ethos of the following decades and left a recognizable trace in the

comic production of the period. As we saw in Solano López's interview, important draftsmen appropriated this perspective to their own ends, with complex outcomes. It is also important to note that other groups followed in Espartaco's footsteps, such as in the case of Gente de Buenos Aires (1960s–mid-1970s), which radicalized the agenda of the former.

11. The issue of "realist comics" in Argentina has been defined against what is known as the "serious tradition of comics" (as opposed to caricature) to which Solano López belongs. This line has its origins in the illustration and adaptions of literature to comics.
12. Sarlo, "Cultural Landscapes," 30.
13. Huyssen, "Authentic Ruins," 18.
14. It is important to note that in many cases electronic fanzines offer a differentiated aesthetic take, with peaceful, romanticized images of cities even when destroyed. In those cases, more often than not, the imaginary worlds represented tend to return to the language of surrealism but organized with the vocabulary and instruments of Renaissance aesthetics, and titles may offer the proper clues for iconographic placement. It is also important to note that the mix of science fiction, horror, and fantasy in these magazines requires a specific approach to its visual imagery, which is aligned with whatever production it is purportedly accompanying, and therefore generates an eclectic collage of vocabularies. In some cases, e-magazines offer access to virtual art galleries where artists (either professionals or fans) exhibit and sell their productions. Lack of space prevents me from analyzing these works here, but I want to point out their importance as symbolic icons. Magazines like *Cuásar* offer a good case study of what I have discussed here, since its life in paper and on the web hints at these aesthetic choices and at the complex transformations of Argentine science fiction publications.
15. For example, consider the often happy, dreamy cities proposed by Xul Solar (1887–1963), whose frequent choice of warm, light palettes suggests optimism.
16. This list is by no means complete but is a sample of works intended to showcase very diverse aesthetic approaches to ruined cities.
17. Sebreli, *Buenos Aires, vida cotidiana*, 243.
18. To mention a few: Gorelick, *Miradas sobre Buenos Aires*; Welch Guerra, *Buenos Aires a la deriva*; and Tella, *Un crack en la ciudad*.
19. Buenos Aires's classification has recently been changed to subtropical due to global warming, although the area still retains some of its older weather features. At the time most of these comics were written, such development could not have been foreseen, so it is important to understand that their view of weather change in one direction or another serves their immediate ideological purposes more than an attempt to forewarn us.
20. Given that Argentine nationalism (and eventually, the radical Left as well as the populist parties that were their direct heirs) was deeply rooted in social organicism and historical determinism, this should not be surprising. I have analyzed elsewhere how this process came into being and will not repeat myself here, but I

would like to point out that the visual imaginary we are discussing belongs to that political strand.

21. It is also important to remember that Argentine comic production at large has been heavily influenced by the French masters of the 1950s and 1960s as well as later periods. So, images of a flooded Buenos Aires almost identically reproduce earlier imageries that appear in series like *Valérian et Laureline* (1967–2010) by Pierre Chrispin (1938–) and Jean-Claude Mézières (1938–), which was originally published in *Pilote* (1959–89). The storyline and structure of *Slot-Barr* is also very close to the saga of Lone Sloane and the *Mystère des Abîmes* originally created and published in 1966 by the already mentioned Druillet, although here the aesthetic register is very far from the French original. The Argentine saga is also a space opera that plays with the planetary romance tradition.

22. For this chapter I have used a later 2001 compilation.

23. On May 1, 1952, shortly before her death, Eva Perón talked in public for the last time. It was the first televised political speech in Argentine history and she improvised most of it. A transcript of the speech can be found in Fernández, *Eva Perón*, vol. 2.

24. Steimberg, "El discurso más allá de las palabras."

25. Such is the case of *El Eternatua II*, published in 1976 by Oesterheld and Solano López.

26. Barreiro and Solano López, *Slot-Barr*, 111.

27. The comic's title is the same as a well-known Silvio Rodríguez (Cuba, 1946) song from his 1984 album, *Tríptico I*. As in the case of the song, the main topic is hope and the individual's ability to overcome hate. Although the similarities end here, it is important to point out this link since Argentine readers understand the cultural reference.

28. Santellán and Serafín, *Reparador de sueños*, 38.

29. Portolano, "The Rhetorical Function of Utopia," 114.

Works Cited

Alonso, Rodrigo. *El futuro ya no es lo que era: Imaginarios de futuro en Argentina 1910–2010; Del 26 de marzo al 30 de mayo de 2009*. Buenos Aires: Fundación OSDE, 2009.

Barreiro, Ricardo, and Francisco Solano López. *Slot-Barr*. Reprint, Buenos Aires: Ediciones Colihue, Colección de Narrativa Dibujada, 2001.

Battistozzi, Ana María. *La ciudad: Arte y utopías*. Centro Virtual de Arte Argentino, July 20, 2016. http://www.cvaa.com.ar/02dossiers/utopia/ 00_actualutopia.php.

Cippolini, Rafael. *Manifiestos argentinos: Políticas de lo visual 1900–2000*. Buenos Aires: Adriana Hidalgo Editora, 2003.

Fernández, Aníbal. *Eva Perón: Discursos completos*. 2 vols. Madrid: Grupo Planeta, 2012.

Freidenberg, Jorge Raúl. "Imágenes con vida humana: Entrevista con Francisco Solano López." *Red Voltaire-Medios*, February 7, 2008. http://www.voltairenet.org/article 155021.html.

Gorelick, Adrián. *Miradas sobre Buenos Aires: Historia y cultura*. Buenos Aires: Siglo XXI, 2004.

Huyssen, Andreas. "Authentic Ruins: Products of Modernity." In *Ruins of Modernity*, edited by Julia Hell and Andreas Schönle, 17–28. Durham, N.C.: Duke University Press, 2010.

Luhmann, Niklas. *Art as a Social System*. Stanford, Calif.: Stanford University Press, 2000.

Montross, Sarah J., Rodrigo Alonso, Miguel Angel Fernández Delgado, and Rory O'Dea. *Past Futures: Science Fiction, Space Travel, and Postwar Art of the Americas*. Brunswick, Maine: Bowdoin College Museum of Art; Cambridge, Mass.: MIT Press, 2015.

Portolano, Marlana. "The Rhetorical Function of Utopia: An Exploration of the Concept of Utopia in Rhetorical Theory." *Utopian Studies* 23, no. 1 (2012): 113–41.

Santellán, Matías, and Serafín. *Reparador de sueños*. Buenos Aires: Ediciones de la Flor, 2012.

Sarlo, Beatriz. "Cultural Landscapes: Buenos Aires from Integration to Fracture." In *Other Cities, Other Worlds: Urban Imaginaries in a Globalizing Age*, edited by Andreas Huyssen, 27–50. Durham, N.C.: Duke University Press, 2008.

Sarmiento, Domingo Faustino. *Argirópolis*. Buenos Aires: Universidad Nacional de la Matanza, 2001.

———. *Facundo o civilización y barbarie en las pampas argentinas*. Buenos Aires: Editorial Kapelusz, 1982.

Sebreli, Juan José. *Buenos Aires, vida cotidiana y alienación seguido de Buenos Aires, ciudad en crisis*. Buenos Aires: Sudamericana, 2003.

Speranza, Graciela. "Wanderers: Surrealism and Contemporary Latin American Art and Fiction." In *Surrealism in Latin America: Vivísimo Muerto*, edited by Dawn Ades, Rita Eder, and Graciela Speranza, 193–211. London and Los Angeles: Tate Publishing in association with Getty Research Institute, 2012.

Steimberg, Alejo. "El discurso más allá de las palabras o el análisis ideológico de historietas: Lecturas de El Eternauta y Slot-Barr." *Camouflage Comics—Dirty War Images*, 2004. http://camouflagecomics.com.

Tella, Guillermo. *Un crack en la ciudad: Rupturas y continuidades en la trama urbana de Buenos Aires*. Buenos Aires: Nobuko, 2007.

Welch Guerra, Max. *Buenos Aires a la deriva: Transformaciones urbanas recientes*. Buenos Aires: Biblos, 2005.

PART III

Digital Textualities, Media, and Editing

8

Discourse or Data?

Theorizing the Electronic Edition of Antonio de León Pinelo's 1629 Bibliography of the Indies

CLAYTON MCCARL

THIS CHAPTER EXPLORES CONCEPTUAL problems in the electronic edition of early modern print bibliographies. I focus on several questions that stem from one central concern: the dual nature of historical bibliographies as linear pieces of discourse and as nonlinear repositories of information. In doing so, I consider the complex relationship between print bibliographies and the "real world" of actual material artifacts (print books and manuscripts), and the threat that a desire to normalize and correct may pose to the integrity of the bibliographic text. This chapter addresses these issues in the context of my ongoing work on a digital version of the *Epitome de la biblioteca oriental i occidental, nautica i geografica* (Summary bibliography of the East and West Indies and the nautical and geographical arts, 1629) by Antonio de León Pinelo (ca. 1590–1660).[1] The thoughts outlined here, however, may have ramifications for other projects involving print bibliographies or, indeed, other types of texts that share similar characteristics.[2]

León Pinelo's *Epitome* contains a listing of approximately one thousand books, including translations, recompilations, and reprints, along with some manuscripts. Often celebrated as the first bibliography of the Americas,[3] the text focuses equally, as the title suggests, on written works dealing with both the East and West Indies, as well as Africa. The *Epitome* forms part of a European tradition of print bibliographies that dates at least to the second century

CE, and is widely regarded as a landmark of European bibliographical and Americanist scholarship.[4] From its publication in 1629 to the present day, the book has served as an essential source for scholars in fields including history, geography, literary studies, and book history. Joseph Sabin, José Toribio Medina, Antonio Palau y Dulcet, and other bibliographers of the Americas turned to León Pinelo's text as a foundational work for their own endeavors, and since the early twentieth century, numerous other scholars have considered the *Epitome*, including Diego Luis Molinari, Raúl Porras Barrenechea, Guillermo Lohmann Villena, Aniceto Almeyda, Agustín Millares Carlo, Isagani Medina, Horacio Capel, Ernesto de la Torre Villar, and Jonathan Carlyon.[5]

Despite the *Epitome*'s importance, however, much work remains to be done regarding this unique text. Many of the aforementioned studies glance peripherally at the *Epitome* as they focus on the *Recopilacion de leyes de los reynos de las Indias* (1681) and other titles for which León Pinelo is perhaps better known.[6] No modern edition of the *Epitome* has been attempted, and as a consequence, researchers continue today to work with the *princeps*, or facsimiles thereof.[7] Likewise, the text has seldom been approached as a book that not only lists other books but also articulates ideas, and few existing studies attempt a close reading of León Pinelo's bibliographic references themselves.[8] With my current project, I seek to address this situation by constructing an edition that increases the usability of the text for twenty-first-century scholars, while at the same time exposing its complexity as a textual object.

A central challenge in editing the *Epitome* results from its existence outside established categories generally embraced by editors. I refer not to the dichotomy between "historical" (or documentary) and "literary" approaches, two broad paradigms through which editorial practice is often viewed. As a print work that is widely available, albeit primarily in facsimile versions, a "documentary" or "historical" approach, as those terms are generally understood, may not offer clear advantages. Methods more along the lines of those traditionally considered "literary" might be appropriate, though we have only the 1629 first edition at our disposal, with no manuscript material. Establishing an ideal text, such as one that might reflect authorial intentions, therefore may not be a productive goal. Certainly, however, as a primary objective of this project is to increase the usability of the text, the creation of a clear, regularized (or partially regularized) version is desirable. In any case, a distinction between models we might label "documentary" and "literary" means increasingly less in a digital age, as recent scholarship by Elena Pierazzo and others seems to suggest.[9]

The real challenge in editing the *Epitome* has more to do with what I will call "multidimensionality." As this chapter attempts to establish, the book is a discursive object in which arguments are articulated in a variety of ways, including through their direct or implicit expression in prose and verse, as well as through the acts of translating, organizing, categorizing, and selectively including or excluding information. Seen through this lens, the *Epitome* is the type of text to which "documentary" and "literary" approaches have historically been applied. At the same time, however, the *Epitome* consists primarily of a listing of books, in entries that are discrete items that need not be accessed in a sequential fashion. In this sense, it is a collection of fragments that can be isolated and manipulated in a variety of ways, existing in an informational domain beyond the linearity of discursive writing. The main problem in the edition of such a text, therefore, resides not in how to approach it as linear discourse (through "documentary" or "literary" approaches) but rather how to manage its dual existence as discourse and as data.

From an editorial perspective, two distinct possibilities offer themselves: on the one hand, to respect the structure of the original, presenting the text sequentially as a continuous piece of writing; and on the other, to transform the document into a set of individual bibliographic entries, to be handled as we would database records. In short, in conceptualizing a project such as this, we find ourselves at the intersection of traditional editorial practice and methods that correspond more to the field of library and information science. We are confronted, consequently, with the need for an editorial approach that may not currently have a name. "Bibliographical" might serve in the case of the *Epitome*, but as such practice might apply to other texts entirely different in terms of content, something like "multidimensional" might be more inclusive.

In the pages that follow, I argue for the validity of understanding the *Epitome* in these two ways—as a piece of linear discourse and as a collection of independent informational units. In doing so, I consider the advantages of approaching the text in a fashion that permits us to interact with it as both a discursive object and as a repository of data. I conclude with some preliminary thoughts about the form that such a hybrid, multidimensional approach might take.

To argue that the *Epitome* can be understood as an aggregation of atomized, nonsequential data is perhaps to belabor an obvious point. Certainly this is how readers have interacted with the book since long before technology made the deliberations in this chapter possible, handling it primarily as a reference work. For proof, we need only look at the manner in which scholars have cited the *Epitome* as a source of historical evidence about particular books—at times, perhaps, in spite of what this chapter argues is the highly problematic nature of the text. The autonomous quality of its bibliographic entries is suggested by the onomastic index, in which each reference points, via the name of an author (or editor, translator, etc.), to an individual bibliographic item, not to the personal names, nor the place-names, that those records might contain internally, as might be the case with less rigidly structured writing. The atomic nature of the entries is indicated as well by their physical layout, with each item formatted as a separate paragraph, as well as by the apparent effort, often frustrated, to include the same categories of information for each. Such an idea is further validated by actual contemporary practice, with print bibliographies serving in part as the basis for relational tools like the online *English Short Title Catalog*, hosted by the British Library.[10] Indeed, we live today in a world in which the autonomy of data and the random access thereof have become in many ways the norm, with our experiences increasingly mediated through digital tools built upon databases.

That the *Epitome* should be thought of as discourse is perhaps less evident. To be sure, the book begins with materials in prose and verse, forms traditionally understood as presenting information to be processed in a serial, word-by-word, line-by-line fashion. The more "standard" nature of these materials should not privilege them, however, as the book in its entirety represents one coherent object that conveys meaning. Whether this is through the sequential presentation of concepts, or through their accumulative repetition, no individual piece can be fully understood outside the context of the larger work.

The strongest evidence that the *Epitome* constitutes a discursive unit with its own internal logic and integrity is found in two central arguments that run throughout, expressed in both the preliminary materials and the bibliographic entries. One of these is autobiographical, consisting of León Pinelo's efforts to promote his own work. He had arrived in Madrid in 1623, following an education and early career in the Americas,[11] and likely saw this text as an opportunity to advance his reputation as an expert on matters related to the Indies. On various occasions, he notes—perhaps hyperbolically—the comprehensive nature of his scholarly efforts. He asserts that the *Epitome* is "the first fruit of his long studies," and suggests that in his book, "there is not one line that didn't cost the reading of many."[12]

This discourse of exhaustiveness continues in the bibliographic entries, where in discussing his work on the *Recopilacion*, for instance, he claims to have read "500 handwritten books of royal decrees," consisting of over 120,000 pages and more than 300,000 documents.[13] In various places, he publicizes the other projects he has in progress, such as in a section listing histories of cities, in which he highlights books about Lima and Potosí.[14] He also locates himself in an inventory of those who collected books about the overseas world, alongside such legendary compilers and editors as Amerigo Vespucci, Giovanni Battista Ramusio, and Theodore De Bry, registering himself as "*Licenciado* Antonio de León, who since he first began to read and write, has busied himself . . . in reading . . . histories . . . of the Indies."[15]

These efforts at self-promotion are echoed in the preliminary materials written by others, who celebrate León Pinelo's erudition and the contribution represented by the *Epitome*. These texts include the laudatory poems by Luis Tribaldos de Toledo and Josef de Valdivielso; the "Apologetic Discourse" by Juan Rodríguez de León, the author's brother; and the certification of the Church's approbation, by Lope de Vega.[16] Though they might be thought of as ancillary, these writings bear a close relationship to the ideas presented in the text itself, and from an editorial viewpoint at least, they can be seen as integral to the *Epitome*.

The other primary discourse that underlies León Pinelo's text is a criticism of indifference in the court toward the study of the overseas world. In his prologue, the author asserts that books about the Indies were the "most forgotten and downtrodden," at a time when scholars valued the study of the ancient world over that of the contemporary overseas empire.[17] Such a lack of interest, he explains, caused him to doubt his ability to prepare the accounting of books about the Indies that his patron had requested: "And thus I resolved myself to print a work whose ideas I feared and whose execution I doubted, because though I dared to imagine this book, it seemed much more difficult to achieve, as there was not in Spain any particular curiosity to guide me, nor—until now—any greater inclination that might inspire me. Such is the quandary faced by one who attempts to know things of other worlds."[18]

Though León Pinelo does not say so directly, the difficulty in writing his book was apparently due in part to a lack of access in Spain to relevant information, during an era in which the centers of nautical and geographical publishing had shifted. In the sixteenth century, texts by Spaniards—and Southern Europeans associated with Spanish voyages—advanced in revolutionary ways European understanding of the physical world and its inhabitants. Toward the end of the century, however, the study of cartography was flourishing instead in the north, and massive collections of nautical texts were being published in England, the Netherlands, and elsewhere.[19] In his "Apologetic Discourse," Rodríguez de León laments this situation, proposing that the Spanish had overlooked the intellectual production surrounding the Americas, distracted by the precious metals that the colonies produced. Such neglect, he proposes, had permitted strangers to become more expert than Spaniards themselves in such matters, with *plumas ajenas*, or foreign quills, metonymically authoring the nautical and geographical books that mattered.[20]

The challenges that León Pinelo faced are reflected in his prologue, where he points to several categories of problematic writers included in his book. One of these involves authors he had found mentioned but whose books he had not seen, and the subjects of which were unknown to him.[21] Another is a set of authors whose identity was in question, though he had seen their works personally, or at least read of them. Here León Pinelo issues an invitation for the reader to intervene: "Thus I leave the names blank. He who may find them can add them, though some will surely defy his efforts, as they have mine."[22]

His struggle to access needed materials is made clear by yet another category not mentioned explicitly, but which nonetheless appears throughout his text. These are works for which León Pinelo had titles or descriptions, and names of authors, but of which he knew only through secondary sources, as in the case of the following: "[Author/s unknown] Twenty-eight books on various topics in Chinese. Fray Juan González de Mendoza lists them by title . . . [and] says they were brought printed from that kingdom."[23] The sources for these secondhand references most frequently are Thomas James, *Catalogvs librorvm*, the first print catalog of the Bodleian Library; and Pierre-François Sweerts, *Athenae Beligcae*, a bibliography of the Low Countries.[24]

A comparison of León Pinelo's entries with those found in such sources supports the idea that he often relied upon them exclusively, as the *Epitome* frequently offers nothing beyond what they contain. For example, León Pinelo lists "Robert of Lincoln. Compendium of the Sphere, printed 1508, according to James," which corresponds to the following entry in the *Catalogvs librorvm*: "Rob. Lincolniesnsis. . . . Cōpen Sphaerae. Ven. 1508. Q.V.3.13."[25] In another instance he cites "Geronimo Verrvcio. Notas a Pomponio Mela, segun Francisco Svveercio," which follows the entry "Hieronymvs Verrvtivs . . . Ad Pomponium Melum Notas" in Sweerts.[26]

At times, León Pinelo's sources for such references are not other bibliographical repertories but rather historiographical texts. For example, he registers in the "Biblioteca occidental" a book by "Juan Flesinge, a native of Antwerp," who, he asserts, wrote about the "coasts and commerce" of the West Indies, after living for many years in that region. The bibliographer cites as his source the fifth volume of the *Historia pontifical* by Fray Marcos de Guadalaxara y Xavier.[27] He follows his source accurately, but the information appears to be spurious. "Flesinge" is almost certainly Jan Huyghen van Linschoten, and the book in question his 1596 journal of his travels to the East Indies (not America) with the Portuguese.[28]

León Pinelo's undertaking was further complicated by the problematic editions that were available to him. For instance, in listing the book resulting from the expedition of Nicolò and Antonio Zeno to the North Sea, he indicates that the journey took place in the year 1200.[29] The Zeno brothers actually traveled in the second half of the fourteenth century, but the date he gives proceeds directly from the version of the story in the *Navigationi et viaggi* of Ramusio, which begins "in the year of our lord 1200."[30]

A similar retransmission of apparently inaccurate information occurs with some of the texts León Pinelo locates in the collections of De Bry. An example is the manner in which he handles the name of Gotthard Arthus (1570–ca. 1630) of Gdánsk (Danzig), the translator of several of the works into Latin. León Pinelo correctly lists him as the translator of an anonymous text from 1600 about Dutch journeys to Africa, following perhaps the title in the *Grands et petits voyages of De Bry*, part 6, where De Bry gathers the Arthus translation, as León Pinelo notes.[31] In other instances, however, León Pinelo lists Arthus ("M. Gotardo Artus Dantiscano," as he refers to him) as the actual author of the respective texts, reproducing the apparent imprecision of the De Bry titles themselves. For instance, following the statement "Auctore M. Gothardo Arthusio Dantiscano" in De Bry, León Pinelo lists Arthus as the author of the published journal of the voyage of Joris van Spilbergen.[32]

Within both the "Biblioteca oriental" and the "Biblioteca occidental," León Pinelo additionally dedicates sections to "authors about whose writings there is doubt."[33] Here he registers writers whose existence he questions, as in the case of a "Pedro Aloisio," the putative author of a book about a nautical journey. As León Pinelo states, "Although Miguel Routarcio cites him thus in chapter 18 of the book he entitled *Oculus historiae*, I believe the author to be suspect."[34] He likewise registers his skepticism about the existence of books themselves, as in the case of an anonymous "three-part history of Perú." As he alleges: "[Antonio] Posevino, the Licenciado Don Francisco Herrera Maldonado, Miguel Routarcio, Doctor Juan Solórzano Pereyra, and now Don Josef Pellicer de Salas mention it, and say it was published in Venice in 1560. None, however, claims to actually have seen it, but rather all reports of the text seem to follow that which Posevino provides, and therefore I'm putting it down as doubtful."³⁵ Such a process of constructing bibliographic entries at a distance, working with indirect or inexact information, highlights the precarious nature of the *Epitome* and, by extension, the complexity of conducting such work in the Spanish court.

León Pinelo also criticizes official apathy by documenting the difficulty that other writers faced in publishing or receiving compensation for their work. For instance, in registering a manuscript treatise on a method for finding longitude at sea by a *Licenciado* Ruiz, León Pinelo offers the following commentary: "He presented it to the Royal Council of the Indies, and, as it appears, still has not been able to successfully make himself understood."³⁶ Regarding the efforts of Juan Arias de Loyola to publish a treatise on the same topic, the bibliographer makes a similar observation: "He presented it in the Royal Council of Indies and the War Council of the Indies. The Council awarded him a subsidy of 1,000 ducados, and promised him six thousand in annual income, and two thousand for life, but he obtained nothing."³⁷ León Pinelo follows with yet another example of a related text by a Luis de Fonseca Coutiño, who delivered his work to the Royal Council of the Indies, after spending 4,000 ducados in its preparation, without receiving anything in return.³⁸

The *Epitome*, then, expresses at least two central arguments: an attempt to elevate the esteem in which the author's intellectual work was held, and a complex, multifaceted criticism of Spain's indifference to the intellectual production surrounding its overseas empire. In addition to these two ideas, other reasons exist to think of the *Epitome* as a discursive object. These include the geographical organization of the text, the internal integrity of the subsections, the fact that much of the text exists in translation, a discourse of absence, the complex relationship between the text and the external world, and the problems inherent in adapting the references in the *Epitome* to a standard bibliographic format. A detailed examination of any of these topics individually lies beyond the scope of the present study, and so each is discussed here only in brief.

The overall organization of the *Epitome* is guided by a European geographical vision of the globe. In naming the two principal sections of the text—the "Biblioteca occidental" and the "Biblioteca oriental"—León Pinelo follows the standard division of the overseas world in the East and West Indies, with Africa grouped with the East Indies as part of the maritime route east. Within those categories, he articulates a further conceptualization of space that surely is not neutral or objective. To divorce the individual bibliographic records from this overarching geographical framework—as we would do when approaching them as individual, nonsequential records—must imply a loss of meaning.

Furthermore, the geographical and other subunits of the *Epitome* are susceptible to a discursive analysis not only for the spatial conceptualization they represent but because they often read as coherent units of meaning. In some instances, this is because the subsections present a running narrative that links the individual entries, as in the case of *título* III of the "Biblioteca náutica," which enumerates the unpublished treatises on finding longitude discussed earlier. Another example is *título* XVI of the "Biblioteca oriental," in which most of the entries refer to a print catalog of authors who wrote about the Indies, mentioned for the first time as part of the second reference in that section.[39] Treating the subsections as linear objects, therefore, allows us to access aspects of the text that approaching the bibliographic entries as independent and atomic entries may not.

The act of translating titles and proper names of people, which León Pinelo does throughout the *Epitome*, must also be regarded as a type of discursive activity. While the meaning of such transformations is a matter for separate investigation, the primary editorial question at hand would seem to be whether to revert these semantic units to the original form they may have taken in León Pinelo's source materials. Unless we could be certain of some type of objectivity and accuracy in León Pinelo' translations—a difficult proposition—surely such enmendation would represent violence to the text. The "correction" or regularization of such titles and names would almost definitely imply a rejection of fundamental facts about the *Epitome* and the worldview it expresses.

The idea of the *Epitome* as a document that must be understood in its totality is not only a function of what it contains but also what it may omit. León Pinelo himself warns us of the incomplete nature of the text, asserting that "many authors are likely missing."[40] For examples, we need only look to the absence of the seminal compilations published by Englishmen Richard Hakluyt and Samuel Purchas, a circumstance that must bear on how we understand the *Epitome*.[41]

A discourse of absence also exists at the level of the individual entries, which often lack not only names and titles but also other information that León Pinelo generally included. A typical example would be his citation of the following book, missing both author and place of publication: "[Anonymous] An account of Japan in French. Printed 1602. Octavo."[42] At a minimum, such problems suggest that this is a book for which León Pinelo had little information, and which he himself likely had not seen. Such gaps and omissions are not merely deficiencies to be remedied through contemporary bibliographic research but rather may themselves convey meaning.

The *Epitome*'s complex relationship to the external world suggests an internal logic that also suggests a type of discursiveness. In his 1979 article "External Fact as an Editorial Problem," G. Thomas Tanselle considers the quandary faced by editors when addressing apparent "errors" in a literary text that result from problematic references to the external world.[43] A central issue, Tanselle's study suggests, has to do with distinguishing whether such "errors" are intentional or unintentional, and determining the type of meaning they should be assumed to convey in either case. If we understand a piece of writing as a self-contained object that defines its own interior reality, emending (or even annotating) such errors may violate the integrity of the text. Such a problem is greatly amplified in the case of the *Epitome*, a work in constant dialogue with an external world of authors and written artifacts. Though to propose a reading of the *Epitome* as an imaginative composition may seem extreme, the elaborate internal discourses and the complex relationship between the text and its external context suggest that the book must be understood on its own terms, much as we would approach works of a more obvious "literary" nature.

Indeed, León Pinelo's book can been seen to engage with discourses about the textual construction of reality that have represented an important thread in Hispanic letters since at least the seventeenth century. The most universally cited figures in this metaliterary tradition are Miguel de Cervantes and Jorge Luis Borges, authors who explore the destabilizing effect of shifting narrative levels and the blurred boundaries between the written text and notions of an objective, external reality. Both writers built texts upon others that are fictitious, and Borges articulated the metaphor of the universe as a library—an idea with immediate relevance to the *Epitome*, a book about books that, in a way, stands in for the world itself.[44] Like these writers, León Pinelo produced a text whose relationship with other writings—real and unreal—is precarious, which posits a reality based on tenuous and uncertain knowledge, and which, as a consequence, poses questions about what we know and how we can know it. In the midst of a reality constructed of books, León Pinelo presents himself as a type of bibliographic antihero, trapped in a labyrinth of false or impossibly vague references. In struggling to discover what cannot be known, he expresses through the *Epitome* a modern yearning for truth in a world where such transcendence seems to be continually beyond reach. Any reading of the *Epitome* that approaches the text uncritically as a mere listing of books, therefore, must clearly be insufficient.

In more prosaic terms, the idea of the *Epitome* as discourse is also supported by the difficulty we might face in actually converting its bibliographic references into a standard format, such as that of MARC records.[45] The incomplete nature of many entries, and the inaccuracies they contain, contributes to the difficulty of this task, as an editor is faced with a choice of either maintaining such "imperfections" or introducing information that is not part of the original text. Another complication lies in the prose format of the entries, from which the extraction of basic bibliographical information is not always a straightforward task, and one that surely cannot be accomplished without losing or altering the facts of the text. The list of errata provided at the beginning of the *Epitome* exacerbates the problem. Can the corrections proposed there simply be effected in our atomized records, or is this list of errors itself a piece of prose? How are we to proceed if the list of errata itself contains errors?

The difficulty and cost of converting León Pinelo's bibliographic entries to standardized fields can be seen in the following example.

> Barrachel Enciso. Of the Island of Santiago. Although in the abovementioned *memoria* it has a name and a title, both are doubtful, as there is no one [in that book] of this last name but he who is mentioned in the *biblioteca* 4—who, for having written about geography, could have addressed the Island of Santiago—and for their being no island by this name in all the Indies so famous that there might be a book about it, this seems all the more doubtful, since those that are known are one among the islands of Caboverde and the other the island of Jamaica, among the Islands of Barlovento.[46]

From this entry we surely can extract "Barrachel Enciso" as author, "Of the Island of Santiago" as title, and "Island of Santiago" as subject. We do not know, however, whether "Barrachel Enciso" is the correct name of the author, whether "Of the Island of Santiago" is an actual title or a description of the content, nor to which island that title refers. We are lacking place and date of publication, and indeed, we do not know whether the book or its alleged author actually exists.

In other words, we face a problem not only in trying to understand the *Epitome* as individual bibliographic records but also in approaching León Pinelo's bibliographic records as separate fields. We must make choices about potentially supplementing missing data and correcting apparently erroneous data, as well as extracting or adapting atomized data from larger prose strings. All are acts that potentially do harm to the text by removing that information from a larger semantic context.

Even were we able to successfully convert these entries into a standardized bibliographic format, we would, it seems, need additional nonstandard fields to qualify the information we are recording. For example, part of the meaning of the entries resides in León Pinelo's expressions of uncertainty, including his doubts about the existence of some authors and books. Where might this fit in a MARC record? To the same point, an issue arises regarding transparency and intentionality. We generally assume that information in standard bibliographic repositories, such as library catalogs, reflects an effort to portray facts about the "real world" of written artifacts. In converting León Pinelo's bibliographic entries into a standardized format, however, we inevitably are creating records that we know to contain information that may do something else. How do we express this? Could such records exist innocently in the larger ecosystem of OCLC records? What would it mean, for instance, for a standardized record like the one we might produce for the Barrachel Enciso entry above to end up somewhere like WorldCat?

All these problems point to reasons why the *Epitome* constitutes a piece of discourse, and cannot be easily approached merely as an accumulation of independent, nonsequential facts. At the same time, however, the benefits of achieving precisely such reformulation are significant. By enabling more flexible and direct ways to interact with the text, we can overcome the many difficulties inherent in consulting the *Epitome* as a static object.

One of these is the challenge in locating particular items. The onomastic index rather unhelpfully lists authors by first name, collapsing foreign names, furthermore, into Hispanized forms. The section listing sixty-eight authors named Pedro, for instance, contains many who surely are Pierre, Pietro, Pieter, Peter, and so on.[47] Foreign last names are likewise transformed, often into forms not immediately recognizable. For example, when Hakluyt does appear (in reference to his 1587 translation of the *Decades* of Peter Martyr), he is Ricardo Hocluito.[48] Even in a clean electronic copy of the text, we would need regularized metadata to find him readily. Within each subsection of the text, entries furthermore follow neither alphabetical nor consistent chronological order.

Another challenge resides in the limitations we face in asking certain types of questions about the *Epitome*. To find all the texts addressing a particular geographical region, for instance, one cannot simply review the corresponding subsection. The inventory for the New Kingdom of Granada ("Biblioteca occidental," *título* XIV), as an example, does not register essential writings that are contained in collections or more general histories—such as those of Gonzalo Fernández de Oviedo, Francisco López de Gómara, and Juan de Castellanos—gathered elsewhere in León Pinelo's repertory.[49] In a similar fashion, we cannot readily interrogate the nonrelational text about books published in a specific language, in a particular place, or within a given range of dates.

An ability to reorder and sort the entries on the basis of such factors—and to register multiple values for certain fields, such as subject, language (for multilingual texts), and region—would therefore imply clear benefits. In addition, the opportunity to interact with the text on the basis of nonstandard metadata—such as fields recording León Pinelo's sources or his degree of doubt—would permit us to see the *Epitome* in entirely new ways. Creating these dynamic capabilities, furthermore, is likely to make possible the asking of questions not yet imagined—surely a desirable goal in any editorial project.

To an extent, the problem presented in this chapter has already been solved by the team editing the financial records of George Washington at the University of Virginia. Jennifer Stertzer notes that the editing of such records differs from the handling of more traditional types of textual material: "Unlike . . . narrative and discursive documents, financial documents are tabular in structure, span decades-long periods of time, are not particularly useful when read from beginning to end, and are uniquely dependent on other documents for full understanding." In conceptualizing an edition of Washington's financial records, her team at the University of Virginia faced the challenge of balancing competing priorities—on the one hand, a desire to provide transcriptions that faithfully represent the information on the page, and on the other, the need to enable researchers to interact with the data in complex, dynamic ways. As Stertzer states the problem: "What is the best way to preserve and present a document both as an object that has been accurately transcribed to mirror the hand-written original, while also providing a way for scholars to analyze the financial content in these records? Quite simply, we need to preserve text and create data."[50]

Stertzer and her team consequently developed an approach that they termed "docs vs. data." In the back end of their edition, they record each transaction two times, once as a transcription of the entry as it appears on the manuscript page, and again as an expanded, regularized set of data that can enable advanced use of the information. Although each transaction is thus articulated twice, the editors consider the two representations of each entry to be inherently linked, since, as Stertzer points out, the individual data records cannot stand alone on semantic terms: "a transaction line taken out of its context—what financial document it comes from, the account it is associated with, where it is located within the financial document (in the case of a ledger, the debit or credit side)—is not only problematic but in many cases unintelligible."[51] For this reason, in the interface to their edition, a user may search for an individual transaction, but the result is never displayed on its own. Instead, it is always shown in the context of the page on which it appears in the transcription.[52]

All the claims Stertzer makes about the nature of financial documents can arguably be applied to the bibliographic material in the *Epitome*, but two items are most relevant. First, she conceptualizes these documents as "tabular," consisting of discrete bits of data divided into columns. Although the bibliographic entries in the *Epitome* appear in a prose format that occupies a single column, they consist of informational subunits corresponding to standardized categories (author, title, etc.) that could be represented—though with difficulty, as we have seen—in a tabular format. Likewise, while readers may consume brief sections of the text in a sequential fashion, reading the entire book front to back is unlikely to be a meaningful exercise in most cases.

Thus, like the financial records in Stertzer's project, the *Epitome* can be thought of as existing in two dimensions, one linear and one relational. Likewise, as in the case of the financial records, the relational dimension cannot exist apart from the linear dimension without losing semantic value. Her team's dual approach to the text, therefore, suggests a possible way to conceptualize an edition of the *Epitome*—a linear presentation of the text itself, with a relational representation of the same data—regularized and made complete, in the background. The relational side might contain fields through which to express the metatextual concerns discussed in this chapter, as well as others not considered here.

The key to this approach is that the two representations of the text are inherently linked in a parallel fashion. While the linear text might exist without the relational version in the background (as indeed it has for several centuries), the same cannot be true of its relational counterpart. We could separate the relational representation from the linear text and interact with it on its own terms, but if we were to do so, we would be dealing with extractive data, or a sort of informational by-product, of the *Epitome* itself. Though the bibliographic records might stand up on their own better than Stertzer's financial records, the same concept of semantic loss applies—the individual records of the *Epitome* lose meaning when removed from the context in which they appear in the original. Were they made complete, and complemented with metadata, they would furthermore contain significant amounts of information not part of the *Epitome*, representing a greater distancing from the text itself, if handled in isolation.

For this reason, the "multidimensional" approach this chapter attempts to envision might better be called "parallel multidimensionality." Such a model not only proposes a way for us to interact with the text in different modalities (linear and relational) but also emphasizes the need to be able to transit across the dimensions seamlessly. This approach suggests the desirability of conceptualizing such a project not as two articulations of the same text, linked in a side-by-side fashion, but rather as a single edition that can project itself into different cognitive realms.

While today such an endeavor may appear to be a novelty, in the future we are likely to see an increasing number of editorial undertakings that wrestle with the basic problem of multidimensionality addressed here. As scholars continue to expand the categories of texts that can be understood as valid objects for electronic editions, this problem may become more prevalent. Furthermore, the mass digitization of books in recent years has created a vast sea of largely uncurated linear data that begs to be understood in new ways, providing a backdrop of general urgency to the need to begin understanding individual texts in ways that can accommodate both their linear and relational existence.

Notes

1. León Pinelo, *Epitome de la biblioteca oriental i occidental, nautica i geografica* (1629). All references to the *Epitome* throughout are to this 1629 first edition. I represent the Spanish title as it appears in the original, without modernizing or adding diacritic marks, as I do with the titles and other bibliographic information throughout for all print books. The English version of the title here is my own. All translations are mine unless otherwise indicated. For *biblioteca* (or *bibliotheca*) as a precursor to the term "bibliography," see Balsamo, *Bibliography*, 5.
2. This chapter limits itself to theoretical considerations, leaving for another occasion a more thorough examination of how to approach these problems in terms of design and technology.
3. See, for instance, Torre Villar, *Antonio de León Pinelo*; Millares Carlo, Introduction.
4. Balsamo, *Bibliography*, 7.
5. Sabin, *A Dictionary of Books Relating to America*; J. Medina, *Biblioteca Hispanoamericana, 1493–1810* and "Estudios biobibliográficos sobre Antonio de León Pinelo," 14–21; Palau y Dulcet, *Manual del librero hispano-americano*; Molinari, Introduction; Porras Barrenechea, Introduction, 1:xv; Lohmann Villena, "Fuentes bibliográficas del *Epítome* de Pinelo," Introduction, and "Un capítulo de eurística peruana"; Almeyda, Introduction, viii–ix; Millares Carlo, Introduction, ix–xxxiv, and *Tres estudios*, 64–113; I. Medina, *Philippine Items*; Capel, Introduction, xi, xiv–xvi; Torre Villar, *Antonio de León Pinelo*; Carlyon, *Andrés González de Barcia and the Creation of the Colonial Spanish American Library*.
6. León Pinelo is considered the central contributor to the *Recopilacion*, a project in which various other individuals were also involved. In 1680, two decades after the

author's death, Carlos II approved the printing of the *Recopilacion*, and the work appeared the following year. See Manzano Manzano, *Historia de las Recopilaciones de Indias*; and Sánchez Bella, Introduction.

7. In the eighteenth century, Andrés González de Barcia produced what he framed as a second edition of León Pinelo's work (1737–38). From the point of view of my current project, however, this radically expanded document must be considered a separate text. In the twentieth century, both versions were reprinted in facsimile—the 1629 edition in Buenos Aires (1919) and Washington, D.C. (1958), and González de Barcia's augmented second edition in Madrid (1973) and Barcelona (1982). A digital facsimile of the 1629 edition is available online through Google Books, but the underlying text is based on the results of an uncorrected optical character recognition (OCR) scan.
8. The exceptions would be Lohmann Villena, "Fuentes bibliográficas del *Epítome*"; and I. Medina, *Philippine Items*.
9. See, for instance, Pierazzo, "A Rationale of Digital Documentary Editions."
10. The *ESTC* is based in part on Wing et al., *Short-Title Catalogue of Books*; and Pollard et al., *A Short-Title Catalogue of Books*. See British Library, "*English Short Title Catalogue*—Content."
11. For León Pinelo's early life through his arrival in the court, see Capel, Introduction, xi; Millares Carlo, *Tres estudios biobibliográficos*, 78–85; and Porras Barrenechea, Introduction, vi–i, among others.
12. León Pinelo, prologue to the *Epitome*, n.p.; León Pinelo, dedication to the Duke of Medina de las Torres in the *Epitome*, n.p. In the prologue, the author explains that the *Epitome* is a summary of a larger work, unknown today, that he planned to publish.
13. León Pinelo, *Epitome*, 123.
14. León Pinelo, *Epitome*, 98.
15. León Pinelo, *Epitome*, 134.
16. "In doctissimi viri Lic[entiati] Antonii Leonis," "Del Maestro Josef de Valdivielso," "Aprobación de Lope de Vega Carpio," and "Del doctor Juan Rodríguez de León," in León Pinelo, *Epitome*, n.p.
17. León Pinelo, prologue to the *Epitome*, n.p.
18. León Pinelo, dedication to the Duke of Medina de las Torres in the *Epitome*, n.p.
19. McCarl, "Ghost Journeys and Phantom Books," 168–69.
20. See "Del doctor Juan Rodríguez de León," in León Pinelo, *Epitome*, n.p.
21. León Pinelo, prologue to the *Epitome*, n.p.
22. León Pinelo, prologue to the *Epitome*, n.p.
23. León Pinelo, *Epitome*, 31.
24. James, *Catalogvs librorvm*; Sweerts, *Athenae Beligcae*.
25. León Pinelo, *Epitome*, 140; James, *Catalogvs librorvm*, 342.
26. León Pinelo, *Epitome*, 160; Sweerts, *Athenae Beligcae*, 347.
27. León Pinelo, *Epitome*, 118–19.

28. León Pinelo's entry is based on Guadalaxara y Xavier, *Quinta parte de la historia pontifical y catholica*, book IV, ch. III, 105–6. Linschoten's text was indeed known to León Pinelo, as he registers it separately in the *Epitome*, 54.
29. León Pinelo, *Epitome*, 44–45. In an example of how problems in the *Epitome* are echoed in other texts, see Seyxas y Lovera, *Piratas y contrabandistas de ambas Indias*, 41, where this error is reproduced.
30. For the history of the Zeno expedition, see Major, Introduction. The original text was first published in 1558. I cite here the English translation by Major in Zeno and Zeno, *Voyages*, 1. For the original, see Ramusio, *Secondo volume delle navigationi et viaggi*, fol. 230, which begins, "Nel mille, & duge[n]to anni della nostra salute." The Ramusio text does not, in fact, propose 1200 as the year of the journey but rather that in which the background story begins, a fact that makes León Pinelo's use of the date even more problematic.
31. See Ludovic, *Grands et petits voyages of De Bry*, 173; and León Pinelo, *Epitome*, 55.
32. Ludovic, *Grands et petits voyages of De Bry*, 151; León Pinelo, *Epitome*, 91.
33. León Pinelo, *Epitome*, 58–60 (Oriental, *título* XVI) and 134–36 (Occidental, *título* XXVII).
34. León Pinelo, *Epitome*, 60.
35. León Pinelo, *Epitome*, 135–36.
36. León Pinelo, *Epitome*, 150.
37. León Pinelo, *Epitome*.
38. León Pinelo, *Epitome*, 150–51.
39. See the repeated references to a "memoria impresa de autores de la India" in León Pinelo, *Epitome*, 58–60.
40. León Pinelo, prologue to the *Epitome*, n.p.
41. Hakluyt, *The Principall Navigations*; Purchas, *Hakluytus Posthumus*.
42. León Pinelo, *Epitome*, 39.
43. Tanselle, "External Fact as an Editorial Problem."
44. I refer, for instance, to the construct of the Cide Hamete Benengeli manuscript in part I, and the apocryphal *Quijote* of Avellaneda in part II, of Cervantes, *Don Quijote de la Mancha*; and such texts by Borges as "Pierre Menard, autor del Quijote," "Examen de la obra de Herbert Quain," and "La biblioteca de Babel," in *Ficciones*.
45. For a definition of the MARC format, see Library of Congress, "MARC Standards."
46. León Pinelo, *Epitome*, 59.
47. León Pinelo, "Catálogo de los autores," in *Epitome*, n.p.
48. León Pinelo, *Epitome*, 72.
49. Fernández de Oviedo y Valdés, *Historia general y natural de las Indias*; López de Gómara, *Historia general de las Indias*; Castellanos, *Primera parte de las elegias de varones illustres de Indias*.
50. Stertzer, "Working with the Financial Records of George Washington."
51. Stertzer, "Working with the Financial Records of George Washington."
52. Stertzer and Cavanaugh, "Creating a Digital Edition of Financial Documents Using Drupal."

Works Cited

Almeyda, Aniceto. Introduction to *Discurso sobre la importancia, forma, y disposición de la Recopilación de leyes de las Indias Occidentales*, by Antonio de León Pinelo, vii–xix. Santiago: Fondo Histórico y Bibliográfico José Toribio Medina, 1956.

Balsamo, Luigi. *Bibliography: History of a Tradition*. Berkeley, Calif.: B. M. Rosenthal, 1990.

Borges, Jorge Luis. *Ficciones*. 1956. Reprint, Buenos Aires: Emecé, 1966.

British Library. "*English Short Title Catalogue*—Content." Accessed November 5, 2016. http://www.bl.uk/reshelp/findhelprestype/catblhold/estccontent/estccontent.html.

Capel, Horacio. Introduction to *Epitome de la bibliotheca oriental, y occidental, nautica, y geografica de don Antonio de León Pinelo... añadido y enmendado nuevamente*, by Antonio de León Pinelo and Andrés González de Barcia Carballido y Zúñiga, viii–xli. Barcelona: Universidad de Barcelona, 1982.

Carlyon, Jonathan. *Andrés González de Barcia and the Creation of the Colonial Spanish American Library*. Toronto: University of Toronto Press, 2005.

Castellanos, Juan de. *Primera parte de las elegias de varones illustres de Indias*. Madrid: En casa de la viuda de Alonso Gomez, 1589.

Cervantes, Miguel de. *Don Quijote de la Mancha*. Edited by John Jay Allen. 2 vols. 1605. Reprint, Madrid: Cátedra, 1992.

Fernández de Oviedo y Valdés, Gonzalo. *Historia general y natural de las Indias*. Seville: Juan Cromberger, 1535.

Guadalaxara y Xavier, Fray Marcos de. *Quinta parte de la historia pontifical y catholica*. Madrid: Por Melchor Sanchez, 1652.

Hakluyt, Richard, ed. *The Principall Navigations, Voiages and Discoveries of the English Nation*. 2 vols. Facsimile of the London 1589 edition. Cambridge: Cambridge University Press, 1965.

James, Thomas. *Catalogvs librorvm*. Oxford: Apud Iosephum Barnesium, 1605.

León Pinelo, Antonio de. *Epitome de la biblioteca oriental i occidental, nautica i geografica*. Madrid: Juan Gonzalez, 1629.

———. *Epítome de la biblioteca oriental i occidental, náutica i geográfica*. 1629. Facsimile of the first edition, with an introduction by Diego Luis Molinari. Buenos Aires: Edición Bibliófilos Argentinos, 1919.

———. *El Epítome de Pinelo, primera bibliografía del Nuevo Mundo*. 1629. Facsimile of the first edition, with an introduction by Agustín Millares Carlo. Washington, D.C.: Unión Panamericana, 1958.

———. *Recopilacion de leyes de los reynos de las Indias*. 4 vols. Madrid: Julian de Paredes, 1681.

León Pinelo, Antonio de, and Andrés González de Barcia Carballido y Zúñiga. *Epitome de la bibliotheca oriental, y occidental, nautica, y geografica de don Antonio de Leon Pinelo... añadido y enmendado nuevamente*. Madrid: F. Martinez Abad, 1737–38.

———. *Epitome de la bibliotheca oriental, y occidental, nautica, y geografica de don Antonio de Leon Pinelo... añadido y enmendado nuevamente*. Facsimile of the augmented 1737–38 edition. Madrid: Gráficas Yagües, 1973.

———. *Epitome de la bibliotheca oriental, y occidental, nautica, y geografica de don Antonio de Leon Pinelo . . . añadido y enmendado nuevamente*. Facsimile of the augmented 1737–38 edition, with an introduction by Horacio Capel. Barcelona: Universidad de Barcelona, 1982.

Library of Congress. "MARC Standards." Accessed November 7, 2016. http://www.loc.gov/marc.

Lohmann Villena, Guillermo. "Fuentes bibliográficas del *Epítome* de Pinelo." *Revista interamericana de bibliografía* 5, no. 3 (1955): 153–64.

———. Introduction to *El gran canciller de las Indias*, by Antonio de León Pinelo, edited by Guillermo Lohmann Villena, vii–clxxxvi. Seville: Escuela de Estudios Hispano-Americanos, 1953.

———. "Un capítulo de eurística peruana: Acotaciones a las fuentes documentales relativas al Perú en el Epítome de León Pinelo." *Revista de Historia de América* 4 (1959): 1–43.

López de Gómara, Francisco. *Historia general de las Indias*. Zaragoça, Spain: En casa de Augustin Milla, 1552.

Ludovic, Earl of Crawford and Balcarres. *Grands et petits voyages of De Bry*. London: Bernard Quartich, 1884.

Major, Richard Henry. Introduction to *The Voyages of the Venetian Brothers, Nicolò & Antonio Zeno, to the Northern Seas, in the XIVth Century*, by Nicolò Zeno and Antonio Zeno. Translated and edited by Richard Henry Major. 1873. Reprint, Works Issued by the Hakluyt Society 50. New York: Burt Franklin, 1964[?].

Manzano Manzano, Juan. *Historia de las Recopilaciones de Indias*. 3rd ed. 2 vols. Madrid: Ediciones de Cultura Hispánica, 1991.

McCarl, Clayton. "Ghost Journeys and Phantom Books: Francisco de Seyxas y Lovera's Elusive Library of Pirates." *Book History* 17 (2014): 165–90.

Medina, Isagani R. *Philippine Items in León Pinelo-Barcia's Epitome 1629 and 1737–38 Editions: A Biobibliographical Study*. Ann Arbor: University of Michigan, Department of Library Science, 1964.

Medina, José Toribio. *Biblioteca Hispanoamericana, 1493–1810*. 7 vols. 1898–1907. Reprint, Santiago: Fondo Histórico y Bibliográfico José Toribio Medina, 1958–62.

———. "Estudios biobibliográficos sobre Antonio de León Pinelo." In *Discurso sobre la importancia, forma, y disposición de la Recopilación de leyes de las Indias Occidentales*, by Antonio de León Pinelo, 5–136. Santiago: Fondo Histórico y Bibliográfico José Toribio Medina, 1956.

Millares Carlo, Agustín. Introduction to *El Epítome de Pinelo, primera bibliografía del Nuevo Mundo*, by Antonio de León Pinelo, viii–xlii. Washington, D.C.: Unión Panamericana, 1958.

———. *Tres estudios biobibliográficos*. Maracaibo, Venezuela: Universidad del Zulia, 1961.

Molinari, Diego Luis. Introduction to *Epítome de la biblioteca oriental i occidental, náutica i geográfica*, by Antonio de León Pinelo. Buenos Aires: Edición Bibliófilos Argentinos, 1919.

Palau y Dulcet, Antonio. *Manual del librero hispano-americano*. 2nd ed. 28 vols. Barcelona: Librería Anticuaria de A. Palau, 1948.

Pierazzo, Elena. "A Rationale of Digital Documentary Editions." *Literary & Linguistic Computing* 26, no. 4 (2011): 463–77.

Pollard, A. W., et al., *A Short-Title Catalogue of Books Printed in England, Scotland, & Ireland and of English Books Printed Abroad 1475–1640*. 2nd ed. 3 vols. London: Bibliographical Society, Oxford University Press, 1896.

Porras Barrenechea, Raúl. Introduction to *El paraíso en el Nuevo Mundo*, 2 vols., by Antonio de León Pinelo, 1:iii–xlv. Lima: Imprenta Torres Aguirre, 1943.

Purchas, Samuel. *Hakluytus Posthumus, or, Purchas his Pilgrimes*. 20 vols. 1624–25. Reprint, Glasgow: J. MacLehose and Sons, 1905–7.

Ramusio, Giovanni Battista. *Secondo volume delle navigationi et viaggi*. Venice, 1583.

Sabin, Joseph. *A Dictionary of Books Relating to America*. 29 vols. 1868. Reprint, Amsterdam: N. Israel, 1961–62.

Sánchez Bella, Ismael. Introduction to *Recopilación de las Indias*, 3 vols., by Antonio de León Pinelo, 1:17–64. Mexico City: Escuela Libre de Derecho, 1992.

Seyxas y Lovera, Francisco de. *Piratas y contrabandistas de ambas Indias, y estado presente de ellas (1693)*. Edited by Clayton McCarl. A Coruña, Spain: Fundación Pedro Barrié de la Maza, 2011.

Stertzer, Jennifer. "Working with the Financial Records of George Washington: Document vs. Data." *SDH–SEMI 2012 Conference Proceedings. Digital Studies / Le champ numérique*. http://doi.org/10.16995/dscn.57.

Stertzer, Jennifer, and Erica Cavanaugh. "Creating a Digital Edition of Financial Documents Using Drupal." Paper presented at the Annual Conference of the Association for Documentary Editing, New Orleans, L.A., August 4–6, 2016.

Sweerts, Pierre-François. *Athenae Beligcae*. Antwerp: Apud Gulielmum Atungris, 1628.

Tanselle, G. Thomas. "External Fact as an Editorial Problem." *Studies in Bibliography* 32 (1979): 1–47. http://www.jstor.org/stable/40371693.

Torre Villar, Ernesto de la. *Antonio de León Pinelo y la primera bibliografía de América*. Supplement to *Anuario* 1986–87 of the Seminario de Cultura Mexicana. Mexico City, 1988.

Wing, Donald Goddard, et al. *Short-Title Catalogue of Books Printed in England, Scotland, Ireland, Wales, and British America, and of English Books Printed in Other Countries, 1641–1700*. 4 vols. New York: Modern Language Association of America, 1994–98.

Zeno, Nicolò, and Antonio Zeno. *The Voyages of the Venetian Brothers, Nicolò & Antonio Zeno, to the Northern Seas, in the XIVth Century*. Translated and edited by Richard Henry Major. 1873. Reprint, Works Issued by the Hakluyt Society 50. New York: Burt Franklin, 1964[?].

9

Do Borges's Librarians Have Bodies?

ZAC ZIMMER

Quizás la historia universal es la historia de la diversa entonación de algunas metáforas.

[Perhaps universal history is the history of the diverse intonation of a few metaphors.]

—JORGE LUIS BORGES, "PASCAL'S SPHERE"

As early as 1960, Jorge Luis Borges himself had noted there no longer existed just one being named "Borges."[1] By the mid-1990s, yet another version of the Argentine author had arrived to the world: Borges the precursor to cyberspace. Interpretations of several of Borges's stories proliferated, not only in literary criticism but also in media studies, technology studies, and new media art. One key touchstone in this line of interpretation has been "The Library of Babel." This chapter will investigate different imaginings and visualizations of Borges's Library as a precursor of the internet. As will become apparent, most of the new media interpretations of Borges operate in a dematerialized register, especially as it relates to the bodies of the Librarians in the Library. I will argue that a renewed focus on body, subject, and place will rescue Borges's story from techno-utopian and new media discourses that have dematerialized "The Library of Babel."

Many of the new media visualizations of Borges's Library prioritize the mathematical and architectural elements of the story, and share a special emphasis on communicating the existential terror of the infinite. This is normally done at the expense of the story's other details, most notably the mundane experiences of the Librarians who inhabit the Library of Babel. The Librarians very rarely appear, for instance, in the many and varied attempts to visualize "The Library of Babel" in digital media. It would seem that Borges's Librarians themselves are absolutely incorporeal. The case of the vanishing Librarians parallels another trend in current technological discourse: a techno-utopian tendency to erase and ignore the particularities of human flesh (meat, body) in the celebration of a newly transcendent virtuality. By returning critical attention to the Librarians who exist within the Library, this chapter asks Borges's Librarians what lessons they can teach us on how to exist in data space as embodied beings. Along the way, I will enlist the help of Bill Viola, whose key question *will there be condominiums in data space?* will flesh out my central inquiry: do Borges's Librarians have bodies?

My task here is not to reinsert the rhythms of Argentine Tango into this particular reading of "Borges the internet precursor,"[2] nor is it to fact-check the mythical foundation of new media studies, but rather to insist on a different kind of materialistic account of "The Library of Babel." Borges equated the universe and the Library back in 1941, when "library" meant something like *brick and mortar construction filled with codex and other material.* Yet somehow one of the most unambiguously textual materialist thinkers of the twentieth century became both prophet of the internet (in the 1990s, as codified in the *New Media Reader*) and prophet of the posthuman (as witnessed by recent critical anthologies like *Cy-Borges: Memories of the Posthuman in the Work of Jorge Luis Borges*). The thing that has been most taken for granted in Borges's Library has become one of the most pressing issues in contemplating the future of media and the future of the species: the body, the librarian, the reader. Beatriz Sarlo reminds us that the only possible activity in the Library is the search for a written sign.[3] But who is doing the searching?

A History of Borges Visualizing the Internet, or Ted Nelson and His Precursors

> Incapable by now of distinguishing between divine omnipotence and the possible omniscience of a perfect combinatorial language handled by man . . .
> — UMBERTO ECO, "BETWEEN LA MANCHA AND BABEL"

In a recent review essay, Andrew Brown proposes a useful concept for thinking about Borges: the Borges-hrönir. Hrönir are those metaphysical materialities that pop up in the later part of Borges's story "Tlön, Uqbar, Orbis Tertius." They are trinkets from the imaginary world, Tlön, that have begun to appear unexpectedly on Earth. Borges defines them as "the duplication of lost objects," but they could also be described as game pieces in Borges's staged battle between nominalist and realist philosophy.[4] Much like those cyclically repeated objects, the Borges-hrönir is the periodic re-creation of Borges by his critics: "we have duplicating criticism that appear, all independent copies of an original in which searchers find that for which they were looking."[5]

It would seem that taking Borges out of context is a prerequisite for any scholarly engagement with the Argentine storyteller, especially given that the celebrated Borges scholar Daniel Balderston titled one of his monographs *Out of Context*. (It does not hurt that Borges's own oeuvre authorizes and encourages that kind of interpretation, even if Balderston's project is to recover a historical and materialist reading of Borges from his more speculative and philosophical commenters.) Nowhere is this more apparent than in the Borges-hrönir that new media studies creates. Borges has ascended to a canonical position in that field, so much so that he is one of the two major thinkers who frame the entire *New Media Reader*.[6] Borges's textual labyrinths have been famously and continuously celebrated as precursors to the internet, and it is to that version of Borges that I now turn my attention.

The introductory sections of the *New Media Reader* posit a structural dichotomy that serves as the scaffolding for the entire volume and, by extension, for media studies in general: the dichotomy between the philosopher and the engineer. The intersection of these two impulses is considered a fork, in the sense of Borges's "The Garden of Forking Paths." Each fork receives a proper name: Borges himself, the storyteller-librarian; and Vannevar Bush, the soldier-scientist.[7] This is, perhaps, the humanist way of phrasing C. P. Snow's 1959 "Two Cultures" argument; in any case, the introductory materials that precede many of the subsequent contributors will locate the authors in relationship to that fork. Murray, in a nod to Borges's "Kafka and His Precursors," absolves this dichotomy of the apparent anachronism: "Bush, of course, is not thinking about the 'computer'—and neither is Borges. Instead they are inventing fantasy information structures—a book-garden-maze, a desk-library-machine—that reflect not a new technology but a change in how our minds are working."[8]

Given his key role in positing the memex—the invention Murray describes as *desk-library-machine*—Vannevar Bush's contribution to new media studies is clear; yet how is it that a short-story writer and librarian from Argentina who died three years before Tim Berners-Lee developed HTTP has become the yin to the analog computer scientist Bush's yang? In another introductory essay, Nick Montfort expands on this unlikely inclusion.

> Borges was no hacker; ... but computers do not function as they do today *only* because of the playful labor of hackers or because of planned-out projects to program, develop, and configure systems. Our use of computers is also based on the visions of those who, like Borges ... saw those courses that future artists, scientists, and hackers might take.[9]

The new media Borges, then, is a visionary, one who not only "predicts" new media but whose imaginings have created a virtual blueprint of the internet's architecture. In Ciccoricco's estimation, "Borges' fictions quickly became superlative examples of hypertextual prototypes, digital fictions ... on the printed page."[10]

The Borges-hrönir who emerges in the pages of the *Reader* appears to have written three stories: "Tlön, Uqbar, Orbis Tertius"; "The Garden of Forking Paths"; and "The Library of Babel." This is not the Borges who authored, for instance, *Evaristo Carriego* or *Fervor de Buenos Aires*, those early celebrations of a vanishing Buenos Aires full of knife fights and *truco*.[11] If the story *The Aleph* is mentioned, the focus is on the single point that condenses all space and time, not on the location of a particular staircase in the basement of a house on Garay Street, nor on Beatriz Viterbo's obscene correspondence.

Yet from just those three stories spring forth several of the main tropes that new media theory investigates. It is as if each story posed a unique but related question about new media and data space. "Tlön" complicates the boundary between the real and the virtual. "The Garden of Forking Paths" teaches its readers how to navigate a hyperlinked space. "The Library of Babel" contemplates the size and scope of dataspace, and wonders how such a space might be organized. The *Reader* reproduces only "The Garden of Forking Paths," but the Garden and the Library have become conflated into an amalgamated vision called *Borges, precursor of the internet*, much like Borges's two different maps from "On Rigor in Science" and "Partial Magic of the *Quijote*" have been conflated into "the Borges map that contains itself."

Many new media practitioners and theorists invoke this Borges. Stuart Moulthrop's "Victory Garden" (included on the CD-ROM that accompanies the *Reader*) is a hypertext homage to Borges, and in his essay on Ted Nelson, Moulthrop specifically compares Nelson's *Xanadu* to the "great hypertextual Library of Babel."[12] Umberto Eco, in a keynote address titled "Between La

Mancha and Babel," repeats the idea that Borges's hypertextuality trained his readers to anticipate networked reading.[13] In all these examples, the hypertextual Garden and the textually infinite Library merge together.

Other media theorists stick closer to the text of these individual stories themselves, as when N. Katherine Hayles uses Borges's Library to make the important point that order is not the same as meaning, or when James Gleick concludes *The Information* by explicitly invoking the Librarians running their fingers along the shelves of the Library of Babel.[14] In a strange twist, some literary theorists even abandon the contents of the Library entirely. Umberto Eco, for instance, reminds readers that Borges's primary concern was never a library but rather infinite, universal, and total knowledge, an omniscience against which any particular book would seem impotent. Eco challenges Borges's readers to recall a few of the titles named within "The Library of Babel." The fact that most readers can't name a single tome makes Borges's Library of a very particular sort; almost everyone who has read Cervantes, for instance, can name at least one or two of the volumes in Don Quixote's library.[15]

"The Library of Babel" has also attracted the attention of mathematicians, who are especially interested in that story's attempt to visualize the ontological terror of infinity.[16] As William Goldbloom Bloch has noted, the ease with which one can note the number of books in the Library betrays the unimaginable magnitude of that number.[17] Bloch outlines a relatively straightforward calculation using scientific notation, yet to actually complete the computation and transcribe the digit would require an enormous amount of computational power and page space: the digit is larger than the estimated number of atoms that compose our universe. Floyd Merrell highlights this as well when he notes that it is less taxing on the mind to imagine an infinite universe than it is to imagine the Library itself. Merrell is as much a fan of paradoxical inversions as Borges, and his postulate that the universe is a condensed metaphor of the Library echoes the opening line of Borges's story.[18]

When it comes to the Librarians themselves, Merrell turns to the second law of thermodynamics, the entropy principle, to interpret their presence in the story. For Merrell, the Librarians represent a pure subjective perspective that exists only to contemplate "a statistical conglomerate, the meaninglessness of which is practically absolute."[19] The Librarians, it seems, are rather disposable. Merrell is not alone in "disappearing" the Librarians: in most of the mathematical and new media accounts of the Library, the Librarians' human bodies might as well be ants crawling along the infinite twist of a Möbius strip.

When the Library's magnitude and geometry are called upon to act as an imaginary architectonics of the internet, the Librarians disappear as embodied beings. While such accounts are fascinating, and further evidence of a certain universality inherent in much of Borges's writing, they sacrifice a particular and important component of the narrative.[20] The new media interpretation identifies the reader as the protagonist of the story, but this at the expense of understanding the Librarians themselves as characters. This phenomenon is even more immediately visible in the remediated attempts to render Borges's Library in visual or virtual form.[21]

The density of Borges's prose complicates any attempt to visually represent the Library. This has led to some confusion, as Antonio Toca Fernández describes in a series of articles.[22] Indeed, Borges corrected the story in a later 1959 edition, changing the geometric description of the hexagonal cells in response to comments from readers. The visualizations accordingly vary based on the edition consulted.[23] None of the images that Toca Fernández reproduces show a single librarian; this is in line with his general interpretation of the story, which reads architecture itself to be the true protagonist (see figure 9.1).[24]

Toca Fernández's visualizations are representative of the broader trends in the architectonic or mathematical visualizations. These images use the diagram

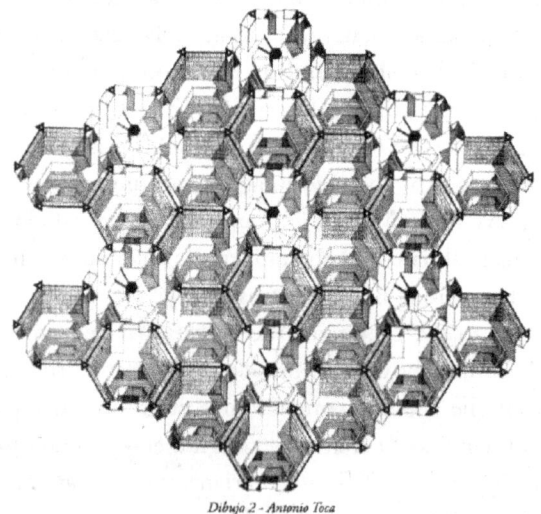

Dibujo 2 - Antonio Toca

FIGURE 9.1 Antonio Toca Fernández, "La biblioteca de Babel," 2009. © Antonio Toca Fernández.

to work out the ambiguities Toca Fernández highlights: the number of shelves on each wall; the number of walls versus the number of doorways that compose the exterior of each hexagon; how the hexagons communicate with one another; and the precise locations of the spiral stairways, the lavatories, and the upright sleeping chambers. An early computer graphics representation at the website HyperDiscordia seems to have been influential in many subsequent versions, and emphasizes the "hall of mirrors" effect (see figure 9.2), while an illustration from a French periodical piles the hexagonal cells into stacks reminiscent of Xul Solar's utopian towers crossed with Bruegel's 1563 *Little Tower of Babel*.[25] A Brazilian researcher created a version of the Library in the 3-D modeling program SketchUp that includes the Librarians, but as abstract shadows, more corporeal placeholders than rendered beings.

Very rarely are the Librarians imagined or represented in ways that reflect the various emotional states narrated in the story itself. There are, of course, exceptions. Some of the most notable are Erik Desmazières's etchings. In Desmazières's beautiful flights of Enlightenment fancy, the Librarians appear studious, reasonable, and quite free of the growing existential dread that haunts Borges's story.[26] While these illustrations are clearly inspired by the story, they do not bring the meticulous diagrammatic attention that has captivated Borges's architectural or mathematic illustrators, and when the Librarians do appear, they are of a very different mindset than that described on the written page. For

FIGURE 9.2 HyperDiscordia, "The Library of Babel," n.d.

Desmazières, the Library is the culmination of the Enlightenment. This differs from many of Borges's more philosophical interpreters, who view the Library's vastness as a high-minded parody of Enlightenment rationality.

Andrew DeGraff's "Library of Babel" chapter in *Plotted: A Literary Atlas* is a much more faithful representation of the existential mindset. DeGraff renders three "plots," each of which correspond to one of the three views he identifies in the story: the individual cell, the knowable world for a typical librarian, and the God's-eye view of the entire universe. The first image is a schematic diagram, accordingly, of a cell; the second illustrates the librarian's world and the story as "philosophical essay," while the third image visualizes the "existential horror story," where man, the imperfect librarian, disappears into a hexagonal abyss.[27] DeGraff's triptych suggests that the progression from the cloistered cell to the infinite expanse is the story's true plot; in that case, the reader him or herself would be the story's protagonist. Borges asks directly: "You, who read me now, are you certain you understand my language?"[28]

The perspective of "You who read me now" has come to dominate the interactive electronic versions of the Library, which culminate in Jonathan Basile's libraryofbabel.info. Basile's website does away with 3-D bookshelves and passageways, instead attempting to render digital manifestations of the contents of each page of every volume in the Library. His unique contribution to the history of the Library-inspired website is the interface. As with previous sites like the now-defunct "Tlön's Library of Babel Simulation," You-the-Librarian can pull up any randomly generated page, but Basile's site allows you to browse the Library with the ease of teleportation.[29] While Borges's Librarians must travel on foot through hexagonal cells and spiral stairways, you can simply click your way around while a backend algorithm seamlessly churns through pseudo-random numbers to offer up endless pages of the twenty-five orthographic symbols.[30] Even more disconcerting is that Basile has included a search feature so that You can locate the precise occurrences of specific strings of characters. For instance, the website tells me that on page 286 of the volume titled *hboonokjndmy*, the ninth book on the first shelf of the first wall of a uniquely identified hexagonal cell (whose unique ID is itself 3,254 characters long), I will find one of the approximately 10^{29} instances of the phrase "oh tiempo tus piramides" surrounded by an otherwise blank page.[31] And yet I could spend a lifetime refreshing my web browser and never once stumble randomly upon any of those 10^{29} pages. The immediate effect of libraryofbabel.info mimics the despair of the Librarian; its ultimate, lasting effect gestures toward an absolute dehumanization. Basile's desired effect is to overwhelm with irrationality, and he ties this irrationality to the hexagonal cells through the image of the beehive: "Bees have represented, throughout a vast history of thought, a society highly organized and hierarchized yet devoid of reason."³² The Library is a honeycombed beehive, and the Librarians are mindless drone-bees: "The random creation of the library's texts shows that even the most complex achievements of human 'reason' are equally possible without any animating consciousness or any intention-to-signify at all."³³ This image could not be further from Desmazières's salon-dwelling Renaissance men. Basile's is perhaps the most absolutely dehumanizing of all Library visualizations, in that beyond being driven to suicidal madness or philosophical resignation, his Librarians have become as devoid of meaning as the gibberish-filled books themselves.³⁴

The vast majority of these visualizations, as should now be clear, fall into one of three categories: those that erase the Librarians' presence; those that plop down generic faceless Librarians to fill an otherwise empty space; and finally, those that directly interpolate the reader as Librarian, with the goal of existentially obliterating the reader into a jumbled mess of incomprehension. Why is it so easy, when the task at hand is to meditate on Borges's Library as a thought-image of dataspace, to discard the Librarians themselves? And, more importantly, how can a different reading of the story—one that pays attention to the embodied Librarians—help reinsert the body and the subject into the technological and new media discourses that have dematerialized "The Library of Babel"?

Posthuman Librarians

> The sin against the body—it was for that they wept in chief; the centuries of wrong against the muscles and the nerves, and those five portals by which we can alone apprehend—glozing it over with talk of evolution, until the body was white pap, the home of ideas as colourless, last sloshy stirrings of a spirit that had grasped the stars.
> — E. M. FORSTER, "THE MACHINE STOPS"

Basile's Librarian-Bee is a clear example of the dematerialized Librarian: the reader becomes an unmarked, unexceptional drone-reader. Neil Badmington understands this bodiless librarian to be an attack on the humanist subject in the Cartesian tradition. A traditional library, Badmington asserts, "conventionally confirms the humanist subject for which it exists. Order orders."[35] Borges's unconventional Library does not confirm the humanist subject but rather unsettles him. To return to Hayles: Order is not the same as meaning. Order can exist independent of a knowing human subject, who "orders" space only by imposing a humanist meaning: "If it were an Order, it would remain one that disorders the security and identity of humanism, for, if the Order only presents itself to an *eternal* traveler, it must be an Order of the infinite. This strikes me as a shattering paradox for the finite humanist subject, simply because the eternal traveler could not possibly be human."[36] Badmington's essay is one of several contributions to *Cy-Borges: Memories of the Posthuman in the Work of Jorge Luis Borges* that imagine Borges's *ficciones* as examples of "a posthumanism without technology."[37] This critical posthumanist line of inquiry takes as its mantra Hayles's invitation: "I see the deconstruction of the liberal humanist subject as an opportunity to put back into the picture the flesh that continues to be erased in contemporary discussions."[38] The Library is a bad, spurious infinity, and the Librarians are dashed upon its frontier, clinging to tattered liberal humanist beliefs like so much intellectual flotsam and jetsam. The melancholy Librarians teach us through their unhappy examples to abandon our pretensions to a rational, ordered, and above all *meaningful* universe. At the very least, critical posthumanist readers can marvel at the paradoxes contained within the Library, even as those paradoxes annihilate the liberal humanist subject.

But there is another line of inquiry that spins out of the *New Media Reader* paradigm, a posthumanism that retains the transcendent subject of Cartesian dualism while leaving behind the body. It is postbody and fully transcendent: thus *transhumanism* of the kind critiqued by Sherryl Vint, which attempts to transmute the entire human experience into information. In transmuting the entire human experience into information, it becomes very easy to forget that *bodies matter*. This is why one should follow in the spirit of Doris Sommer's advice and proceed with caution when engaging the posthuman. In order to assure that You, the Reader, are following a critical posthumanist—and not a techno-utopian transhumanist—line of inquiry, you must be clear in your own thinking whether the *human* will become some other kind of embodied subject, or whether, alternatively, the *human* will be transcended through a separation of flesh and mind, and a transubstantiation into virtuality.

If *human* names a given amalgamation of particularities (for instance: the *white property-owning cisgendered heterosexual male* who so dominates the liberal humanist imaginary), then posthumanism would define itself against those universalized particularities. But if, conversely, *human* names the being that changes and adapts, then I think posthumanism is a misnomer, a self-negating attempt to supersede the very things—desire, technology, and an adaptable body—that most define our species. We are the being who self-consciously claims as its own the otherwise illusory power to define and change itself, both in body and in species-being. As Vint explains in *Bodies of Tomorrow: Technology, Subjectivity, Science Fiction*:

> It is important to return to a notion of embodied subjectivity in order to articulate the ethical implications of [bodily] technologies. Technological visions of a post-embodied future are merely fantasies about transcending the material realm of social responsibility....
>
> The only viable posthumanism is one that goes back to the liberal humanist subject and starts anew, moving beyond the exclusions of the false universality of the humanist self and beyond the moral vacuity of the excessive individualism of the liberal self.[39]

As Vint and others have argued, transhumanism, like many of liberalism's other ideologies, is a juvenile fantasy based on a particular claim of false universality. That troublesome claim is made in a two-step move. First, uncritical liberal humanism posits a particular body type as ideal. Second, technological transhumanism proclaims the immanent transcendence of that idealized body type. Nonconforming bodies become doubly erased: at first, they are historically and materially excluded by an abstract liberal humanist discourse (slave-owning misogynists proclaiming *All men are created equal*, for instance); Wendy Brown describes this as difference disappearing into neutral standard of the same.[40] Then those bodies are told that, in fact, the body no longer matters, as it is simply a matter of time before consciousness is uploaded to the cloud.

It is high time for us as a species to figure out how to exist as material bodies in cyberspace, as beings who exist in meat space *and* data space. Bodies matter. That sentence condenses the wisdom of Isaac Newton and Donna Haraway, of Judith Butler and Albert Einstein. In the service of this task, Borges's Library can serve as a beta user's guide to bodies in dataspace. But like all beta versions, it is an incomplete user's guide, for its users are still very narrowly conceived. Borges's readers become very invested in whether the *knowledge* contained in the Library is representative of human experience, usually at the expense of an attention to whether the *bodies* in the Library are representative of human experience. If we redirect this attention to the Librarians themselves, new trends emerge.

Beyond their clear duty of attending to the books and the hexagons, I have found six general characteristic behaviors of the Librarians. They satisfy their physical necessities and they travel, sometimes arduous distances. They theorize their environment on multiple scales. They express a small range of deeply felt emotions. They reproduce across generations, although it is unclear how. Finally, they theologize their environment through myths. Many Librarians seek personalized *Vindications*: the singular tome that will impose a narrative, and a true meaning, upon their lives.[41] This search has been recognized as futile for as long as the narrator can recall, although knowledge of the search's ultimate futility has done little to discourage the searchers.

The Library is adapted to allow for "the physical necessities," but it is certainly the Librarians' three-dimensional travel across the hexagonal cells and along the spiral staircases that allow for even the most rudimentary theorizations of the space (see figure 9.3a and b).[42] Early on, an announcement rings through the corridors and stairwells: "The Library contains all books."[43] In response, the Librarians form ideological sects based on their locations in the Library, and the different sects begin to diverge linguistically. This linguistic localization is regional; the many accents and dialects vary across space, which

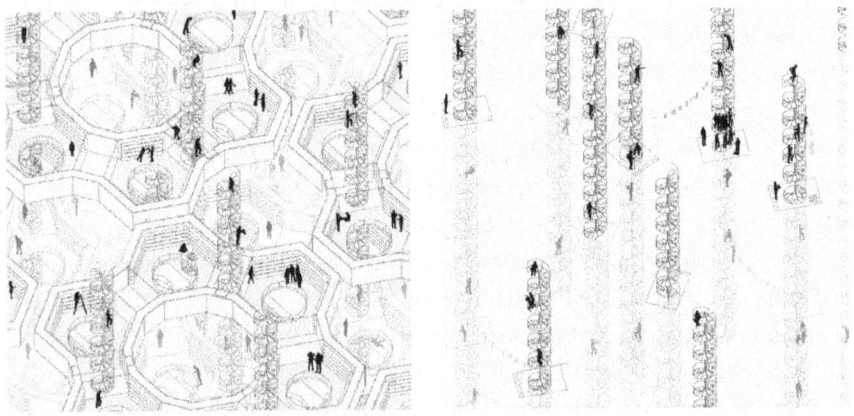

FIGURE 9.3A AND B "The Universe" (*left*) and "Travelers and Inquisitors" (*right*), 2013. © Rice+Lipka Architects. Images courtesy Rice+Lipka Architects.

would properly be called "bibliographic space" since the *geo* of the Library's geography is *biblios*, "of the book."

The bibliographic revelation that the Library contains all books inspires some of the story's most strongly expressed emotions. The Librarians feel an initial joy, which compels them, as noted above, on the vain quest to find their *Vindications*. Some Librarians despair, which leads to violence and murder among themselves. Alas, the Library is not free of crime, although most motives can be traced back to fits of the characteristic "hygienic, ascetic rage" that periodically overcomes the Librarians.[44] Others devote themselves to antiquated sects while hidden in the water closets, where they clandestinely match the throw of dice to the pages of an apocryphal divination text. Love is notably absent from their emotional repertoire, as is bodily desire (unless these are included in the "physical necessities"—*necesidades finales*—attended to in the water closets). The narrator mentions a father, but the mechanics of reproduction are obscure, especially since there is no mother to speak of.

The total exclusion of female Librarians begs the question: is the Library a space of genderless reproduction? At the very least it is dominated by masculine reading practices, emphasizing mastery over pleasure. Are the *bibliotecarias* specifically excluded, or simply erased? Perhaps the *bibliotecarias* are silent wives, hidden within the "two-person single career" phenomenon that Barbara Tedlock discusses in regard to anthropologists. In Tedlock's examples of twentieth-century anthropologist couples, "the affected women are not only muted, in that their work is subsumed into the corporate body and identity of their husbands, but their presence in the field is often unacknowledged."[45] Borges's Librarians are readers of culture, much like Tedlock's anthropologists; do the *bibliotecarias* follow around the Librarians with notepads, tea cakes, and a reading lamp? Or perhaps the Library only exists in the gaze of the Librarians, while other female bodies perceive the space as completely "other," as a jungle, or a spaceship. The difficulty involved in imagining female librarians moving through the Library in full "bodily involvement and maternal nurturing" is symptomatic of a gendered space, and when Borges's Library is "ported" to the internet, masculinity is hard-coded into the build.[46]

Beyond these hidden gender politics, the Library is governed more by theology than any form of political or civil society. Death is ceremonial, as Tristán Bauer's film *Los libros y la noche* (*The Books and the Night*, 1999) illustrates with a terrifying scene of the Library's traditional "burial" rights. Librarians hoist their defunct colleague over the short railing into the abyss between hexagonal cells: "When I am dead, compassionate hands will throw me over the railing; my tomb will be the unfathomable air, my body will sink for ages, and will decay and dissolve in the wind engendered by my fall, which shall be infinite."[47] Other than pneumonia and the stray strangulation, suicide is the leading cause of death, a statistic that casts a macabre glow over the bibliography. Even the officially appointed searchers, the *Inquisitors*, are mere transients, arriving to new cells with a resigned exhaustion and departing again after merely flipping through a few pages of the nearest book. The source of their authority is opaque, but that authority is sovereign enough to define and ban blasphemous sects while cursing their names. The most notorious of these sects, whom the narrator calls the fanatical *Purifiers*, roamed the Library and destroyed any books they did not comprehend, and all books they judged unnecessary. Their act of destructive purification was perhaps even more pointless than the *Inquisitors'* searching, since even though "every volume is uniquely irreplaceable, there are always several hundred thousand imperfect facsimiles, other tomes who only differ by a single letter or comma."[48]

As the Librarians do not read for pleasure, and are baffled by their universe and its contents, all eventually turn to despair. They are indeed philosophically exhausted as they ponder the innumerable hexagons, but they are far from static. Some ceaselessly wander the corridors; others attack and destroy the very books that compose their universe. They find solace in crafting mythologies. These myths and theologies (the differences between the two are adjudicated by the *Inquisitors*) vary in depth and complexity. The most basic are youthful cults who kiss undecipherable books and bow in illiterate worship. Others attempt a more positivistic theologization of their environment through cryptographic interpretations, while the mystics resort to dream analysis and cabbalistic speculation. "The Book Man" is the Library's monotheistic deity: he who has read the catalog of catalogs, and accordingly ascended to divine status. And yet all these theologies and mythologies are but mere distractions to the fact that "the human species—the *only* species—teeters on the verge of extinction."[49] An infinite universe whose only conceivable purpose is to confound the finite beings who dwell within it: it is a realization that occurs only where flesh meets mind, where Librarian ponders Library, where a mortal body exists within an incomprehensible data space. Barrenechea has expressed the paradox with grace: Borges conjures the madness-inducing nightmare of the infinite within the confines of the finite human imagination.[50]

Viola, Visualization, and Vindication

> Thus we have been witnessing two seemingly contradictory projects of "embodying" the spirit: one actually reducing it to the body as traditionally (i.e., biophysically) understood, the other upgrading the body to the traditional (i.e., cultural-theological) status of "spirit."
> — EDUARDO VIVEIROS DE CASTRO, *COSMOLOGICAL PERSPECTIVISM*, 117

The question of the Librarians' bodies, then, unfolds into a profound attempt to imagine an embodied data space. How do these bodies perceive, and what do they experience in the Library? An analogous question is ostensibly the topic of Bill Viola's "Will There Be Condominiums in Data Space?," reprinted in the *New Media Reader*. Viola is a video installation artist who creates "total environments that envelop the viewer in image and sound," exploring "sense perception as an avenue to self-knowledge."[51] Viola works in the mystical register, and he has dedicated pieces to San Juan de la Cruz, Rumi, and other figures from a variety of spiritual traditions. As an early experimenter with video technology, Viola helped legitimize a new artistic medium. His persistent engagement of embodied sense perception and his insistence on massive physical installations set him apart from other new media artists of his generation, and earned his enigmatic essay on "Data Space" a slot in the *New Media* anthology.

Although I have not found anywhere that Viola refers explicitly to Borges, we might say that Borges is the camel to Viola's Koran.[52] In another essay, "The Porcupine and the Car," included in *Reasons for Knocking at an Empty House*, Viola describes a failed art project that resonates with one of Borges's favorite themes. Viola had come into the possession of a large number of spare audio cassette tapes. His vision was to "create a sort of stream-of-consciousness parallel world to the present, but displaced in time."[53] The first step in the project was to record all sonic activity in his home on those tapes. After accumulating a full day's worth of audio, Viola had a revelation.

> I would need 24 hours, exactly the time it took to record, to play all this stuff back. Furthermore, if I kept this up, say, for a year, I would have to stop after six months to begin playing back, and if I got really ambitious and made it my life's work, I would have to stop my life when it was only half over to sit down and listen to all the material for the rest of my life, plus a little additional time for rewinding

all the cassettes. It was a horrible thought, so I took down my tape recorder and immediately stopped the project.[54]

The artist's terror when confronted by the sublimely banal accumulation of sensory data–paired with the realization that the project would all at once be boring, dehumanizing, and impossible—resolves him to abandon the endeavor.

In "Funes el memorioso," Borges tells a similar tale. Funes, the story's protagonist, suffers a childhood accident that graces him with total recall (while leaving him crippled and immobilized). Not only does Funes remember every single event; he remembers every single perception, so that it is a struggle for him to understand why two different image-impressions of a dog at different times of the day, or at different angles, are regarded as the same being. Inspired (or tormented, as the case may be) by the same muse that spoke to Viola, Funes

> resolved to reduce every one of his past days to some seventy thousand recollections, which he would then categorize by numbers. Two considerations dissuaded him: the realization that the task was interminable, and the realization that it was pointless. He saw that by the time he died he would still not have even finished classifying all the memories of his childhood.[55]

The specter of mortality haunts both of these tales. Funes's implacable memory registered his every single perception, yet his perfect doubling of experience is meaningless to all others, and vanished with his bodily death.[56] In a moment of resignation, Funes declares, "My memory, sir, is like a garbage heap."[57] Perhaps Viola was thinking of Funes when he called video archives "a sort of magnetic city dump."[58] In any case, the sentiments are analogous. Whether the sensory data is recorded in memory or on magnetic tape, its expansive proliferation robs the material of meaning, and any attempt to order the chaos would subsume and negate the life of the very subject doing the ordering.

In attempting to reproduce what it *feels like* to inhabit a particular space of perception, Viola's art runs the risk of duplicating the very world itself. Borges's literary aesthetics confronts this challenge directly. To return to the "Library of Babel": those innumerable, nonsensical tomes exist *within* a space.[59] Viola's "Will There Be Condominiums in Data Space" helps bring this to the surface.

> The interesting thing about idea spaces and memory systems is that they presuppose the existence of some sort of place, either real or graphic, which has its own

structure and architecture. There is always a whole space, which already exists *in its entirety*, onto which ideas and images can be mapped, using only that portion of the space needed.[60]

As the Library's narrator postulates: *The Library has existed ab aeterno*. But Viola does not go so far as Borges's narrator. Viola proclaims that the *need* to install ideas and memories into a place is universal, but the architectures of such spaces—whether material or virtual—vary across historical, cultural, and spiritual traditions. His essay is his attempt to interpret that tendency, while his video installations are aesthetic creations meant to push the viewer up to the limits of such constructed spaces. The titular question *will there be condominiums in data space?* asks the reader to consider the specifics of constructed virtual space through the question of dwelling. It prepares the reader for Viola's embodied meditation on infinite virtual worlds by insisting on a seemingly incongruous thing: a condominium.

The main concern of the essay, however, has little to do with real estate. Viola is ultimately interested in the meeting of body and spirit, although in proper mystical fashion he uses riddles to express and explore this theme. He focuses the bulk of his attention on how the merging of computer and video technologies will change aesthetic possibilities for artists and perception for viewers. "The eye," Viola says, "is being reattached to the brain."[61] This is not only a technological change but a perceptual change as well. (Accordingly, artists are as necessary as engineers, to return to the *New Media Reader*'s structuring dichotomy, since media technologies change the very structure and function of mind itself.)

Thus *data space* implies not only the storage space for digital information but also the perceptual and psychic space of its inhabitants.[62] In order to map the point where information meets perception, Viola turns to Indian Tantric doctrine, specifically the relationship between the anthropomorphic image, the geometric energy diagram (or *yantra*), and the sonic representation (*mantra*). These three different spiritual/aesthetic forms are all equal outward expressions of the same underlying thing: the place where the material and immaterial collide.[63] He gives examples: the memory palaces evoked by Francis Yates's study *The Art of Memory* as anthropomorphic images, the branching or matrix diagrams of database structures as mandalas or yantra, and the sonic environments of his own installations as mantra. Visual and sonic representations merge with abstract mental diagrams to create the contours of virtual space. Data space is both information *and* practice, body *and* spirit, sensory stimulation *and* sense organs. Its map must orient the archive of knowledge but also the repertoire of bodily practice and performance.[64] Viola's essay closes with a warning: "development of self must precede development of the technology or we will go nowhere—there *will* be condominiums in data space."[65]

Borges's Library, and the many diagrams and images that have sprung from its pages, are glimpses of what condominiums in data space might look like. They all represent an ordered space that completely lacks human scale and meaning, spaces constructed for the bare minimum of human body. The Librarians will never transcend the Library, nor will an individual Librarian ever find her or his *Vindication* (other than in death). The Librarians will never become books; there is an unbridgeable gap between life and volume, and yet body and text exist only and exclusively in relationship to one another. The refusal to accept this truth will only lead to annihilation. This is how to interpret the enduring image of an expired body hurling through the infinite void of the Library's empty space. Borges's story is an invitation to think the very thing the total Library seeks to erase. What is the space of data space? Where are the bodies? This, perhaps, can be Borges's true contribution to visualizing the internet: Borges is always, in Sarlo's words, a writer on the edge, on the periphery. *The Aleph* is always located in an unassuming basement on Garray Street. *The Book of Sand* is always hidden within the Biblioteca Nacional on Calle México in Buenos Aires. Borges's stories always map the universal pretensions of philosophical paradoxes onto the cartographies of marginal places. To ignore these particular geographies, or the bodies contained within them, is to reduce the Library to nothing more than a bland repeating series of frivolous hexagonal condominiums.

Notes

An early version of this research was presented in 2016 at the Latin American Studies Association conference in Lima, Perú; thanks to Anita Say Chan for including me in the multipanel session on Latin American Digital Humanities. The chapter epigraph is a translation by Eliot Weinberger from Borges, *Selected Non-fictions*, 353. I have provided published translations when available; all other translations are mine unless otherwise indicated.

1. "Borges and I," in Borges, *Collected Fictions*, 324.
2. To do so would be to ignore one of Borges's profound insights: "The Argentine cult of local color is a recent European cult that nationalists should reject as foreign import." Borges, "The Argentine Writer and Tradition," in Borges, *Selected Non-fictions*, 423.
3. Sarlo, *Borges, un escritor en las orillas*, 165.

4. "Tlön, Uqbar, Orbis Tertius," in Borges, *Collected Fictions*, 77. See Fishburn, "Digging for Hrönir"; and Zamora, "Borges' Poetic Objects."
5. J. Brown, "Retasking Borges," 238.
6. The *New Media Reader* (2003), edited by Noah Wardrip-Fruin and Nick Montfort, was the first attempt by MIT Press to develop a canon for the emerging fields of new media art and criticism. Its impact has been profound. David Ciccoricco also comments on the centrality of Borges to the *Reader*; his "Borges, Technology, and the Same Infinite Substance as the Night" is an attempt to rescue literature, and a literary Borges, from what I am calling the new media Borges-hrönir. For other new media readings of Borges's Library, see Bolter, "Interactive Fiction"; Boulter, "Partial Glimpses of the Infinite"; Hoyos, "Review"; Lapidot, "Borges"; Rowe, "The New Library"; and Tuckey, "The Imaginative Mathematics."
7. Murray, "Inventing the Medium," 3–5.
8. Murray, "Inventing the Medium," 3.
9. Montfort, "Introduction," 29–30.
10. Ciccoricco, "Borges, Technology, and the Same Infinite Substance as the Night," 77–78.
11. For critical readings of *that* Borges, see Sarlo, *Borges, un escritor en las orillas*.
12. Moulthrop, "You Say You Want A Revolution?," 6.
13. Eco, "Between La Mancha and Babel," 61.
14. Hayles, "Subversion," 151–52; Gleick, "After the Flood," 397.
15. Eco, "Between La Mancha and Babel," 52.
16. Castellón Serrano, "Letizia, Borges y el infinito," 504.
17. Bloch, *Unimaginable Mathematics*, 22.
18. Merrell, "The Universe as Library," 128. "The Library of Babel" memorably begins, "The Universe (which others call the Library) . . ." Borges, *Collected Fictions*, 112. Much of Merrell's textual analysis, which is on the whole a vindication of the imaginative thought experiment as the science of the nonempirical, seems to own a profound debt to Barrenechea's *La expresión de la irrealidad en la obra de Borges*, although that book is only cited twice, and in translation.
19. Merrell, "The Universe as Library," 129–32. Bloch has a related interpretation of the Library and the Librarian together embodying "a Turing machine, running an unimaginable program whose output can only be interpreted by a godlike external observer. A user. A reader." Bloch, *Unimaginable Mathematics*, 125.
20. My understanding of "embodiment" relies on N. Katherine Hayles's definition, articulated in "The Materiality of Informatics": "Embodiment never coincides exactly with 'the body,' however that normalized concept is understood. Whereas the body is an idealized form that gestures toward a Platonic reality, embodiment is the specific instantiation generated from the noise of difference" (196). Hayles is Borges's most inspired reader in the Anglophone new media tradition.
21. On remediation, see Bolter and Grusin, *Remediation*.
22. See Toca Fernández, "La biblioteca de Babel," in addition to his 1984–85 articles cited therein.

23. In the article, Toca Fernández himself offers Borges one additional, albeit posthumous, copyedit, with the elegantly gentle suggestion that "this variation, as simple as it seems, would clarify some confusion that I am certain that Borges would not have wanted in his arbitrary universe" (78).
24. Toca Fernández, "La biblioteca de Babel," 79.
25. See HyperDiscordia, "The Library of Babel," http://hyperdiscordia.crywalt.com/library_of_babel.html; and Jean-François Rauzier, *Bibliotheque Babel*, 2016, http://hyper-photo.com/selection/04_selection-bibliotheques_12-bibli-babylon/index.html.
26. See Desmazières's drawings in the 2000 edition of Borges, *The Library of Babel*.
27. DeGraff, "Infinite Intelligence."
28. Borges, "The Library of Babel," in *Collected Fictions*, 118.
29. "Tlön's Library of Babel Simulation" is no longer hosted on the original server, but it can be accessed via Mark Marino's "Marginalia in the Library of Babel" project.
30. As readers of "The Library of Babel" will remember, one of the two fundamental axioms of the Library is "There are twenty-five orthographic symbols." Borges, *Collected Fictions*, 113.
31. See Basile, https://libraryofbabel.info/bookmark.cgi?hboonokjndmy286; the Library does not contain written accent marks, thus "piramides" instead of "pirámides."
32. Basile, "Why Hexagons pt. 2," https://libraryofbabel.info/theory2.html. "The most important experience the library can offer us is that of being overwhelmed by irrationality." Basile, "Grains of Sand," https://libraryofbabel.info/theory4.html.
33. Basile, "Why Hexagons pt. 2."
34. One additional group of artists, whom Garrett Stewart has named the bibliobject artists, deserves its own separate essay. These artists use Borges's Library as inspiration for media-specific installations. Many of these works were collected in a 2007 University of Iowa show curated by Buzz Spector titled *One More Thing Added to the World: The Borges Effect in Contemporary Artists' Books*. These book artists tend to turn the Library's paradoxes inward, not toward a regressive subjectivity driven mad by spurious infinity but rather into the materiality of the book object itself. Perhaps the most mind-bending manifestations of bibliobject art are Matej Kren's instalations *Book Cell* (Centro de Arte Moderna, Lisbon, 2006) and *Passage* (City Gallery, Bratislava, 2004), both of which give architectural form to the subjective and psychological elements of Borges's Library. On these installations, see http://www.matejkren.cz/cs/book-cell/ and http://www.matejkren.cz/cs/passage/, respectively. See also Spector, ". . . One More Thing"; and Stewart, *Bookwork* and "Lector/Spector."
35. Badmington, "Babelation," 65.
36. Badmington, "Babelation," 65–66.
37. Herbrechter and Callus, *Cy-Borges*, 27.
38. Herbrechter and Callus, *Cy-Borges*, 149, along with several other references across the edited volume.
39. Vint, *Bodies of Tomorrow*, 8, 13.
40. See W. Brown, *States of Injury*.

41. Would one Librarian's Vindication be the opaque, indecipherable jumbles that make up an identity's digital trace in the mediascape? Would it be a transcription of an individual's atmospheric impressions within the carbon footprint? Would it be an archaeological account of an individual's detritus fossilized in the anthropocene? All of these and more, a multi-tome Vindication? Who, in these scenarios, are the librarians?
42. Borges, "The Library of Babel," in *Collected Fictions*, 112. Another illustration in the Rice+Lipka series also diagrams the physical "necessities"; see Bernheimer and Bernheimer, "Fairy Tale Architecture."
43. Borges, "The Library of Babel," in *Collected Fictions*, 115.
44. Borges, "The Library of Babel," in *Collected Fictions*, 116.
45. Tedlock, "Works and Wives," 269–70. Borges's own meditation on anthropology and universal knowledge is best captured by his short story "El etnógrafo." It is a deeply masculine portrait of the limits of language at the encounter with the Other. See Borges, *Collected Fictions*, 334–35.
46. Tedlock, "Works and Wives," 271. Borges is not the only author used to such ends in the *New Media Reader*, but the editors also include other contributors like Critical Art Ensemble and Donna Haraway who privilege the body as a site of technological experience and knowledge.
47. Borges, "The Library of Babel," in *Collected Fictions*, 112.
48. Borges, "The Library of Babel," in *Collected Fictions*, 116.
49. Borges, "The Library of Babel," in *Collected Fictions*, 118.
50. Barrenechea, *La expresión de la irrealidad en la obra de Borges*, 60.
51. Bill Viola, "Artist's Bio," accessed May 14, 2018, http://www.billviola.com/biograph.htm.
52. "Gibbon observes that in the Arab book *par excellence*, the Koran, there are no camels; I believe that if there were ever any doubt as to the authenticity of the Koran, this lack of camels would suffice to prove that it is Arab." Borges, "The Argentine Writer and Tradition," in Borges, *Selected Non-Fictions*, 423.
53. Viola, "The Porcupine and the Car," in *Reasons for Knocking*, 59.
54. Viola, "The Porcupine and the Car," in *Reasons for Knocking*, 59.
55. Borges, "Funes the Memorious," in *Collected Fictions*, 136.
56. In a coincidence that is almost certainly intentional, Funes—like many of the deceased Librarians—ultimately succumbed to a fatal respiratory infection.
57. Borges, "Funes," in *Collected Fictions*, 135.
58. Viola, "History, 10 Years, and the Dreamtime," in *Reasons for Knocking*, 125.
59. In the final footnote to "The Library of Babel," Borges refers to an idea he will explore in a later story, "The Book of Sand": a single volume with infinitely thin pages that, in essence, contains every possible page of the Library between its covers. The story narrates how that book ended up in Buenos Aires' national library, creating yet another *mise en abyme* within a specific and peripheral library.
60. Viola, "Will There be Condominiums in Data Space?," in *Reasons for Knocking*, 100.

61. Viola, "Condominiums?," in *Reasons for Knocking*, 106.
62. Recall Vint's warning about reducing embodied subjectivity to just one more common piece of "information."
63. Viola, "Condominiums?," in *Reasons for Knocking*, 107.
64. Taylor, *Archive and Repertoire*.
65. Viola, "Condominiums?," in *Reasons for Knocking*, 110.

Works Cited

Badmington, Neil. "Babelation." In *Cy-Borges: Memories of the Posthuman in the Work of Jorge Luis Borges*, edited by Stefan Herbrechter and Ivan Callus, 60–72. Lewisburg, Penn.: Bucknell University Press, 2009.

Balderston, Daniel. *Out of Context: Historical Reference and the Representation of Reality in Borges*. Durham, N.C.: Duke University Press, 1993.

Barrenechea, Ana María. *La expresión de la irrealidad en la obra de Borges*. Buenos Aires: Paidós, 1967.

Basile, Jonathan. *The Library of Babel*. Accessed May 14, 2018. https://libraryofbabel.info.

Bauer, Tristán, dir. *Los libros y la noche*. 1999; Ennetbaden, Switzerland: Trigon-Film, 2008. DVD.

Bernheimer, Kate, and Andrew Bernheimer. "Fairy Tale Architecture: The Library of Babel." *Places Journal*, December 2013.

Bloch, William Goldbloom. *The Unimaginable Mathematics of Borges' Library of Babel*. Oxford: Oxford Univeristy Press, 2008.

Bolter, Jay David. "Interactive Fiction: Borges and Exhaustion in Print." In *Writing Space: The Computer, Hypertext, and the History of Writing*, 137–39. Mahwah, N.J.: Lawrence Erlbaum Associates, 1991.

Bolter, Jay David, and Richard Grusin. *Remediation: Understanding New Media*. Cambridge, Mass.: MIT Press, 1999.

Borges, Jorge Luis. *Collected Fictions*. Translated by Andrew Hurley. New York: Penguin, 1998.

———. *The Library of Babel*. Illustrated by Erik Desmazières. Translated by Andrew Hurley. Boston: David R. Godine, 2000.

———. *Selected Non-fictions*. Edited by Eliot Weinberger. Translated by Esther Allen, Suzanne Jill Levine, and Eliot Weinberger. New York: Penguin, 1999.

Boulter, Jonathan Stuart. "Partial Glimpses of the Infinite: Borges and the Simulacrum." *Hispanic Review* 69, no. 3 (2001): 355–77.

Brown, J. Andrew. "Retasking Borges: Technology and the Desire for a Borgesian Present." *Variaciones Borges* 28 (2009): 231–40.

Brown, Wendy. *States of Injury: Power and Freedom in Late Modernity*. Princeton, N.J.: Princeton University Press, 1995.

Castellón Serrano, Alberto. "Letizia, Borges y el infinito." *Boletín de la Real Academia de Extremadura* 16 (2008): 503–29.

Ciccoricco, David. "Borges, Technology, and the Same Infinite Substance as the Night." In *Cy-Borges: Memories of the Posthuman in the Work of Jorge Luis Borges*, edited by Stefan Herbrechter and Ivan Callus, 73–87. Lewisburg, Penn.: Bucknell University Press, 2009.

DeGraff, Andrew. "Infinite Intelligence." In *Plotted: A Literary Atlas*, 84–89. San Francisco: Pulp Books, 2015.

Eco, Umberto. "Between La Mancha and Babel." *Variaciones Borges* 4 (1997): 51–62.

Fishburn, Evelyn. "Digging for Hrönir: A Second Reading of 'Tlön, Uqbar, Orbis Tertius.'" *Variaciones Borges* 25 (2008): 53–67.

Forster, E. M. "The Machine Stops." In *Collected Short Stories*, edited by David Leavitt and Mark Mitchell, 91–123. New York: Penguin, 2002.

Gleick, James. "After the Flood: A Great Album of Babel." In *The Information: A Theory, a History, a Flood*, 373–97. New York: Pantheon, 2011.

Hayles, N. Katherine. "The Materiality of Informatics." In *How We Become Posthuman*, 192–221. Chicago: University of Chicago Press, 1999.

———. "Subversion: Infinite Series and Transfinite Numbers in Borges's Fiction." In *The Cosmic Web: Scientific Field Models and Literary Strategies in the Twentieth Century*, 138–67. Ithaca, N.Y.: Cornell University Press, 1984.

Herbrechter, Stefan, and Ivan Callus, eds. *Cy-Borges: Memories of the Posthuman in the Work of Jorge Luis Borges*. Lewisburg, Penn.: Bucknell University Press, 2009.

Hoyos, Héctor. "Review of *Cy-Borges*." *Comparative Literature Studies* 48, no. 4 (2011): 593–96.

Lapidot, Ema. "Borges Between the Printing Press and the Hypertext." In *Jorge Luis Borges: Thought and Knowledge in the XXth Century*, 327–51. Frankfurt: Iberoamericana Editorial Vervuert, 1999.

Marino, Mark. "Marginalia in the Library of Babel." Accessed May 14, 2018. http://markcmarino.com/diigo/webarchive_org_tlon_simBabel.html.

Merrell, Floyd. "The Universe as Library." In *Unthinking Thinking: Jorge Luis Borges, Mathematics, and the New Physics*, 103–32. West Lafayette, Ind.: Purdue University Press, 1991.

Montfort, Nick. "Introduction: The Garden of Forking Paths." In *The New Media Reader*, edited by Noah Wardrip-Fruin and Nick Montfort, 29–30. Cambridge, Mass.: MIT Press, 2003.

Moulthrop, Stuart. "You Say You Want a Revolution? Hypertext and the Laws of Media." *Postmodern Culture* 1, no. 3 (1991).

Murray, Janet H. "Inventing the Medium." In *The New Media Reader*, edited by Noah Wardrip-Fruin and Nick Montfort, 3–11. Cambridge, Mass.: MIT Press, 2003.

Rowe, Christopher. "The New Library of Babel? Borges, Digitisation, and the Myth of the Universal Library." *First Monday* 18, no. 2 (2013).

Sarlo, Beatriz. *Borges, un escritor en las orillas*. Buenos Aires: Ariel, 1998.

Spector, Buzz. ". . . One More Thing Added to the World . . . : The Borges Effect in Contemporary Artists' Books." *Variaciones Borges* 24 (2007): 167–72.

Stewart, Garrett. *Bookwork: Medium to Object to Concept to Art.* University of Chicago Press, 2011.

———. "Lector/Spector: Borges and the Bibliojet." *Variaciones Borges* 24 (2007): 173–96.

Taylor, Diana. *The Archive and the Repertoire: Performing Cultural Memory in the Americas.* Durham, N.C.: Duke University Press, 2003.

Tedlock, Barbara. "Works and Wives: On the Sexual Division of Textual Labor." In *Women Writing Culture*, edited by Ruth Behar and Deborah A. Gordon, 267–81. Berkeley: University of California Press, 1995.

Toca Fernández, Antonio. "La biblioteca de Babel: Una modesta propuesta." *Casa del tiempo* 2, no. 24 (2009): 77–80.

Tuckey, Curtis. "The Imaginative Mathematics of Bloch's Unimaginable Mathematics of Borges' Library of Babel." *Variaciones Borges* 30 (2010): 1–12.

Vint, Sherryl. *Bodies of Tomorrow: Technology, Subjectivity, Science Fiction.* Toronto: University of Toronto Press, 2007.

Viola, Bill. *Reasons for Knocking at an Empty House: Writings 1973–1994.* Cambridge Mass.: MIT Press, 1995.

Viveiros de Castro, Eduardo. *Cosmological Perspectivism in Amazonia and Elsewhere.* HAU Masterclass Series 1. Manchester: HAU Journal of Ethnographic Theory, 2012.

Wardrip-Fruin, Noah, and Nick Montfort, eds. *The New Media Reader.* Cambridge Mass.: MIT Press, 2003.

Yates, Frances A. *The Art of Memory.* Chicago: University of Chicago Press, 1966.

Zamora, Lois Parkinson. "Borges' Poetic Objects." Section 2 of *Swords and Silver Rings: Objects and Expressions in Magic Realism and the New World Baroque.* University of Houston, n.d. Accessed May 14, 2018. http://www.uh.edu/~englmi/ObjectsAndSeeing_2.html.

10

Between Street and Book

Textual Assemblages and Urban Topologies in Graphic Fiction from Brazil

EDWARD KING

THE GRAPHIC NOVEL FORM OCCUPIES an important position in the contemporary media ecology in Latin America, which is characterized by increasing fluidity between genres, producers, and consumers as well as between textual, visual, and audio media. In a study of what he calls "late book culture" in Argentina, Craig Epplin examines the porous and constantly mutating boundaries between books and the "volatile media landscape" in which "the ways readers gain access to written words, the nature of the assemblages that connect books to other media and the very definition of the book seem to be in a state of flux."[1] Media culture is in a period of transition between print and the digital world in which the "status of the book as a literary medium is increasingly uncertain."[2] It is in this context of transition and instability that the graphic novel has risen to prominence across Latin America, receiving ever-increasing critical and popular attention. The production of visually and conceptually sophisticated book-length comics has risen dramatically across the region with areas of especially intense production emerging in Mexico, Chile, Uruguay, and Brazil. These publications have thrived in the cracks of the edifice that Ángel Rama once called "the lettered city," the historical conjunction between the written word and political power in the region.[3] As Héctor Fernández L'Hoeste and Juan Poblete argue, comics in Latin America have long occupied an interstitial space between elite literary and popular visual cultures and as such became important vehicles for national-popular imaginaries throughout the twentieth century.[4] In the context of neoliberal globalization, they have become a point of contact between national-popular and "international popular" cultures.[5] The most popular genres of graphic novel published in the region have explored this point of contact, whether it be through popularizations of literary texts (in 2012 the Mexican comics publishers Editorial Resistencia published a graphic version of Manuel Payno's 1891 novel *Los bandidos de Río Frío*) or the parodying of North American genre conventions (such as the satire of postmodern science fiction in *Planeta Extra* [2009] by Argentine artists Diego Agrimbau and Gabriel Ippóliti). Graphic novels also often position themselves within what Epplin describes as the "assemblages" of texts and readers produced by a rapidly changing media ecology, tapping into the networks of fans and modes of readership made possible by digital technologies.[6] Comics and graphic novel creators in Brazil, the focus of this chapter, have been particularly active in using the form to explore intersections between literary and popular cultures (for example, Fábio Moon and Gabriel Bá's 2007 adaptation of the Machado de Assis short story "O alienista") as well as between local aesthetic traditions and global genres (in *Estórias Gerais* [2007] Wellington Srbek and Flávio Colin revisit the genre conventions of the Western through a visual style reminiscent of the popular book-block printing techniques used in the northeast of the country).

Comics and graphic novels have also become more prominent objects of interest for literary and visual culture studies that are increasingly interested in the study of texts in relation to the discursive and material networks that subtend them. Yasco Horsman connects the rise of critical interest in the graphic novel form with a change in the humanities from "a study of works as self-contained texts to a (self-aware) attentiveness to their roles in various transmedial networks."[7] Due to their constitutive intramedial connections between word and image coupled with their tendency to become vehicles for narratives that develop across different media platforms (which Henry Jenkins terms "transmedia narratives"), graphic fictions are laboratories for experimentations with connections between media.[8] Jan-Noël Thon, meanwhile, ascribes "graphic narrative" a position of central importance to the emerging discipline of what he calls "transmedial narratology," a critical approach that has become necessary due to a "highly interconnected media landscape," which has been shaped by "the move of media conglomerates from vertical to horizontal integration."[9] The comics industries in Latin America have been quick to make use of transmedial strategies. For example, in 2015 Maurício de Sousa Produções in Brazil, the most popular creators of childrens' comics in the region, launched a series of anime spin-offs for their teen series *Turma da Mônica Jovem*, which started in 2008.[10] However, most intermedial experimentations have emerged from independent collaborations, such as that between André Diniz and photographer Maurício Hora in *Morro da Favela* (2011) and the connections between electronic music, art performance, and comic books forged in Edgar Franco's multimedia science fiction universe "Aurora pós-humana" (started in 2004 and ongoing).

This chapter focuses on the connections between street art and comic book textuality staged in the 2015 graphic novel *Zé Ninguém*, part of the ongoing street comics project by Alberto Serrano, the graffiti artist known as Tito na Rua (Tito on the Street). *Zé Ninguem* performs a parallel between the assemblages that connect books to other media and an urban context that is composed of assemblages connecting local actions and events with global flows of images as well as human with nonhuman forms of agency. The book is composed of photographs of a series of street art interventions by Serrano onto walls, doorways, and underpasses in the city of Rio de Janeiro, all of which revolve around a homeless character called Zé. Serrano produced almost 150 pieces in isolated spots in and around the city, from the prosperous Leblon neighborhood in the Zona Sul to the Comlexo da Maré favela in the Zona Norte. The book's photographs turn the street art pieces into panels, which are then assembled into a narrative that recounts Zé's search for his lost love Ana and his battle against a multinational pharmaceuticals company that ruined his life. In what follows, I argue that the intermedial textuality of the project performs a topological conception of the city of Rio de Janeiro, characterized by a mutual imbrication of virtual and material space. The Tito na Rua project builds on the tradition of comics in Latin America to contribute to the demise of the power edifice of the lettered city; it constructs a perspective on life in Rio de Janeiro that decenters human subjectivity by placing it in relation to locally and globally connected networks of human and nonhuman agency.

Urban Topologies and Comic Books

Serrano's book *Zé Ninguém* stages a complex interface between the street comics and the textuality of the graphic novel. On the one hand, it could be argued that the book form produces an effect of containing the excesses of graffiti practice within the strictures of print. The street comics are "read" by the inhabitants of the city of Rio de Janeiro in a partial, fragmentary, and nonlinear way. According to this interpretation, whereas reading the street comics is embodied and carried out in movement (from the vantage point of a passing bus or while walking along a street), reading the graphic novel is disembodied and static. No one experience of reading the street comics is the same, since there is no prescribed order and, due to the constitutive evanescence of graffiti, some works disappear soon after they are produced. The book, by contrast, imposes an order on the different image-texts, which have now been transmuted into panels. Furthermore, the book form attempts to package the transitory experience of the street comics as a commodity. To use Michel de Certeau's terms, which have been central to a number of scholars' conceptualization of the transgressive textuality of street writing, whereas graffiti is a "tactic," the book form is a "strategy." Andrea Mubi Brighenti, in his discussion of graffiti in Italy, argues that walls in cities are "strategies" of power "aimed at controlling people and their activities by means of a control of space," which graffiti writers "subject to tactical uses."[11] Tactics denaturalize workings of power by drawing them into the foreground and using them against the grain of their strategic intentions. The producers and consumers of street comics exist at the level of what de Certeau describes as "the ordinary practitioners of the city . . . whose bodies follow the thicks and thins of an urban 'text' they write without being able to read it"; a text, that is, that "elude[s] legibility."[12] Following this line of argument, the genre of the graffiti book would be considered a strategy in that it encourages a controlled, detached perspective on street art and carries out a form of disciplinary domestication of street writing, reducing it from an experience or process to a form of visual art. *Zé Ninguém* recontextualizes the street works and arranges them into the grid structure of the comic form. In the process, it appeals to the "scopic drive" of the "totalizing eye" by "mak[ing] the complexity of the city readable, and immobiliz[ing] its opaque mobility in a transparent text."[13] By producing a book version of the Tito na Rua street comics, its makers could be accused of fetishizing the visual end product of graffiti and in the process obscuring graffiti as a practice that brings together an assemblage of bodies and material and is part of an ongoing transformation of city space. Jeff Ferrell points out that with the growing trend of coffee-table books on the work of individual artists, graffiti and street art "com[e] unstuck from their situations of production" and as a result "become free-floating signifiers, increasingly available for inclusion in advertising campaigns, public service announcements, television shows, and films."[14] The production of books such as *Zé Ninguém* could be viewed as part of a wider process of gentrification in which graffiti and street art "are used as valuable markers of urban desirability and vitality."[15] This process has been particularly visible in Brazil, where, in March 2009, the federal government passed a law that makes street art on buildings and monuments legal if it is done with the consent of the owners.

However, a closer look at the specific textuality of the graphic novel reveals that its relationship with the street comics project is not one of containment (imposing linearity on nonlinear reading paths), stability (fixing the movement intrinsic to the reading experience of street comics), and dematerialization (from unprogrammed embodied instantiations of the narrative to the ideal text implied by the editing process). By inserting the photographs of Alberto Serrano's street art interventions into the textual arrangements of the graphic novel, the book draws attention to the topological assemblages that constitute urban space. Jason Dittmer and Alan Latham explore the connection between the production of space both on and off the comics page and examine the "symmetry" between the formal properties of graphic narrative and recent theoretical accounts of space as "not a thing but a performance" that is "emergent through the relations between different entities."[16] As opposed to topographical understandings of space, grounded in the fixities of Euclidean geometry, the topological perspective is interested in figures in processes of change. In her analysis of topological constructions of the city in Hollywood cinema, Anna Secor defines topology in contrast to a topographical understanding of space. Topographical approaches are grounded in "discrete points, regions, or territories."[17] By contrast, topology "deals with surfaces and their properties, their boundedness, orientability, decomposition, and connectivity"—that is, sets of properties that retain their relationships under processes of transformation—and is "defined in terms of processes and relations."[18] Rob Shields argues that only topology provides an adequate vocabulary for conceptualizing the distributed and decentralized workings of power in the digital age. Conceptual commonplaces for thinking about globalization, such as David Harvey's "time-space compression," evoke not Euclidean space but a "rubber sheet geometry" that "is only possible in an elastic topological space."[19] Dittmer and Latham argue that space in comic books is also a relational entity. It is emergent from a multiplicity of connections between pages, panels, images, and words both within and outside the text. The production of space in the comic follows the "plurivectorial" process of reading, a term that comics scholar Thierry Groensteen uses to describe the way the reader is encouraged to "weave" paths through the text, making connections between and within panels that are not reducible to the linear progression of the plot.[20] Comic texts, Dittmer and Latham argue, can be likened to the experience of art installations in that they encourage readers to think critically about space as relational and in a state of constant becoming rather than a fixed, given entity.

The structure of *Zé Ninguém* produces the conditions for the reader to make connections between and among the panels in a way that mirrors the nonlinear reading experience of the street comics. The way the narrative overlays the physical space of the city produces a dynamic that pulls against the grain of the progressive sequentiality of the panels. Readers familiar with the streets, buildings, and underpasses that form the material substrate of the images make connections between their locations. These connections set up a constant underlying tension with the narrative. Rather than constituting a fixed map of the city in a way that "immobilizes its opaque mobility," the project renders it mobile by producing topological folds in urban space. By placing in sequence images that were taken at different points (and at different times) in the city, *Zé Ninguém* resembles the crumpled handkerchief, Michel Serres's metaphor for topological space. Just as the urban text of the street comics haunts the reading experience of *Zé Ninguém*, the graphic novel haunts the streetwalker's experience of Serrano's street art interventions by evoking the specter of connections with multiple other points in the city.

The connections forged by the book exist in a virtual relation to the individual works. In this respect, the relation of the book to the street comics resembles that of "augmented reality" technologies that in an age of mobile computing increasingly mediate our experience of urban space. Mark Graham, Matthew Zook, and Andrew Boulton use the term to conceptualize the way in which urban experience is increasingly the product of an "indeterminate, unstable, context dependent . . . material/virtual nexus mediated through technology, information and code, and enacted in specific and individualized space/time configurations."[21] The connection between street-level experience and the information accessed via augmented reality technologies is recursive since this information is constantly updated to reflect new experiences.[22] The relationship between the street comics and *Zé Ninguém* is also recursive since the graphic novel provides narrative for the individual artworks seen on the street, while the physical placement of the artworks in the street comics sets up a tension with the linear construct of the narrative by the graphic novel readers.

Rather than an anomaly, the recursive connections between Tito na Rua's street comics project and the graphic novel draw attention to the way in which much street art now exists in conjunction and dialogue with its "extensions" in other globally networked media, in particular through the internet. Increasingly, graffiti and street artists produce work to be photographed and posted online. The demands of online platforms, whether it is the photo-sharing app Instagram or a street art forum, actively shape the work rather than merely providing a neutral vehicle for it. Artists increasingly produce images that are easily "shareable" and "tagable." Ferrell argues that "this widespread digitization of graffiti and street art does more than record actions and images, and elongate their presence; it feeds back into the very process through which such actions and images unfold, and alters their essential meaning."[23] Global media networks such as Instagram not only influence the distribution of graffiti but increasingly shape its aesthetic, complicating at its root the notion of street art as a local embodied experience. Since the works preempt the logic of "tagability," the local consumption of these works at the street level is always shot through with the global. The connective logic of social media is thematized in *Zé Ninguém*. Zé is only reunited with Ana when a selfie with a street cleaner becomes an internet meme and goes viral. In one panel, the street cleaner is shown attaching a series of hashtags to the image while in a later panel he is depicted triumphantly exclaiming, "Nossa selfie bombou!" (Our selfie has gone wild!).[24] Furthermore, the ecological message carried by the narrative (which is discussed later in this chapter) functions as a metaphor for the global connectivity of the media ecology.

One of the dangers of the genre of the graffiti book is that the editing process risks effacing the multifarious materiality of the work on the street in the name of producing the ideal work. In her discussion of shifting modes of textuality from print culture to the digital age, N. Katherine Hayles argues that texts have been thought of as essentially immaterial entities in the dominant modes of textual criticism in the humanities for the last two centuries. Debates about copyright in the eighteenth century "elided or erased material and economic considerations ... in favor of an emphasis on literary property as an intellectual construction that owed nothing to the medium in which it was embodied."[25] Although this privileging of the immaterial has been repeatedly challenged by movements such as futurism and imagism, "the long reign of print made it easy for literary criticism to ignore the specificities of the CODEX book when discussing literary texts."[26] The definition of editing complicit with this notion of the literary work is conceived as a process of convergence on the ideal work. Hans Zeller argues that "the editor searches in the transmitted text for the one authentic text, in comparison with which all else will be a textual corruption."[27] The danger that the conception of the ideal text will be reinforced in the production of *Zé Ninguém* is all the stronger considering the ephemerality of the source material. Once the works on the street have faded or been painted over, the book will survive as a lasting testimonial to their ideal incarnations. However, the way in which *Zé Ninguém* is edited places an emphasis on the materiality of both the graffiti and the graphic novel. In her introduction to the book, the editor Renata Nakano draws a parallel between how the specific materiality of books is frequently ignored through the persistence of certain print conventions and how familiarity renders buildings, trees, and street corners invisible as we follow habitual routes through the city on a daily basis. Just as we fail to notice "as pequenas diferenças de cada dia" (the small everyday differences) in the city, the book becomes transparent through familiarity: "O livro é um objeto familiar a todos nós. Tão familiar que já não percebemos sua singularidade. . . . Essa familiaridade transforma o livro em algo transparente, que não se vê" (The book is a familiar object to all of us. So familiar that we no longer notice its singularity. . . . This familiarity transforms the book into something transparent, which we do not see).[28] Graffiti, she goes on to point out, is a practice that renders the invisible materiality of the city visible. It highlights walls the city inhabitants take for granted and draws attention to the interstitial gaps that normally go unseen: concrete motorway partitions and underpasses inhabited by the homeless.

The graphic novel *Zé Ninguém* echoes the process of rendering visible the invisible corners of the city not only through the narrative focus on the homeless, which is discussed later in this chapter, but also through its structure. Like graffiti, the graphic novel is a medium that draws attention to its own materiality. The overt incorporation of paratextual design elements into the construction of meaning is a common strategy in graphic novel production. As Charles Hatfield explains in his discussion of the work of Chris Ware and other artists emerging from the North American indie comics scene, "many comics make it impossible to distinguish between text per se and secondary aspects such as design and the physical package, because they continually invoke said aspects to influence the reader's participation in meaning-making."[29] The graphic novel incorporates into its structure the preexisting but equally artificial divisions in the built environment of Rio de Janeiro. The interplay between the street art and the context of the graphic novel medium repeatedly draws attention to the role of central structuring elements such as panel and page. This is principally achieved through the inconsistency of structuring strategies and the layering of framing devices. The frames of panels are provided by the edges of city walls and doorways, the camera, ink-drawn borders on the page, and the edges of the page itself. Often, these frames are layered over one another. In the first few pages of the narrative proper, the image of the protagonist Zé is depicted on the concrete columns supporting the network of roads around the city's downtown bus station, Terminal Rodoviário Novo Rio (see figure 10.1). The images that appear in the book function through a double framing. The columns frame the individual images of Zé together with speech bubbles and thought balloons. The camera frames the column together with the surrounding environment to place Zé in the context of the bus station and to depict him together with other inhabitants of the city. Some pages capture two figures on separate columns (for example, Zé and his dog), creating the effect of two different panels in the same photograph (see figure 10.2). When Zé and his dog chase after a pigeon that has taken his last 100 reais note, the action is depicted in several stages across the same wall. The different moments in time are not separated by panel divisions

FIGURE 10.1 Zé lost near the Terminal Rodoviário Novo Rio. Detail from Tito na Rua [Alberto Serrano], *Zé Ninguém* (Rio de Janeiro: Edições de Janeiro, 2015), 15. Image courtesy of Alberto Serrano.

FIGURE 10.2 Zé in search of his dog. Detail from Tito na Rua [Alberto Serrano], *Zé Ninguém* (Rio de Janeiro: Edições de Janeiro, 2015), 19. Image courtesy of Alberto Serrano.

in a way that evokes screen fold or tapestry techniques.[30] At other points, the use of panel borders is part of the street artwork itself and not just the result of its subsequent textual emplacement. These panels sometimes follow preexisting divisions. For example, a sequence in which Zé uses a remote-controlled helicopter to chase the pigeon is painted over a gateway that is divided into nine equal sections. Serrano divides these sections into three differently sized panels (see figure 10.3). Elsewhere, panel borders are painted over blank walls. However, although these walls are often whitewashed, their textures always show through the artwork in the form of outlines of bricks or weeds breaking through walls. The intermedial connections that haunt both the street comics and the graphic novel reinforce the emphasis on materiality by highlighting the constraints that govern both media. Hatfield's focus on the influence of the physical package of comics and graphic novels on the reading experience is part of a wider turn toward the haptic in comic book scholarship. Ian Hague, for example, argues that the readers of comics and graphic novels do not interact with the texts at the level of the visual alone. Rather, the reading experience is

FIGURE 10.3 Zé building a pigeon-catching robot. Detail from Tito na Rua [Alberto Serrano], *Zé Ninguém* (Rio de Janeiro: Edições de Janeiro, 2015), 33. Image courtesy of Alberto Serrano.

a "performance" that involves the whole body: "The physicality of comics, their embodiment, is a crucial element of what they are and what they can be; how they do work and how they could work."[31] The emphasis on the textures of the surfaces visible beneath Serrano's painting encourages the reader of *Zé Ninguém* to connect this to the materiality of the graphic novel.

The use of divisions in the physical structures of the city as panel borders within the graphic novel evokes connections between urban space and comic book form made by a number of critics. The essay collection *Comics and the City* explores various ways in which the medium reflects the context of its emergence in the urban centers of the nineteenth century. Jens Balzer argues that the amalgamation of word and image in the pioneering work of Richard F. Outcault in the "Hogan's Alley" series (first published in *New York World* between 1895 and 1898) demands what Walter Benjamin described as the "distracted" gaze of the flâneur in the modern city. By denying primacy to either word or image, the eye of the reader of Outcault's comics is "constantly in motion": "Their distraction is the mirror image of the endless restlessness confronting the gaze in the modern cities."[32] Ole Frahm, meanwhile, argues that early comics such as

Little Nemo by Windsor McCay and *Krazy Kat* by George Herriman "enable an optical knowledge of the city" that sets in tension and "play" the conflicting modes of perception identified by de Certeau: the topographical perspective of the panoptic gaze and the immersion of the street walker.[33] For the reader of the comics page, "the gaze is forced to move and develops its own rhetoric of ambivalence between control and the loss of control."[34] The Tito na Rua street comics project literalizes these connections between urban form and comic book form. The graphic novel *Zé Ninguém* does not carry out a topographical reading of the cityscape but immerses the reader into the complex interrelations between the material and the virtual that characterize a topological spatial logic. As one element in a wider assemblage of globally connected media, the book not only carries out a distraction of the gaze but, as we will see in the next section, constructs a perspective on the city that displaces the centrality of human subjectivity and draws into view the networks of human and nonhuman agencies that determine urban life.

Posthuman Textuality and New Visibilities

Serrano's intermedial textual assemblage provides a useful perspective on debates about textualities of the posthuman. The Tito na Rua project performs a number of the processes of what Hayles describes as a "Work as Assemblage." Hayles proposes this term as a textual corollary of the metaphor that Gilles Deleuze and Félix Guattari construct for the transindividual posthuman flows of desire that proliferate in machinic connections, the Body without Organs.[35] The Work as Assemblage is not "bound into the straightjacket of a work possessing an immaterial essence that textual criticism strives to identify and stabilize."[36] Rather, it moves "fluidly among and across media" while "its components take forms distinctive to the media in which they flourish."[37] The subjectivity implied by this form of textuality is not the unified, bounded, and immaterial entity of humanistic traditions but one determined by material externalities. As Hayles explains the concept, "humans are conceived as mutating assemblages that can absorb a variety of entities into their environments, including both machines and organic matter."[38] Debates about changing human and posthuman subjectivities tend to play themselves out around the transition from paper-based to digital writing practices. However, although the two main elements of the Tito na Rua assemblage are the "old" media of city walls and printed books, they stage a digital network logic both through the aesthetic of "tagability" and by the way the connection between the street comics and the graphic novel repeats the dynamics of augmented reality. As Kiene Brillenburg Wurth argues, some of the most interesting posthumanist texts occupy the in-between spaces of a transitional media culture, "where visual, textual, and graphic figurations interact and resonate."[39] As well as this network aesthetic, the specific properties of graffiti writing also contribute to the posthuman quality of the project's textuality. In her study of graffiti in early modern England, Juliet Fleming argues that the then-common practice of writing on a wide variety of objects and surfaces—including cabinets, walls, and roof beams—challenges our dominant conceptions of what a text is. In this writing economy the material support for texts is not taken for granted and therefore "those supports remain importantly visible."[40] What modern graffiti has in common with these writing practices is that it "announces itself as being written 'on' something."[41] Fleming argues that one of the dimensions of these forms that constitutes a conceptual challenge for a contemporary readership is that they were "readily perceived by [their] practitioners as tending towards non-subjectivity—that is, towards a writing that requires no subjective position of enunciation."[42] In contrast to the forms of poetry that replaced it, for which "the presupposition of an originating human presence [is] more or less coterminous with the suppression of matter," the graffiti poetry practices explored by Fleming "call language into being as a tangible thing."[43]

Modern graffiti vacillates between the assertion and suppression of a subject of enunciation. On the one hand, some contemporary graffiti practices are premised on the assertion of an individual voice or identity. The rise of graffiti auteurism has taken place in conjunction with a shift in the focus of scholarship from ethnographic studies of gang-based graffiti to aesthetic and political engagements with the work of individual artists.[44] On the other hand, because much graffiti practice takes place at the fringes of legality, anonymity is still a prized quality among taggers and street artists. The reception of graffiti and street art in Brazil reflects this ambiguity. Artists such as Osgemeos (The twins), the artistic name for brothers Gustavo and Otavio Pandolfo, have achieved celebrity status and international renown. Their work has become among the most important tourist attractions in São Paulo. By contrast, the tagging practice of *pixação*, which is also associated with São Paulo, is treated as an anonymous cry of pain from the disadvantaged occupants of the city's peripheries. The distinctiveness of pixação derives from a standardization of the letters, which are uniformly elongated with straight lines and sharp edges, giving them a "jagged look."[45] This standardization reflects the fact that *pixadores* work in groups rather than as individuals. The Tito na Rua project also contains this ambiguity.

For example, Serrano has also become something of an international celebrity. Based in both Rio and New York, Serrano has appeared in newspapers speaking out against the gentrification of the Bronx, and he regularly appears at public events in which he paints in front of an audience.[46] However, the Tito na Rua project emphasizes anonymity. The images spring up in obscure corners of the city, behind public trashcans and down dark alleyways, unpropitious platforms for a high-profile artist. Anonymity is emphasized at the levels of both form and content. The fact that the artist behind the images remains anonymous for the vast majority of passersby in Rio de Janeiro reflects the anonymity of their protagonist, Zé Ninguém. A second multitemporal sequence that borrows from the tapestry technique described above is inscribed over a wall on one side of a main road (see figure 10.4). Four separate images of Zé being thrown out of a moving car and bouncing painfully along the road appear in and among the familiar sight of tags. At the moment in the narrative in which Zé is made homeless, his image is presented as just one of a number of tags that exist on the cusp between visibility and invisibility. Tags paradoxically carry out an assertion

FIGURE 10.4 Zé being thrown out of a moving vehicle. Detail from Tito na Rua [Alberto Serrano], *Zé Ninguém* (Rio de Janeiro: Edições de Janeiro, 2015), 74. Image courtesy of Alberto Serrano.

of selfhood against the anonymity of the city (the signing of a name) and an effacement of this selfhood. The seriality and repetition of tags reveals this assertion of selfhood to be a performance; the name is a code designed to frustrate the state's attempt to connect it with its actual living, prosecutable author.

However, the centrality of human subjectivity is undermined in the Tito na Rua project not just through the emphasis on anonymity in graffiti writing but also through the foregrounding of assemblages between networks of humans and nonhuman objects. The project presents itself as an assemblage, in the sense that Hayles uses the term, by emphasizing the materiality behind both the street interventions and the graphic novel, and it draws attention to the distributed agency of these assemblages at the level of narrative. The plot of *Zé Ninguém* contains a strong ecological message that presents nature and the built urban environment as mutually entangled. The middle section of the graphic novel recounts the backstory to Zé's homelessness and his split from his beloved Ana. "Years" previous to the frame narrative, the reader learns, Zé and Ana are living in an unspecified city in the north of Brazil. Their happy life together is interrupted when Ana gets a job working on a nature reserve with endangered species of turtles in Rio de Janeiro. Zé is teaching science at a school to fund his PhD and, since he has only one year left of his research project, he decides to finish it before joining Ana in Rio. Before this comes to pass, Zé is kidnapped by the shadowy agents of a multinational corporation who coerce him into finishing his research in their laboratory by threatening to contaminate Ana's reserve. The corporation steals Zé's research and then dumps him, homeless and alone, on the streets of Rio. In the final third of the book, which returns to the frame of the narrative present, Ana is kidnapped by the same multinational corporation, only to finally be rescued and reunited with Zé. The effect creates a parallel between a narrative connectedness, in which the various characters are all bound together in webs of causality, and an environmental connectedness in which the boundaries between human and nonhuman environment are shown to be porous. This is emphasized through the characterization of Zé as human waste. Just as in the street comics project the human figure of Zé is merged with the physical infrastructure of the city (the images of him routinely reveal the shapes and textures of the walls and doors they are painted on), the narrative centers on the merging of human with environment. Not only is Zé discarded by the corporation like a waste product, but during his time in the city he is repeatedly placed behind trash cans alongside the unwanted dejecta of the city. Zé survives by merging with the disavowed ecosystems of waste in

Rio. He inhabits the city's rubbish dumps and assembles robots and machines from the discarded matter to help him in his quests. Furthermore, as an inventor who assembles machines from waste, Zé functions as a diegetic stand-in for the graffiti artist Alberto Serrano himself, who, rather than godlike author, is a connector who, by drawing together disparate points in the city separated in space and time, lends visibility to both the material dejecta of the city and the "wasted lives" embodied by the figure of Zé.[47]

From Community to Assemblage

The complex textuality of *Zé Ninguém*, and the wider Tito na Rua project of which it forms a part, constitutes an intervention into two of the dominant discourses surrounding street art in Brazil. One of the main arguments in favor of the decriminalization of street art in Rio in 2009 was that these works contribute to a sense of local community. Community street art projects such as Projeto Queto, centered in the Sampaoi favela in Rio's Zona Norte, place the emphasis on graffiti not as a finished work of art but as an ongoing collaborative engagement with the local community as well as with the buildings and streets that they inhabit.[48] Some critics have described graffiti as a symptom of the fragmentation of traditional notions of community. In her discussion of pixação in São Paulo, Teresa Caldeira argues that these practices, which she describes as "new visibilities," express an emerging and long-repressed political subjectivity that does not quite fit the mold of official political institutions or identity discourses in Brazil. By "articulating anew the profound social inequalities" that have marked urban space (in particular the construction of fortified spaces for the rich such as high-end shopping malls protected by private security guards), interventions such as pixação "not only give the subaltern new visibility in the city but also express new forms of political agency."[49] The parallel between the posthuman ecologies that are the focus of the narrative and the displacement of human agency in the textual ecology of the Tito na Rua project, produces a map of the sociotechnological assemblages that have taken the place of community. These assemblages are connected at both local and global levels and are characterized by complex interaction between the material infrastructure of the city and the virtual digitally accessible information that flows around and through it. The "new forms of political agency" to which the project gestures emerge as epiphenomena of the multiple connections that constitute these assemblages.

The effect of *Zé Ninguém*'s intervention into Rio de Janeiro is not simply to lend visibility to the marginalized populations in the city. Rather, the book employs the formal specificities of graphic fiction to encourage readers to think about their role in the complex assemblages of power in the city.

Notes

1. Epplin, *Late Book Culture in Argentina*, 4.
2. Epplin, *Late Book Culture in Argentina*, 3.
3. Rama, *La ciudad letrada*.
4. Fernández L'Hoeste and Poblete, Introduction, 5.
5. Renato Ortiz uses the term "international popular" in his study of culture and globalization, *Mundialização e cultura*, 105.
6. Epplin, *Late Book Culture in Argentina*, 4.
7. Horsman, "The Rise of Comic Studies," 149.
8. Jenkins, *Convergence Culture*, 20. A number of prominent scholars have argued that the inclusion of both words and images is not an essential characteristic of comic book texts. Ann Miller, for instance, proposes the following influential definition: "As a visual and narrative art, [comics] produce meaning out of images which are in a sequential relationship, and which co-exist with each other spatially, with or without text." Miller, *Reading Bande Dessinée*, 75.
9. Thon, *Transmedial Narratology and Contemporary Media Culture*, 1.
10. Querino, "Após mini-episódios."
11. Brighenti, "At the Wall," 322–33.
12. De Certeau, *The Practice of Everyday Life*, 93.
13. De Certeau, *The Practice of Everyday Life*, 92.
14. Ferrell, "Foreword," xxxiv.
15. Ferrell, "Foreword," xxxv.
16. Dittmer and Latham, "The Rut and the Gutter," 431–32.
17. Dittmer and Latham, "The Rut and the Gutter," 435.
18. Secor, "Topological City," 431–35.
19. Shields is referring to a metaphor used by anthropologist Edmund Leach in the 1960s to convey the idea that what is significant in topological understandings of space are not distances and shapes so much as what holds them together or connects them. Shields, *Spatial Questions*, 9. The metaphor is echoed by the image of a crumpled handkerchief in Michel Serres's application of topological thought to understandings of time. Time according to this conception is not the linear, forward-moving time of progress but is multidirectional, bifurcating and connecting seemingly disparate points into adjacency. Serres and Latour, *Conversations on Science, Culture, and Time*, 60–61. The term "time-space compression" is from Harvey, *The Condition of Postmodernity*, 284–307.
20. Groensteen, *The System of Comics*, 108.

21. Graham, Zook, and Boulton, "Augmented Reality in Urban Places," 465.
22. In his account "iPhone City," Benjamin Bratton uses the example of consumers who choose a restaurant via a reviews app such as Yelp and, after their meal, update the app with their own review that will in turn affect the choices of future consumers and therefore shapes their interaction with the city. Bratton, "iPhone City," 94.
23. Ferrell, "Foreword," xxxiv.
24. Serrano, *Zé Ninguém*, 98. All translations are mine unless otherwise indicated.
25. Hayles, *Writing Machines*, 31.
26. Hayles, *Writing Machines*, 31.
27. Zeller, quoted in Hayles, *My Mother Was a Computer*, 94.
28. Nakano, Introduction, 4.
29. Hatfield, *Alternative Comics*, xiv.
30. In *Understanding Comics*, Scott McCloud describes both Mexican pre-Conquest codices and the Bayeux Tapestry as comics avant la lettre in which "there are no **panel borders** per se, but there are clear divisions of scene by **subject matter**." McCloud, *Understanding Comics*, 13; bold in original.
31. Hague, *Comics and the Senses*, 7.
32. Balzer, "'Hully Gee, I'm a Hieroglyphe,'" 30–31.
33. Frahm, "Every Window Tells a Story," 34.
34. Frahm, "Every Window Tells a Story," 43–44.
35. Deleuze and Guattari, *Anti-Oedipus*, 9.
36. Hayles, *My Mother Was a Computer*, 106–7.
37. Hayles, *My Mother Was a Computer*, 107.
38. Hayles, *My Mother Was a Computer*, 173.
39. Wurth, "Posthumanities and Post-Textualities," 126.
40. Fleming, *Graffiti and the Writing Arts of Early Modern England*, 9.
41. Fleming, *Graffiti and the Writing Arts of Early Modern England*, 33.
42. Fleming, *Graffiti and the Writing Arts of Early Modern England*, 41.
43. Fleming, *Graffiti and the Writing Arts of Early Modern England*, 22.
44. Ross, "Introduction," 3.
45. Siwi, "Pixação." The term *pixação* is derived from the Portuguese word *piche*, meaning pitch or tar.
46. Gonzalez, "On a Wall in the West Bronx, a Gentrification Battle Rages."
47. Bauman, *Wasted Lives*.
48. See Young, "The Legalization of Street Art in Rio de Janeiro, Brazil."
49. Caldeira, "Imprinting and Moving Around," 385.

Works Cited

Agrimbau, Diego, and Gabriel Ippóliti. *Planeta Extra*. Barcelona: Planeta DeAgostini, 2009.

Ahrens, Jörg, and Arno Meteling, eds. *Comics and the City: Urban Space in Print, Picture and Sequence*. New York: Continuum, 2010.

Balzer, Jens. "'Hully Gee, I'm a Hieroglyphe': Mobilizing the Gaze and the Invention of Comics in New York City, 1895." In *Comics and the City: Urban Space in Print, Picture and Sequence*, edited by Jörn Ahrens and Arno Meteling, 19–31. New York: Continuum, 2010.

Bauman, Zygmunt. *Wasted Lives: Modernity and Its Outcasts*. Malden, Mass.: Polity Press, 2003.

Bratton, Benjamin H. "iPhone City." *Architectural Design* 79, no. 4 (2009): 92–97.

Brighenti, Andrea Mubi. "At the Wall: Graffiti Writers, Urban Territoriality, and the Public Domain." *Space and Culture* 13, no. 3 (2010): 315–22.

Caldeira, Teresa P. R. "Imprinting and Moving Around: New Visibilities and Configurations of Public Space in São Paulo." *Public Culture* 24, no. 2 (2012): 385–419.

de Certeau, Michel. *The Practice of Everyday Life*. Translated by Steven Rendall. Berkeley: University of California Press, 2011.

Deleuze, Gilles, and Félix Guattari. *Anti-Oedipus: Capitalism and Schizophrenia*. Translated by Robert Hurley, Mark Seem, and Helen R. Lane. New York: Continuum, 2004.

Diniz, André. *Morro da favela*. Photographs by Maurício Hora. São Paulo: Barba Negra / Leya Editora, 2011.

Dittmer, Jason, and Alan Latham. "The Rut and the Gutter: Space and Time in Graphic Narrative." *Cultural Geographies* 22, no. 3 (2015): 1–18.

Epplin, Craig. *Late Book Culture in Argentina*. New York: Bloomsbury, 2014.

Fernández L'Hoeste, Héctor, and Juan Poblete. Introduction to *Redrawing the Nation: National Identity in Latin/o American Comics*, edited by Héctor Fernández L'Hoeste and Juan Poblete, 1–16. New York: Palgrave Macmillan, 2008.

Ferrell, Jeff. "Forword: Graffiti, Street Art and the Politics of Complexity." In *Routledge Handbook of Graffiti and Street Art*, edited by Jeffrey Ian Ross, xxx–xxxviii. New York: Routledge, 2016.

Fleming, Juliet. *Graffiti and the Writing Arts of Early Modern England*. London: Reaktion Books, 2001.

Frahm, Ole. "Every Window Tells a Story: Remarks on the Urbanity of Early Comic Strips." In *Comics and the City: Urban Space in Print, Picture and Sequence*, edited by Jörn Ahrens and Arno Meteling, 32–44. New York: Continuum, 2010.

Gonzalez, David. "On a Wall in the West Bronx, a Gentrification Battle Rages." *New York Times*, November 29, 2015.

Graham, Mark, Matthew Zook, and Andrew Boulton. "Augmented Reality in Urban Places: Contested Content and the Duplicity of Code." *Transactions of the Institute of British Geographers* 38, no. 3 (2013): 464–79

Groensteen, Thierry. *The System of Comics*. Translated by Bart Beaty and Nick Nguyen. Jackson: University Press of Mississippi, 2007.

Hague, Ian. *Comics and the Senses: A Multisensory Approach to Comics and Graphic Novels*. New York: Routledge, 2014.

Harvey, David. *The Condition of Postmodernity*. Oxford: Blackwell, 1989.

Hatfield, Charles. *Alternative Comics: An Emerging Literature*. Jackson: University Press of Mississippi, 2005.

Hayles, N. Katherine. *My Mother Was a Computer: Digital Subjects and Literary Texts*. Chicago: University of Chicago Press, 2005.

———. *Writing Machines*. Cambridge, Mass.: MIT Press, 2002.

Horsman, Yasco. "The Rise of Comic Studies." *Oxford Art Journal* 38, no. 1 (2015): 148–52.

Jenkins, Henry. *Convergence Culture: Where Old and New Media Collide*. New York: New York University Press, 2006.

McCloud, Scott. *Understanding Comics: The Invisible Art*. New York: HarperPerennial, 1993.

Miller, Ann. *Reading Bande Dessinée*. Bristol: Intellect, 2007.

Moon, Fábio, and Gabriel Bá. *O alienista*. São Paulo: Agir, 2007.

Nakano, Renata. Introduction to *Zé Ninguém*, by Tito na Rua [Alberto Serrano], 4. Rio de Janeiro: Edições de Janeiro, 2015.

Ortiz, Renato. *Mundialização e cultura*. São Paulo: Editora Brasiliense, 1994.

Payno, Manuel, and F. G. Haghenbeck. *Los bandidos de Río Frío*. Mexico City: Editorial Resistencia, 2012.

Querino, Rangel. "Após mini-episódios, Cartoon lança 'Turma da Mônica Jovem' em versão oficial." *RD1*, October 21, 2015. http://rd1.ig.com.br/apos-mini-episodios-cartoon-lanca-turma-da-monica-jovem-em-versao-oficial.

Rama, Ángel. *La ciudad letrada*. Hanover, N.H.: Ediciones del Norte, 1984.

Ross, Jeffrey Ian. "Introduction: Sorting It All Out." In *Routledge Handbook of Graffiti and Street Art*, edited by Jeffrey Ian Ross, 1–10. New York: Routledge, 2016.

Secor, Anna. "Topological City." *Urban Geography* 34, no. 4 (2013): 430–44.

Serres, Michel, and Bruno Latour. *Conversations on Science, Culture, and Time*. Translated by Roxanne Lapidus. Ann Arbor: University of Michigan Press, 1995.

Shields, Rob. *Spatial Questions: Cultural Topologies and Social Spatialisations*. London: SAGE, 2013.

Siwi, Mario. "Pixação: The Story Behind São Paulo's 'Angry' Alternative to Graffiti." *Guardian*, January 6, 2016.

Srbek, Wellington, and Flávio Colin. *Estórias gerais*. São Paulo: Conrad Editora, 2007.

Thon, Jan-Noël. *Transmedial Narratology and Contemporary Media Culture*. Lincoln: University of Nebraska Press, 2016.

Tito na Rua [Alberto Serrano]. *Zé Ninguém*. Rio de Janeiro: Edições de Janeiro, 2015.

Wurth, Kiene Brillenburg. "Posthumanities and Post-Textualities: Reading 'The Raw Shark Texts and Woman's World.'" *Comparative Literature* 63, no. 2 (2011): 119–41.

Young, Michelle. "The Legalization of Street Art in Rio de Janeiro, Brazil." *Untapped Cities*, February 13, 2012. http://untappedcities.com/2012/02/13/the-legalization-of-street-art-in-rio-de-janeiro-brazil.

Afterword

Texts, Coding, and Translation

SARA CASTRO-KLARÉN

Since the publication in English of Roger Chartier's *The Order of Books: Readers, Authors and Libraries in Europe Between the Fourteenth and Enlightenment Centuries* in 1994, we have been looking at books in a different way. Our attention now encompasses not only the book and the prose on the page but its entire materiality as a physical and social object. Inquiries into the history of the book and print's transformative power for language and visual objects in Europe and the rest of the globe's modernity have illuminated the growth and circulation of cultural objects with a new sense of complexity: highlighting the materiality of objects, their place in society, their meaning-making possibilities, as well as their reception and consumption by the reader-viewer. Book history studies look back into medieval times in Europe, the period of handmade codices, and gaze into classical times when the word was recorded on scrolls that, given their physical characteristics, were stored and organized in ways different from what books eventually permitted librarians to do with the square or rectangular bricks that the bound, printed pages became. Greek and Roman reading of prose graphed onto scrolls invited comparison with the operations of writing and reading scrolls in Chinese, which as we know does not move the eye from left to right but from top to bottom.

Perhaps nothing underscored the materiality of writing more than the discovery and decoding of Maya glyph writing, not only because the Maya did not necessarily write from left to right but also because glyphs represented a completely different way of capturing and representing word and speech on the surfaces on which they were drawn. Of course, any ideographic or semasiographic writing system challenged our assumption that writing, and thus the book, captures the word in its orality. Walter Ong, among others, has shown that writing does not render orality onto the written page but is rather a technology of its own that registers language-based thinking in its own coordinates and parameters.

The key text in this discussion on the materiality of the book and its relation to writing was offered by Elizabeth Hill Boone and Walter Mignolo in their seminal *Writing Without Words: Alternative Literacies in Mesoamerica and the Andes*, where they challenge the idea that all writing deployed alphabetic writing in order to capture words, and that writing could not occur when the system for recording thought was not language-based. The limits of the theory of writing as alphabetic- and language-based technology was not only shown to stand in the way of decoding other systems of notation and representation but also prevents us from considering that other forms of visuality could be capable of conveying information and thought without necessarily representing language. With this and other studies, our understanding of the book became increasingly complex indeed, as it also made room for a reconsideration of our age, aptly called by Walter Ong a "second orality," due to the overwhelming presence of television and other similar products and technologies in which silent reading does not play the fundamental role of making meaning.

The focus on the history of the book as a social and aesthetic object calls attention to manuscripts and their peculiarities, not so much as writing before print but rather as writing on all kinds of surfaces besides paper. This perspective opens the way for the study of writing in caves, on ancient and modern walls, on murals, and, of course, graffiti (as in Edward King's study of a Brazilian graffiti project in chapter 10). Having enlarged the concept of writing beyond its historical European modalities as alphabetic writing, writing on Chinese, Maya, and European vases could now be examined as the interaction between graphs representing words and images, telling stories on the shared surface. One of the major consequences of this theoretical opening was the ability to read Nahua and Mixtec *amoxtli* (accordion-fold codices) as well as Maya vases and murals, thus recovering an essential part of the history of knowledge and creativity in ancient Amerindian civilizations. When the coding of knowledge is separated from the written page whose marks represent language, and we move onto other surfaces and signs, the decoding of the *khipu* system begins to take shape. Here we do not have paper. Instead we have wool or cotton fibers highly spun to produce different and contrasting or complimentary colors, thicknesses, and lengths. In these cords, as Gary Urton has shown in his studies on khipus, threads can be twisted in different directions and, of course, knotted in many different ways with a variety of colors, shapes, and sizes standing for quantities, ideas, and even items in narratives.[1] The creativity of the khipu stands as the ultimate challenge to the paper- and ink-based idea that alphabetic writing is the only proper name for a book, an artifact and technology conceived to record and store information and ideas, and also make aesthetic statements. What signifies are structure, organization, and textuality.

With Chartier's emphasis on the materiality of the book and perhaps also with Roland Barthes's extension of the idea of textuality to visual (but not written) objects, the concept of textuality as a weaving of different discursive possibilities and signifying strands acquired a new analytical power that could bring almost any symbolic object under its parameters. The emphasis on the materiality of the book and the image brought about a sense of thickening that enhanced the object's tactile and sensorial aspects, its dimensions, irregularities, weight, precedence of the materials necessary for its making, price in the marketplace, and patterns of circulation and consumption. With these considerations in mind, books, films, and radio programs became objects whose physicality not only commanded our attention but whose texture also made a difference in our assessment of its meaning and place in society. Manuscripts, codices, cheap editions, and facsimile and even *amoxtli* could now all be placed on the same table to examine their materiality as part of a cultural history in which objects rivaled ideas.

Needless to say, in this brief sketch delineating the amplification of the concept of text beyond its deep association with the written page and the book, we see the work of many disciplines beyond literary criticism and intellectual history. Complementing each other, we detect the work of semiotics, linguistics, archaeology, critical theory, and what is now labeled digital humanities. In order to address this amplification, the editors of this volume open their introduction with a definition of textuality as "the conditions in which a text is created, edited, archived, published, disseminated, and consumed." Following the work of D. F. McKenzie, the term "text" also includes "visual, oral, and numeric data, in the form of maps, prints, and music, or archives of recorded sound, of films, videos, and any computer-stored information, everything in fact from epigraphy to the latest forms of discography."[2] With this all-encompassing definition, one capable of bringing any communication-based object under scrutiny, the editors have assembled a variety of theoretically well-grounded chapters that examine with acumen the history of texts and textual ties thus far only lightly studied.

More specifically, the interplay of text as a material object and its social contexts are emphasized in this collection of very granular chapters. Studies move from a possible item of postcolonial contact in Cuzco—European costume books that Felipe Guaman Poma de Ayala may have seen (chapter 4)—to Jorge Luis Borges's "library" of Babel as a mathematical proposition with respect to the infinite (chapter 9). Along with what texts Guaman Poma may have seen and how he may have translated them onto the page as he drew portraits of Incas, conquistadors, clergymen, and bureaucrats, we find a chapter not on translation itself but on how influential Argentine publishing houses concentrated on translating the works of French and German writers into Spanish (chapter 3). In this chapter, José Enrique Navarro highlights the movement of capital and knowhow from the Catalan publishing industry to Argentina. This consolidation of both financial and symbolic capital resulted in unprecedented dissemination of European literary and philosophical works in Spanish America. Curiously, it also impacted Spain, for the books translated here were sold in the Franco-regimented book market that restricted the translation of some of these groundbreaking writers. In examining the vicissitudes of these Argentine presses, Navarro's chapter contributes to learning more about the financial and social aspect of book publishing and the formation of publics for certain kinds of contents and styles, and also illuminates the intimate connection built between the translator, often a writer him or herself, and the text being translated. This kind of analysis adds much to the spotty account we have of the dimensions and role of translation of European literature in Spanish America from the late eighteenth century—when it became easier to circumvent Spanish inquisitorial censorship—to the present.

Considering the cultural as well as linguistic aspect of translation, the enterprise of translating Quechua oral texts into Spanish achieves two towering exemplars in the work of the Inca Garcilaso de la Vega (1539–1616) and Guaman Poma (1535–1616). But multiple others were and continue to be involved in this centuries-old enterprise. The lawyers and historians employed by the Viceroy Francisco de Toledo (1515–82), for instance, also engaged the vicissitudes of translation not only from one archive into another but from an oral tradition into the parameters of writing. However, accurate translation was only a secondary objective for Toledo and his circle of *letrados* in Cuzco. His intent was to render Inca history as taken from the oral account of informants into a narrative that would serve to delegitimize Inca rule and justify deep colonization. In *The Narrow Pass of Our Nerves: Writing, Coloniality and Postcolonial Theory*, I showed that colonization is nothing short of cultural war on the local archive, its modes of assemblage, and rhetorical deployment. Under colonial rule, collecting materials and assembling them into dictionaries, vocabularies, maps, and other texts is not simply a documentary or interpretative labor. Walter Mignolo, among others, has written with acumen on the social and epistemological dimensions of composing dictionaries, as in the case of Antonio de Nebrija and making maps in German map-making shops.[3] We know today that each linguistic object or text, be it dictionary, catechism, prayer book, letter of inquiry, or questionnaire, is a political document as well. Thus these texts reverberate and in fact are fully meaningful when placed in the complete cultural and political ambiance from which they draw their breath. Establishing the grammar of a foreign language is no less fraught with ideological dangers than writing grammar books of one's own language, or tweeting.

But what makes establishing a grammar book for Quechua, as Catalina Andrango-Walker discusses in chapter 1, in the light of unexamined European models and molds doubly precarious is the fact that several translations are going on at the same time. First, in the colonial claim or assumption that Quechua "resembled" Latin, there is developed a comparison to a master text—Latin—assumed to contain all multiple explanatory registers for understating Quechua "grammar." In other words, if you knew Latin, and only if you knew Latin, you could then be translating the grammar of Quechua into Spanish grammar, itself invented by the Spanish grammarians based on the Latin model. So what we have here is a first translation or comparison to Latin. This first translation serves as the foundation upon which the second translation of Quechua into Spanish can take place, even though Spanish grammar no longer resembles Latin grammar. Implicit in these linguistic exercises is an unacknowledged model translation. What constitutes a silenced dimension of the text is the multiplicity of comparative maneuvers at work which, rather than facilitate understanding on the workings of the language being translated, end up obfuscating its grammar and logic. The difference is thus reduced to the number of possibilities as understood to exist in the master text or model. This event in the history of colonization of Amerindian languages by Latin-centric grammarians is partially brought out again in Andrango-Walker's chapter when she states that, "unlike Friar Domingo, González Holguin's conception of Quechua grammar no longer depends on Latin, although frequently he makes comparisons *to help* the student understand concepts that are already familiar to him" (36; emphasis added).

Just as the Quechua grammarians thought of their audience as largely native Spanish speakers, it is clear that when the Inca Garcilaso and Guaman Poma embark on their separate enterprises of "writing" the Andean past by drawing from the oral tradition as each received it, both men conceived of their audience as made up mainly of European readers who had already been propagandized by the negative views of Amerindian civilizations circulating in Europe after 1492. Both seem to be aware of the key points they needed to address in order to make the case that Andean societies were indeed worthy of being called civilizations, partly because they enjoyed long traditions of oral language-based textuality as well as other modes of producing and recording memory, such as architecture, song, and theater. The archive that the two men handled was therefore truly enormous.

What unfolds in the work of these two men is a huge comparative examination of costumes and mores on two separate continents. Both intellectuals understood that in order for the comparison to be effective, they must first start by showing that they were more than familiar with the European objects or forms, be it language, political organization, religion, modes of writing, painting, and so on. Once the European text has been put forward but unexpectedly misplaced and dis-placed—for it has been moved from the matrix of its European archive to an Andean colonial archive—both men proceeded to read the world "differently," from another epistemological perspective. This maneuver on their part, to put the European object in front so the reader knows what the discourse is going to be about, is often taken by scholars as a call to find the "sources" in Guaman Poma or the Inca, because without the European object or form in *our* hands we feel lost as to what they could possibly have meant, given the fact that we do not have dominion over Inca culture. Thus, despite his familiarity with Inca culture, John Murra suggests that Guaman Poma must have had access to some great European library in Cuzco, for how else can we explain his seemingly being so versed in the discussions and textualities of his time.[4]

Tom R. Zuidema, like Murra, never neglects the European archive but he also engages in material studies of the remaining Inca objects, such as the road system, the ceque system of huacas, which he walked in almost its entire network of routes; and tactile examination of surviving Inca, Huari, and Paracas textiles. In the many investigations concerning the possibility that the Inca wrote not only with khipu, archaeologists and ethnographers have attempted to read the *tokapus* on the surviving Inca tunics. Zuidema performs one such reading when he studies the tokapus on the tunics of the Incas as portrayed by Guaman Poma and determines that types of dress portrayals do indeed carry information about each Inca and his deeds.[5] Of course, Guaman Poma's Andean sources were not only his own memory of Inca tunics but the materiality of the tunics worn by the surviving Inca nobility and high-rank *kurakas* on Catholic festivity days when the Panacas regaled the Cuzco public with the splendor of their royal dress. The heads of the Panacas even contracted with painters to have their portraits done and paint in detail the tunics (rank, gender, and descent) that they still possessed and wore. We know from many studies by ethnohistorians how important weaving, design, color, and quality were in Andean society. Precious clothing was as valuable and important in Andean society as it was in Europe, and Guaman Poma's interest in vestments is a necessity in his portrayal of Andean society. However, as we know, Guaman Poma never passed up an opportunity to criticize and ridicule the excess of Spanish grandees, soldiers, or clergy. It is possible then that if he came across German and Italian costume books, as George Antony Thomas argues in chapter 4, he may have taken a twist or two as an aid to portray clergymen in unbecoming sumptuous costume; although, of course, as in the case of the Inca tunics, he could plainly observe the clergy wearing their regalia in festive dates and rituals. My point here could be supported by Thomas's assertion that "the first costume books printed in Spanish appeared *well after* the composition of his manuscript" (100; emphasis added). Thus Murra's suggestion that Guaman Poma had access to a library in Cuzco where German (Protestant) books may have been available to Andeans leads to more speculation about interesting sources with actual textual manifestations.

Many of the chapters in this volume move beyond print technology and thus the book. The materiality of the image not just in photography but also in comic books (see chapter 7 by Silvia Kurlat Ares) speaks of newly formed canvases in Latin American culture as new technologies create and find their publics and consumers, and thus challenge the hegemony of print and the book. The appearance of the phonograph, as Sam Carter notes in chapter 5, marks another pivotal point in the history of communication as people now not only capture language-based memory but can in fact preserve and store the voice itself. Even when they sound old and raspy, listening to the voice of Carlos Gardel and Enrico Caruso gives the listener a feeling of being in touch and in the presence of a past that feels more physical and material than print text. With this new technology for the storage and transportability of the voice, a new sort of orality begins to circulate. As in the case of music, the introduction of the voice with phonograph technology pushes literacy aside. As Carter argues, "these confluences of print and political power that partly defined the *letrado*" begin to fade (114). The advent of radio will, of course, cut even more deeply into the hegemonic realm of writing. In some cases, radio will serve, paradoxically, as the stimulant for the creation of new literacies in Amerindian languages, for the voice will reformulate the oral beginnings of elementary school. Night school on the radio will acquire publics of its own and this mixed textuality where people learn to read by attending radio school will change the face of the electorate in some communities.

Perhaps the most sui generis text discussed in this volume is the case of Antonio de León Pinelo as letrado beyond compare in the composition of his many-faceted and omnivorous bibliography. Clayton McCarl, in chapter 8, discusses the problem of "converting" or translating this "bibliography" put together in the most idiosyncratic form possible into a digital format that will not only recode and store the data, if not its form, and actually make it available for searches. *Epitome de la biblioteca oriental i occidental, nautica i geografica* (1629) is a book that is a list of other books. In addition, it is a text that "articulates ideas" and in doing so, exceeds the idea of a bibliography that lists existing objects but is not a disquisition that involves various processes of translation (178). Transposing this bibliography, with its appended articulation of ideas, to digital form calls for both interpretation of the text as well as a recording of its order and thus producing a new textuality that readers and users of digital formats can access and manipulate. McCarl's discussion of the granular qualities of this epitome, the "autonomous quality of its bibliographic entries" when the author claims to have read five hundred handwritten books and *cedulas reales* (180), brings to the fore the categorical problem fictionalized by Borges in "Funes the Memorious."

Curiously, with the *Epitome* we enter in this volume into the Borgean world of "The Library of Babel," one of his many stories that would seem to stand at the opposite end of thinking about the materiality of objects, narratives, and no doubt authors. The questions of the virtual, the double, the copy without an original, and the simulacrum have been explored by Borges repeatedly and always in provocative ways that deepen inquiry while refusing a definitive answer. It is thus at once surprising but predictable to see that the theorists of new media have found grounds for claiming Borges as one of the precursors of the nature and dimensions of cyberspace. In his discussion of this finding in new media theory, Zac Zimmer points out that Borges's predilection for playing with mathematical puzzles enables his readers to see in his speculative worlds anticipations of techno-utopian cyberspace. Zimmer sees in this reading of Borges a tendency to dematerialize the coordinates of the "world" of "The Garden of the Forking Paths" and "The Library of Babel," to name just two stories in which mathematical conundrums constitute an integrative part of plot and form. Zimmer sets out to restore the corporality of the Librarians in "The Library of Babel," but at this twenty-first-century point in the discussion it is not clear what is virtual and what is material, especially with regard to textualities and their intrinsic status as systems of coding.

According to Zimmer, for new media theorists, Borges is "a visionary, one who not only 'predicts' new media but whose imaginings have created a virtual blueprint of the internet's architecture" (200). A transformation is operable in Borges's "The Library of Babel" when understood as ciphered, that is, as a hypertext. Somehow, I see that a translation operation is also necessary here, for only those readers who master the language or see and understand the architecture of the internet can detect the codes hidden in the text we "normally" interpret and decipher with human and not posthuman understanding. With Zimmer's thesis at hand, and even with a "human" perspective alone, it has always been hard to envision the materiality of the librarians, unless another translation operation takes place in the decoding of this text. Zimmer points out that for Umberto Eco, this Borgean text was not about libraries but rather about the terror of the infinite, infinite omniscience, a total knowledge that would render any reader of all the books impotent (201). This reader is not unlike Funes; and we remember, Funes's problem is the absence of categorical capacity, which stands for the beginning of thinking in human terms. Back to back, the conceit of "The Library of Babel" and "Funes the Memorious" seems to stand for the oppositional play between categorical thought and infinite recollection. It would seem that if the library is not about books but rather about the terror of the infinite, then it would follow that, as Floyd Merrell argues in "The Universe as Library," the Librarians "represent a pure subjective perspective that exists only to contemplate 'a statistical conglomerate, the meaninglessness of which is absolute'" (Zimmer, 201, quoting Merrell). I am not sure that such mathematical rendition of the Borgean puzzle leaves much room for exploring the questions of textuality the various insightful chapters in this volume have articulated.

Whether we read in "The Library of Babel" a metaphysical or mathematical intertext—the term is a Borgean contribution to hermeneutics—or as cybernetic codings, what we end up doing is searching inside the trap of one of Borges's labyrinths, which are designed to resist interpretation due to both his dense intertextual weaving and the infinite possibilities for decoding that the Borgean text unleashes. It is interesting to see that some of his interpreters posit a terror of the infinite as the meaning of the library metaphor while others offer a cool, unemotional contemplation of a statistical game. Neither possibility offers the human consolation of finding meaning, one of the objectives I believe is part of the all-too-human search for understanding the materiality of life and within that frame, the human production and consumption of an infinite variety of cultural objects, a search that is manifested in the excellent display of scholarship in this volume.

Notes

1. Urton, *Inka History in Knots*.
2. McKenzie, *Bibliography and the Sociology of Texts*, 13.
3. Mignolo, *The Darker Side of the Renaissance*.
4. Murra, "Guaman Poma's Sources."
5. Zuidema, "Guaman Poma and the Art of Empire." Tokapu refers to the geometric design on an Incan textile or drinking vessel. It is thought to contain either heraldic information or else a fully developed writing system, as yet undeciphered.

Works Cited

Castro-Klarén, Sara. *The Narrow Pass of Our Nerves: Writing, Coloniality and Postcolonial Theory*. Frankfurt: Vervuert; Madrid: Iberoamericana, 2011.

Chartier, Roger. *The Order of Books: Readers, Authors, and Libraries in Europe Between the Fourteenth and Eighteenth Centuries*. Translated by Lydia G. Cochrane. Stanford, Calif.: Stanford University Press, 1994.

Hill Boone, Elizabeth, and Walter Mignolo, eds. *Writing Without Words: Alternative Literacies in Mesoamerica and the Andes*. Durham, N.C.: Duke University Press, 1994.

McKenzie, D. F. *Bibliography and the Sociology of Texts*. Cambridge: Cambridge University Press, 1999.

Merrell, Floyd. "The Universe as Library." In *Unthinking Thinking: Jorge Luis Borges, Mathematics, and the New Physics*, 103–32. West Lafayette, Ind.: Purdue University Press, 1991.

Mignolo, Walter. *The Darker Side of the Renaissance*. Ann Arbor: University of Michigan Press, 1995.

Murra, John. "Guaman Poma's Sources." In *Guaman Poma de Ayala: The Colonial Art of an Andean Author*, edited by Mercedes López-Baralt, 60–66. New York: Americas Society.

Ong, Walter. *Orality and Literacy: The Technologizing of the Word*. New York: Routledge, 1991.

Urton, Gary. *Inka History in Knots: Reading Khipus as Primary Sources*. Texas: University of Texas Press, 2017.

Zuidema, R. Tom. "Guaman Poma and the Art of Empire: Toward an Iconography of Inca Royal Dress." In *Transatlantic Encounters: Europeans and Andeans in the Sixteenth Century*, edited by Kenneth J. Adrien and Rolena Adorno, 151–202. Berkeley: University of California Press, 1991.

Contributors

Heather J. Allen (editor) is associate professor of Spanish at the University of Mississippi. Her research and teaching focus on early modern Spanish American historiography and the cultural history of print. Her recent publications include articles on indigenous and European reading practices as portrayed in New Spanish historiography, weeping in conquest histories, early modern Mexican print culture, and reported speech as a rhetorical device in mestizo-authored conquest narratives. They appear in journals including *Colonial Latin American Review* and *Revista de Estudios Hispánicos*, and edited volumes from various publishers.

Catalina Andrango-Walker is associate professor of Spanish at Virginia Tech. Her research and teaching focus on early modern Spanish American literature and culture. Her book *El Símbolo católico indiano (1598) de Luis Jerónimo de Oré: Saberes coloniales y los problemas de la evangelización en la región andina* (2008) focuses on criollo identity in the first book for evangelization by a Peruvian-born author printed in Peru. Her recent publications include articles on gender, race, and criollo intellectual production in the Andean region. Her work appears in such journals as *Revista Candiense de Estudios Hispánicos*, *Latin American Literary Review*, *Chasqui*, and *Symposium*.

Sam Carter is a PhD candidate in the Department of Romance Studies at Cornell University. Engaging sound studies, photography, and the digital humanities, his research addresses questions concerning the relationship between text and technology with a particular emphasis on the effects of reproduced sound on literary form in early twentieth-century works from the Southern Cone.

Sara Castro-Klarén is professor of Latin American literature and culture at Johns Hopkins University. She specializes in modern Latin American literature, cultural and postcolonial theory, and colonial studies. In 2017 she received the Order of the Sun of Peru, the highest civilian award conferred by the Peruvian government, for her outstanding scholarly contributions to the study of Peru's literary and cultural history as well as to the field of Latin American studies at large. She received her PhD in Hispanic languages and literatures from the University of California, Los Angeles in 1968. She taught at Dartmouth College from 1970 to 1983 and chaired the Department of Spanish and Portuguese between 1979 and 1982. She was the chief of the Hispanic Division of the Library of Congress for three years before joining the Hopkins faculty in the spring of 1987. In 1988 she cofounded the Program in Latin American Studies and has been the director of the program two times since its inception. From 2007 to 2009 she was chair of the Department of Spanish and Portuguese at the University of California, Irvine. Professor Castro-Klarén has received a number of teaching awards and, in 1993, the Foreign Service Institute conferred upon her the title of "Distinguished Visiting Lecturer." In 1999 then-president Bill Clinton appointed her to the Fulbright Board of Directors. She has been and is a member of numerous editorial boards of professional journals and associations. Most recently, she has been a member of the Kluge Board at the Library of Congress.

Edward King is a lecturer in the School of Modern Languages, University of Bristol. His research focuses on interconnections between culture and technology in Latin America, concentrating on how cultural texts are used to question the shifting power dynamics of the digital age. He has published two monographs, *Science Fiction and Digital Technologies in Argentine and Brazilian Culture* (2013) and *Virtual Orientalism in Brazilian Culture* (2015), and a book co-authored with Joanne Page, *Posthumanism and the Graphic Novel in Latin America* (2017).

Rebecca Kosick is a lecturer in translation studies and a member of the Department of Hispanic, Portuguese, and Latin American Studies at the University of Bristol. Her research focuses on the poetry and poetics of the Americas, with interests in visual and textual studies, poetic materiality, and experimental approaches to the practice and theory of translation. Her recent and forthcoming publications include a study of poetics and relation in Juan Luis Martínez's *La nueva novela* and a call for increased attention to the materiality of language in translation theory today.

Silvia Kurlat Ares specializes in Southern Cone literature, with a particular interest in the relationship between culture and politics. Kurlat Ares has been visiting professor at George Mason University and Johns Hopkins University. From 2003 to 2006 she was associate director/postdoctoral fellow in the Latin American Studies Program at Johns Hopkins University, where she developed the research for her forthcoming book, *A Persistent Illusion: Science Fiction in Argentina*. She has also edited several dossiers and collective volumes for such academic journals as *Revista Iberomericana* and *Alter/Nativas*. She has founded and chaired the Mass Media and Popular Culture Section of LASA (2012–15). She is the co-editor of a book in progress titled "The Peter Lang Companion of Latin American Science Fiction Studies."

Walther Maradiegue is a PhD candidate in the Department of Spanish and Portuguese at Northwestern University. He received his master's in anthropology with a focus on Andean studies from the Pontificia Universidad Católica del Perú. His doctoral research focuses on the role and influence of diverse discursive technologies—textuality, orality, visuality, and materiality—in framing indigeneity, indigenous literacies, and the politics of history-writing in late nineteenth-century Peru.

Clayton McCarl is associate professor of Spanish at the University of North Florida, where he directs the Digital Humanities Institute and leads coloniaLab, a workshop for the collaborative electronic edition of manuscripts and rare print books related to colonial Latin America. His research focuses in part on the textual products of maritime exploration and piracy in the sixteenth through eighteenth centuries. In 2011 he published the first edition of Francisco de Seyxas y Lovera's 1693 treatise, *Piratas y contrabandistas de ambas Indias*. His work has also appeared in the journals *Colonial Latin American Review*, *Book History*, and *Scholarly Editing*, and he has articles forthcoming in *Quaerendo* and the *Journal of Academic Librarianship*.

José Enrique Navarro is assistant professor of Spanish at Wichita State University. His area of expertise is contemporary Spanish American literature and culture and transatlantic studies. His research interests include publishing history, cultural globalization, politics of memory, and graphic novels. He has published on such issues as the impact of stronger copyright laws in the republication of certain literary works, on authorship and the literary market in contemporary Spanish and Spanish American literature, and on blogs and collaborative authorship. His works have appeared in such journals as *Anales de la Literatura Española Contemporánea, Hispanic Issues Online,* and *Ciberletras.*

Andrew R. Reynolds (editor) is associate professor of Spanish at West Texas A&M University. He is author of *The Spanish American Crónica Modernista, Temporality, and Material Culture* (2012) and co-editor of *Behind the Masks of Modernism: Global and Transnational Perspectives* (2016). He has recently published articles on modernismo, visual cultures, and periodical studies in such journals as *Modern Languages Open, Revista Iberoamericana,* and *Decimonónica.* Reynolds also serves on the Executive Board of the Society for Textual Scholarship (STS).

George Antony Thomas is professor of Spanish and chair of the Department of Hispanic Studies at the University of Northern Colorado, Greeley. His research interests include early modern women writers, indigenous studies, and colonial Latin American print culture. He is the author of *The Politics and Poetics of Sor Juana Inés de la Cruz* (2012) and has also published articles in the journals *Dieciocho: Hispanic Enlightenment, Hispania,* and *Letras Femeninas.*

Zac Zimmer is assistant professor of literature at the University of California, Santa Cruz, and faculty affiliate with Latin American and Latino studies. His research explores questions of literature, aesthetics, politics, and technology in Latin America. His current project is a comparative study of Latin American science fiction and narratives of the sixteenth-century conquest of the Americas; previous publications have appeared in *Latin American Research Review, Technology and Culture, Chasqui, Modern Language Notes, Revista Hispánica Moderna,* and *Revista Otra Parte.*

Index

Acosta, José de, 27–29
Adorno, Rolena, 101n1, 101n5, 102n17
advertising, 66, 74, 108, 110, 113, 116–18, 122n2, 142, 163, 224
Agrimbau, Diego, 222
Alcatena, Enrique, 154, 158
American Printing History Association (APHA), 19n3
Anderson, Benedict, 50
antipoetry, 128, 130–31, 133, 136–37, 147
archive, 9–11, 18, 66, 214, 244–46; digital, 10
Arciniegas, Germán, 75, 77
Asimov, Isaac, 164
Assis, Machado de, 222
aural, 53
authorship, 57, 59, 131–32, 236
avant-garde, 68, 71, 77–78, 112, 125n48
Ayala, Guaman Poma de, 85–104, 244, 246
Aymara, 29–31

Bá, Gabriel, 222
Badmington, Neil, 205–6
Balzer, Jens, 231
Barletta, Leonidas, 77
Baroja, Pío, 71

Barreiro, Ricardo, 152, 157–58
Barrenechea, Ana María, 210, 215n18
Barthes, Roland, 145, 243
Basile, Jonathan, 204–5, 216n31
Battista Ramusio, Giovanni, 181
Bauer, Tristán, 209
Benjamin, Walter, 231
Benson Latin American Collection, 9–11, 21n23
Bernández, Francisco Luis, 77
Berni, Antonio, 153
Betanzos, Juan de, 28
Bloch, Ernst, 169, 215n19
blog, 10
bibliography, 177–79, 187–90, 210, 248
Binns, Niall, 135
Bioy Casares, Adolfo, 72, 157
Bolter, Jay David, 215n6, 215n21
book, 129, 177, 180, 182, 209–10, 214, 221–28; bestselling, 86; block printing, 222; collections, 101; digital, 133; disappearance of, 133; edition, 74, 89, 141, 158, 177–79, 189–91, 202, 243; history, 4, 19n2, 19n6, 85, 132, 241–47; jackets, 74, 153; library, 208; markets, 15, 66–69; sellers, 100

Borges, Jorge Luis, 7, 16, 71–72, 118, 186, 197–214, 244, 248–50
Bottaro, Raúl, 78n3, 79n11
Boulton, Andrew, 226
Bourdieu, Pierre, 72
Brasilica, 31
Breccia, Enrique, 154
Brillenburg Wurth, Kiene, 233
Brokaw, Galen, 19n2, 101n4
Brown, Andrew, 198
Brown, Wendy, 207
Buenos Aires, Argentina, 108, 115, 123n16, 124n22, 125n37, 156, 158–59, 161, 170n4, 172n19, 173n21, 192n7, 214
Bullrich, Silvina, 77, 80n34
Burkhart, Louise, 30
Burtonio, Ludovico, 31, 32
Butler, Judith, 207

Caldeira, Teresa, 236
canon, 68, 86, 92, 157, 199, 215n6
Cañizares-Esguerra, Jorge, 20n4
Caras y Caretas, 108, 110, 121, 124n22, 152
Cárcova, Ernesto de la, 152
Caruso, Enrico, 247
catechism manuals, 31, 245
Catholic: clergy, 49, 90, 93–95; conversion, 99; doctrine, 31; images, 96
CD-ROM, 200
cell phone, 16
Cerrón-Palomino, Rodolfo, 39n1, 41n28, 42n48, 42n57
Cervantes, Miguel de, 186, 193n44, 201
Chartier, Roger, 20n6, 242–43
Chichoni, Oscar, 154, 159–60
Christianity, 8; colonial explanations of, 35; conversion to, 30; doctrine of, 28; spread of in the Americas, 27–28
chronicle genre, 6, 99
Ciccoricco, David, 200, 215n6
codex, 9, 128–29, 132–33, 136, 145–47, 198, 227
Codex Foundation, 19n3

Colin, Flávio, 222
collage, 130, 141, 172n14
comics, 152–54, 157, 165, 221–23, 226, 230, 235
Cornejo Polar, Antonio, 5, 20n14, 48
Cortázar, Julio, 7, 72–73, 75, 77, 80n33, 80n34
Costa, René de, 134
costume book, 85–104, 246–47
creationism, 134–35, 148n7
criollo, 29, 48–49
Cros, Charles, 112, 125n33
cubism, 153
cultural industry, 66, 69, 79n11
Cummins, Thomas, 88, 100, 102n11, 102n29, 104n38, 104n42
Cuzco, 30, 34, 85, 90, 244, 247
cyborg, 160

Dada, 153
data, 16, 121, 179–80, 187–90, 198–200, 207, 211–13, 243, 248
database, 3, 179–80, 213
De Bry, Theodore, 181, 183
de Certeau, Michel, 224, 232
decolonialization, 4
Degraff, Andrew, 204
de la Cruz, Sor Juan Inés, 7–11, 21n23, 21n26
Deleuze, Gilles, 232
Desmazières, Erik, 203
Dittmer, Jason, 225–26
Dominicans (religious order), 28, 31
Druillet, Phillip, 154
dystopia, 152, 156–58, 160, 169

Eco, Umberto, 198, 200–201
Edison, Thomas, 112, 114, 116, 124n27
editing, 77, 178, 189, 227–28 digital, 16
editor, influence of, 10; policies of, 66–71, 179–81, 185–87
ebook, 133
Einstein, Albert, 144, 207
engraving, 101, 104n41, 110

Epplin, Craig, 19n2, 221–22
Estenssoro, Juan Carlos, 35
eurocentrism, 4

facsimile, 9, 21n23, 128, 178, 192n7, 210, 243
Faulkner, William, 71
Fernández L'Hoeste, Héctor, 221
Fernández Moreno, César, 77, 81n36
Ferreira, Domingo, 154
Ferrell, Jeff, 224
Fleming, Juliet, 233
font, 129, 133, 139
Forner, Raquel, 153
Forster, E.M., 205
Foucault, Michel, 145
Frahm, Ole, 231
Franciscans, 31
Franco, Edgar, 223
Franco, Orlando, 77
Fuentes, Carlos, 77

Gándara, Carmen, 77
García, Eustasio A., 78n3, 79n11
García Márquez, Gabriel, 7, 72, 75, 77, 80n33, 80n34
Garcilaso de la Vega, Inca, 41n26, 244. 246
Gardel, Carlos, 247
Generation of '27, 72
Giménez, Juan, 158
Giri, Alberto, 77
Girondo, Oliverio, 68, 77, 118
Gitelman, Lisa, 110, 123n9
Gleick, James, 201
globalization, 152, 222
Goldbloom Bloch, William, 201
Goligorsky, Eduardo, 157
González Echevarría, Roberto, 13
González Holguín, Diego, 27, 31–32, 36–39
González Lanuza, Eduardo, 118–21, 125n48
Google Books, 192n7
gothic, 152, 154
Gottlieb, Marlene, 130, 148n5
graffiti, 223–36, 242

Graham, Mark, 226
grammar books, 27, 31, 33, 245
gramophone, 108, 110, 118, 121, 122n2, 123n7
graphic novel, 3, 18, 152–65, 169, 221–35
Groensteen, Thierry, 225
Gruzinski, Serge, 20n5, 20n13
Guaraní, 31
Guattari, Félix, 232
Guibovich Pérez, Pedro, 40n6, 40n8
Gutiérrez, Fermín Estrella, 77

Haraway, Donna, 207, 217n46
Harrison, Regina, 35–36
Harvey, David, 225, 237n19
Hatfield, Charles, 228, 230
Hayles, N. Katherine, 201, 206, 215n20, 227, 232
Hebrew, 36, 124n22
hegemony, 49, 54, 96, 247
Herbert, Frank, 164
Hernández, Felisberto, 77
Hernández, José, 112, 113
Herrera, Yuri, 16–17
Herriman, George, 232
heterogeneity, 3–6, 20n14, 31, 47
high art, 130, 153
Hill Boone, Elizabeth, 19n2, 20n5, 242
Hincks, Edward, 112
Hogar, El, 116
Hora, Maurício, 223
Horsman, Yasco, 222
Huari, 246
Huidobro, Vicente, 134–37, 148n7
humanism, 206–7
Huyssen, Andreas, 157
hyperlink, 10, 200
hypertext, 200–201, 249

Ibáñez Langlois, José Miguel, 128
Ibarbourou, Juana de, 76
Ilg, Ulrike, 102n18
Inca, 29–45, 244–47; dress, 89–90, 97; queen, 89; rulers, 88–90, 97, 247

index, 67, 74, 180, 188
indigenismo, 5, 49
indigenous: authors, 86; representations during colonialism, 97, 99; cultures, 28; groups as subaltern, 48; languages, 32, 47, 50; men, 99; orality, 31; populations in Peru, 95; readers, 85; information technologies, 63; textuality, 3–6, 101n4, 242; traditions, 48; use of Spanish, 47; women, 46, 97, 99
indio, 38, 56, 60, 62
Instagram, 227
Ippóliti, Gabriel, 222

Jakobson, Roman, 142
Jenkins, Henry, 222
Jerónimo de Oré, Luis, 31, 41n26
Jesuits, 29–32, 36, 38–39, 102n17
Jodorowsky, Alejandro, 130
Jones, Ann Rosalind, 91, 102n9
journalism, 47–48

khipu, 4, 101n4, 242–43, 247
Kittler, Friedrich, 110
Kosice, Gyula, 153

Lang, Fritz, 168
Lange, Norah, 118
Larraz, Fernando, 72, 76, 79n11
Latham, Alan, 225–26
Latin, 33, 245
Latin America: the arts in, 102n6; colonial, 85, 93, 246; colonization of, 4–6, 69, 93; history of, 11, 18; invention of, 4; lettered authority of, 55; literary Boom of, 75, 80n33; racist discourses in, 62; studies, 5
Lauer, Mirko, 48
León-Cáceres, Samuel, 138
León Pinelo, Antonio de, 177–191
lettered city. *See* Rama, Ángel
letrado, 6, 53, 56, 100, 104n37, 114, 244, 248
library, 10, 21n23, 85–86, 100, 186, 197–214, 244–50

librarian, 203–5, 249
Lihn, Enrique, 130
Lima, 49–54, 103n23, 181; cathedral of, 28; publications in, 31; Third Council of, 29, 39, 40n6
Lindstrom, Naomi, 78
literacy, 53–54, 100, 110, 248
Loayza, Jéronimo de, 28
low art, 153
Ludmer, Josefina, 63n3, 123n12
Luis de Diego, José, 67

MacCormack, Sabine, 34–35
Madrid, Spain, 70, 180, 192n7
magazine, 15, 50, 118, 121n1, 122n4, 125n37, 154, 157, 172n14
Mallea, Eduardo, 71, 76, 80n34
Malraux, André, 159
Manco Capac, 34
manuscript, 9–10, 66, 85–86, 89–90, 133, 177–78, 242–43
MARC, 187–88
Marcuse, Herbert, 169
Marechal, Leopoldo, 73, 75, 77, 80n34, 118
Martí, José, 6, 123n11
masses, 46, 55–56, 63, 156
materiality. *See* textual materiality
Matto de Turner, Clorinda, 49
Maya, 241–42
McCay, Windsor, 232
McKenzie, D.F., 18n1, 243
media, 13, 47–48, 54, 68–69, 197–206, 232; audio, 221; digital, 133, 197; culture, 221; ecology, 114, 221, 227; mass, 74; new, 202; platforms, 222; scape, 217n41; social, 21n28; studies, 197; theory, 120, 200, 249; visual, 153, 221; visualizations, 197
Mendoza, Viceroy Antonio de, 28
Merrell, Floyd, 201, 215n18, 249
metaliterature, 186
Mexico City, Mexico, 21n26
mesztizo, 29

Mignolo, Walter, 4, 20n5, 40n23, 242, 245
Millares Carlo, Agustín, 19n2, 191n3
Mixtec, 242
Mochica, 31
modernism, 132, 148n10, 154
modernismo, 132, 137, 148n10
modernity, 15, 47, 53–55, 152–53, 157, 242
modernization, 56, 151–52, 169, 170n1
Molina, Enrique, 77
Montevideo, Uruguay, 115, 124n30
Montfort, Nick, 200, 215n6
Moon, Fábio, 222
Morales, Leonidas, 131, 142
Moyano, Daniel, 77
Mubi Brighenti, Andrea, 224
Mújica Laínez, Manuel, 73, 77, 80n34
multimedia, 18, 68, 130, 223
Muñoz Lareta, Helena, 77
Murra, John, 85–86, 100, 101n5, 246–47

Nahuatl, 30, 242
Nakano, Renata, 228
naturalism, 55
Nebrija, Antonio de, 32–33, 36, 41n43, 245
neorealism, 152, 156
Nestárez, Francisco, 54–62
newspaper, 3, 11, 48–53, 114, 116, 122n4, 124n22, 130
Newton, Isaac, 207
New York, 51, 54, 234
Nietzsche, Friedrich, 162
Niño-Murcia, Mercedes, 64n13, 101n4
Nouzeilles, Gabriela, 55, 63

Ocampo, Silvina, 77
Ocampo, Victoria, 68, 79n19
Ochoa Gautier, Ana María, 49, 123n15
OCLC, 188
OCR, 192n7
Oesterheld, Héctor G., 154, 157, 166
Olivera, Lucho, 158
Ong, Walter, 63n1, 242
orality, 12, 39, 48–49, 57, 100, 101n4, 242, 248

Osgemeos, 233
Outcault, Richard F., 231

Pacaritambo, 34
Paracas, 246
Paris, France, 112, 135, 166–67
Parody, Guillermo, 112, 123n11
patriarchy, 163
Payno, Manuel, 222
Paz, Octavio, 6
Perón, Eva, 162, 173n21
Philip II, King, 33, 39
Philip III, King, 88, 95, 100
phonograph, 3, 110–21, 247
photography, 74, 115, 152, 155, 227, 247
Pierazzo, Elena, 178
Pinedo, Rafael, 157
Pitman, Isaac, 112
Pius X, Pope, 110
Pizarnik, Alejandra, 77
Poblete, Juan, 221
poets.org, 10
Portolano, Marlana, 169
positivism, 61–62, 210
postcard, 128–47
posthumanism, 206–7
postmodernity, 160
Potosí, 30
Pratt, Mary Louise, 96
pre-Colombian, history, 97; manuscripts, 86; mythology, 54
Prieto, Adolfo, 19n2, 71, 122n4
print, 3–4, 28–29, 46–51, 95–96, 110, 114–21, 132, 177–82, 228 culture, 86, 99–101; limits of, 47–48, 119, 242
publisher catalogs, 66–78
Pukina, 31

Quechua, 49, 244–46; as a field of study, 28; evangelization with, 30; grammar of, 32, 36; printing in, 29; proficiency tests of, 28; religious texts in, 31; sophistication of, 28, 37; speakers of, 29;

Quechua (*continued*)
  standardization of, 31; translations of Spanish into, 31, 35

race, 55, 63, 138
radio, 118–21, 125n48, 243, 248
Rama, Ángel, 6, 19n2, 48, 53, 100, 104n37, 221, 223
Ramos, Julio, 55
Rappaport, Joanne, 100, 104n38
readership, 6, 15, 69–70, 100, 137, 206, 222, 226, 233
reading, 10, 15, 46, 122n4, 123n15, 147, 190, 201, 209, 224–26, 230, 241–242
realism, 48, 78, 152–56, 163
renaissance, 172n14, 205
Ricardo, Antonio, 29, 40n6
Rio de Janeiro, 223–24, 228, 234–37
Risso, Eduardo, 158
Rivera, Jorge B., 78n3, 79n11
robot, 164, 166, 231, 236
Rodó, José Enrique, 6
Rodríguez, José María, 51
Roman Empire, 88–89
Romero, Silvio, 7

Sabato, Ernesto, 73, 75, 77, 80n34
Saer, Juan José, 77
Sagastizábal, Leandro de, 67, 79n11
Said, Edward, 69
Salomon, Frank, 19n2, 30, 64n13, 101n4
Sánchez de las Broza, Francisco, 36
Sánchez Vigil, Juan Miguel, 74, 78n1
Santa María, Cristián, 132, 148n8
Santellán, Matías, 152
Santiago, Chile, 130
Santo Tomás, Fray Domingo de, 27, 31–39, 42n48
São Paulo, 233, 236
Sarlo, Beatriz, 19n2, 156, 198, 215n11
Sarmiento, Domingo Faustino, 151, 156, 158, 170n1
Saturninus, Augustinus, 36

Scafati, Luis, 154
Schiaffino, Jorge, 162
Schmidhuber de la Mora, Guillermo, 9
Schons, Dorothy, 9–10, 19n2, 21n23
science fiction, 151–70
Scott, Edouard, 112
Scott, Ridley, 168
Sebreli, Juan José, 158
Secor, Anna, 225
Segui, Antonio, 152
selfie, 227
Serafín, Pablo Guillermo, 152
Serrano, Alberto, 223, 231–36
Serres, Michel, 226, 237n19
Shields, Rob, 225, 237n19
Society for the History of Authorship, Reading and Publishing (SHARP), 19n3
Society of Textual Scholarship (STS), 19n3
Solano López, Francisco, 152, 157, 162, 165
Solar, Xul, 172n15, 203
Sommers, Doris, 206
sound, 33, 36, 123n15, 132–33, 135–36, 243; technologies, 110–20, 123n9
Spain, 32, 69–70, 79n11, 244; court of, 184; inquisition of, 95
Spanglish, 144
Spanish language: spoken, 49; standardization of, 32
Srbek, Wellington, 222
Steimberg, Alejo, 163
Stertzer, Jennifer, 189–90
Sur, 68, 79n19, 120, 125n38
surrealism, 153–54, 160, 168, 171n7, 172n14

Tanselle, G. Thomas, 186
Taylor, Gérald, 41n38, 41n40
Tedlock, Barbara, 209
Tejeda, Guillermo, 128, 131
telegraph, 151
text, 3–4, 6, 9–10, 13–18, 20n14, 112; access to, 136; definition of, 3; devotional, 27–29; European, 246; found, 131, 147;

history of, 3–18; image and, 130, 138, 223; non-print 90; printed, 132
textual: artifact, 67, 129, 133, 177; circulation, 70, 132, 136; consumption, 52; layout, 180; materiality, 6, 9–13, 16, 67–68, 133, 151, 160, 198, 227, 232, 235, 242–43; objects, 121, 178; notation, 100; production, 3–5, 8, 15–16, 39, 55; studies, 4, 227; transmission, 55, 115, 120
textuality, 3–14, 47, 121, 223–25, 243; definition of, 3; digital, 9–10, 15, 157, 222, 248; diversity of, 63; indigenous, 101n4; intermedial, 223
Thompson, Lawrence S., 19n2, 104n42
Thon, Jan-Noël, 222
Toca Fernández, Antonio, 202–3, 215n22, 216n23
Toledo, Viceroy Francisco de, 28
Toribio Medina, José, 19n2, 40n8
Torre Revello, José, 19n2, 104n42
Torres Rubio, Diego de, 31, 32
train, 52
transcription, 48, 50–51, 57–59, 113, 119, 123n15, 189–90, 217n41
translation, 29–31, 35–36, 48, 67–72, 77–78, 96–97, 100, 244–45, 248–49
travelogue, 55
Trillo, Carlos, 158
Twitter, 16–17

Universidad Católica de Chile, 130
Universidad de Alcalá de Henares, 41n43
University of San Marcos, 28
University of Texas, 9–11, 21n23
urbanism, 159
Urton, Gary, 243

vampire, 164, 167
Van Hoott, Karen S., 129–30
Vargas Llosa, Mario, 77, 80n33
Vecellio, Cesare, 88–90
Vega, Lope de, 181
Vespucci, Amerigo, 181
Villaroel, Gabriel, 139, 146–47
Vint, Sherryl, 206–7, 218n62
Viola, Bill, 198, 211–14
virtual, 3, 200, 202, 213, 223, 232, 236, 248–49
Viveiros de Castro, Eduardo, 211

Wagner, Richard, 114
Ware, Chris, 228
Washington, D.C., 192n7
Washington, George, 189
web browser, 204
Weinberger, Eliot, 135
Werner, Liz, 135
Wilcock, Juan Rodolfo, 77
Wilde, Eduardo, 114–15
Willmann, Travis, 10, 21n25, 21n27
Wilson, Bronwen, 97
Woolf, Virginia, 71
WorldCat, 188
World War I, 69

Yates, Francis, 213

Zanotto, Juan, 158
Zeller, Hans, 227
Zemon Davis, Natalie, 57
Zook, Matthew, 226
Zuidema, R. Tom, 41n30, 89–90, 246–47